Cinema and Cultural Identity

Cinema and Cultural Identity

REFLECTIONS ON FILMS FROM JAPAN, INDIA, AND CHINA

EDITED BY
WIMAL DISSANAYAKE

UNIVERSITY
PRESS OF
AMERICA

Lanham • New York • London

Copyright © 1988 by

University Press of America,® Inc.

4720 Boston Way
Lanham, MD 20706

3 Henrietta Street
London WC2E 8LU England

All rights reserved

Printed in the United States of America

British Cataloging in Publication Information Available

Co-published by arrangement with the East-West Center,
Institute of Culture and Communication

Library of Congress Cataloging-in-Publication Data

Cinema and cultural identity : reflections on films from Japan, India,
and China / edited by Wimal Dissanayake.
p. cm.
Includes index.
1. Motion pictures—Asia. 2. Motion pictures—Japan. 3. Motion pictures—India. 4. Motion pictures—China. 5. Japan—Civilization—20th century. 6. India—Civilization—20th century. 7. China—Civilization—20th century. I. Dissanayake, Wimal.
PN1993.5.A75C56   11988
791.43'095—dc 19   88–5467 CIP

All University Press of America books are produced on acid-free paper which exceeds the minimum standards set by the National Historical Publications and Records Commission.

Contents

Acknowledgments	v
Cultural Identity and Asian Cinema: An Introduction	1
WIMAL DISSANAYAKE	

PART 1. JAPAN 13

1. Viewing Japanese Film: Some Considerations 19
   DONALD RICHIE

2. The Destiny of Samurai Films 33
   MICHITARO TADA

3. The Multilayered Nature of the Tradition of Acting in Japanese Cinema 45
   TADAO SATO

4. Japanese Film Genres 53
   AUDIE BOCK

5. Change in the Image of Mother in Japanese Cinema and Television 63
   TADAO SATO

PART 2. INDIA 71

6. Innovation and Imitation in the Indian Cinema 77
   MIRA REYM BINFORD

7. Art, Vision, and Culture: Satyajit Ray's Apu Trilogy Revisited 93
   WIMAL DISSANAYAKE

8. The Woman: Myth and Reality in the Indian Cinema 107
   ARUNA VASUDEV

9. The Painted Face of Politics: The Actor Politicians of South India 127
   CHIDANANDA DAS GUPTA

10. Songs in Hindi Films: Nature and Function 149
    TERI SKILLMAN

PART 3. CHINA 159

11. The Chinese Film in the 1980s: Art and Industry 165
    MA QIANG

12. The Sinification of Cinema: The Foreignness of Film in China 175
    PAUL CLARK

13. The Position of Women in New Chinese Cinema 185
    TONY RAYNS

14. Chinese Films Amidst the Tide of Reform 199
    SHAO MUJUN

Index 209

Acknowledgments

I WISH to thank all the distinguished contributors to this volume. A number of the articles in this book have been previously published. "Viewing Japanese Film: Some Considerations" by Donald Richie, "The Destiny of Samurai Films" by Michitaro Tada, "The Position of Women in New Chinese Cinema" by Tony Rayns, "Chinese Film Amidst the Tide of Reform" by Shao Mujun, and my own "Art, Vision, and Culture: Satyajit Ray's Apu Trilogy Revisited" were first published in the *East-West Film Journal,* which I edit. An earlier version of Chidananda Das Gupta's "The Painted Face of Politics: The Actor Politicians of South India" appeared in *Film Comment.*

To Dr. Mary Bitterman, director of the Institute of Culture and Communication at the East-West Center, I owe a deep debt of gratitude for her interest in the publication of this book. I also wish to express my thanks to Michael E. Macmillan for his assistance and advice.

Cultural Identity and Asian Cinema: An Introduction

WIMAL DISSANAYAKE

THE CONCEPT of cinema as an art form was introduced to Asia from the West. It took root in many Asian countries, such as Japan, India, and China, and cinema began to evolve into a medium capable of giving artistic expression to the deeper currents and shaping influences of culture. However, there was a constant tussle between the imported nature of the medium and the unyielding will to bend it in the service of exploring indigenous experiences and culturally sanctioned values, beliefs, and lifeways. As a consequence of this conflict, the concept of cultural identity assumed great importance both in serious filmmaking and in film discussion. The objective of this collection of essays is to examine from diverse angles the concept of cultural identity as it manifests itself in the cinema of Japan, India, and China. Many of the authors in this book commenting on the various aspects of cultural identity in relation to the cinemas of their chosen countries are internationally acclaimed critics and scholars.

Some months ago, I was in Kuala Lumpur having dinner with some of the leading filmmakers and top officials involved with the film industry. The conversation invariably veered toward the question of cultural identity in cinema and the process of internationalization, with its overt and covert threats to indigenous culture, which is rapidly taking place over the face of the planet. This conversation reminded me of similar discussions I had had with Japanese, Indian, and Chinese filmmakers. Clearly, there is no unanimity of opinion, no convergence of viewpoints, on this issue. While some underline the imperative need for a sense of cultural identity in cinema, others brush it aside as misplaced patriotism, a gratuitous anachronism. Some perceive it to be an ideal consciously to be pursued, while others see it as

I

only a by-product of serious filmmaking. Some see the process of internationalization, which is threatening to obliterate cultural identity, as wholly detrimental to the growth of an indigenous cinema art and industry; others discern in this phenomenon a great potential for invigorating, creative growth. Opinions may be divided, but the topic is critically important.

This book is committed to the task of investigating the manifold ways in which cultural identity finds creative expression in the cinemas of Japan, India, and China. First of all, I think, we need to attain a clear understanding of the concept of cultural identity—a concept that figures prominently in the humanities and the social sciences alike. In general conversation, the two terms "national identity" and "cultural identity" are used interchangeably. However, it is useful to distinguish between these two concepts. National identity can be defined very broadly as the recognition of a given territory as one's homeland and the recognition that one's personal identity is largely determined by one's identification with that homeland. Political, social, economic, cultural, and psychological questions of varying magnitude enter into this conceptualization.

Cultural identity, in many ways, forms a part of the larger entity called national identity. A nation may consist of several different cultures, each with its own sense of history, myth, ritual, and uniqueness. The national identity, on the other hand, is often the result of artificial and arbitrary lines of demarcation drawn on the surface of the earth by colonial powers as in Asia and Africa. In some countries (for example, Japan, which comes close to possessing a sense of cultural homogeneity within its national boundaries), the terms "national identity" and "cultural identity" can be used almost synonymously. On the other hand, in countries like India, Malaysia, and Indonesia, where different ethnic groups with their own distinctive cultures exist and thrive within the national boundaries, a clear distinction needs to be made between national and cultural identity.

To understand the complications of cultural identity, we must first understand the meaning of culture. Clearly, culture is one of those slippery terms that defy easy formulation. However, for the purpose of the present analysis, I should like to define culture as the system of meanings by which human beings externalize and communicate the significances that they attach to their own actions as well as those of others and to the environment that they inhabit. Hence the notion of meaning systems is central to the concept of culture. To know a culture is to know its systems of meanings articulated through symbolic forms. Clifford Geertz (1973) remarks that culture is the webs of significance that human beings have spun around themselves. Therefore, it is these webs of significance that should command our attention. As Greg Dening (1980) observes, cultural things are signs and symbols of something else. Being cultural means being able to read the signs not for the unambiguously unitary meanings they display but for the meaning upon meaning that is piled up by context and condition. As Dening goes on to observe, a cultured person, for example, reads the symbols of religious ritual not only for the explicit meaning they are deemed to contain, but also for the meanings of status and power, of wealth and status, of belief and disbelief that all those who take part betray in their voice and gesture, their body language and dress, their use of space. Understanding a culture, therefore, entails the understanding of the ways in which different groups construct, maintain, and respond to meaning systems.

Cultural identity needs to be perceived as the way in which these meaning systems and their symbolic forms invest a given group with a readily identifiable distinctiveness. Rituals, symbols, material artifacts, forms of worship, norms of conduct, and the like are the externalized forms of a culture's meaning system, and when one is concerned with the investigation into the cultural identity of a given community, these demand the closest attention. The question of cultural identity takes on added significance during periods of culture contact, and in the present-day world, which is witnessing an inevitable process of globalization and internationalization, cultural identity has become a focal point for analysis.

The question of cultural identity assumes great importance in Asian cinema for a number of reasons. The concept of cinema as an art form bears the imprint of its Western origin. Asian filmmakers are interested in converting cinema into a more indigenous instrument of communication by drawing on the strengths and vitality of traditional culture. (One has only to examine the work of Yasujiro Ozu or Satyajit Ray to realize the truth of this statement.) The effect is to endow cinema with a distinct cultural identity. Moreover, Asian filmmakers are deeply concerned with the multifarious social forces that impinge on individual lives. One issue in particular that has engaged their profoundest interest is the clash of tradition and modernity. Indeed, this is probably the single most dominant theme in Asian cinema. Asian societies are being rapidly modernized as a consequence of the impact of the West and technology; traditional values are being called into question, if not totally obliterated; there is an uncertainty about future direction. As a consequence, serious filmmakers, who are in many ways the most sensitive instruments of society, have been continually addressing their minds to this question and seeking to examine the feasibility of drawing on traditional cultures as a means of overcoming some of the uncertainty of aim and confusion of direction. This effort, too, has had the effect of lending a greater sense of cultural identity to Asian cinema.

How does cultural identity manifest itself in cinema? Here I wish to call attention to two main aspects of cinema: cinema as art and cinema as industry. Both of these aspects, which, in many ways, interpenetrate each other, have a crucial bearing on the question of cultural identity. Let us first consider cinema as art. In this regard, three areas present themselves as worthy of closer study: content, style, and vision. I believe that all good artistic films, through conscious design or not, reflect a sense of cultural identity. (This quality is not, of course, confined to artistic films alone. Popular films, which have no pretensions to artistic excellence, also display some of these characteristics. The popular Indian cinema is a case in point.) First, let us consider the question of content. By content, I mean the basic human experience contained in a film—the human interactions and conflicts that form the bedrock of any movie. Clearly, the works of some directors bear more strongly the imprint of the culture from which these works draw their emotional sustenance and imaginative power than do the works of others. However, the content of most films can be usefully examined for its relation to the cultural identity. A filmmaker like Yasujiro Ozu deals with experiences—family life in Japan—that are distinctly Japanese. This depiction of the experiences of a distinct culture is true of many other Asian film directors. Let us now consider the question of form and style. A film by Ozu or Ray has a readily identifiable and distinct cinematic style, inextricably and vitally connected with the culture that constitutes its backdrop. Ozu's films are characterized by a sense of serenity and restraint, which remain highly prized qualities in Japanese culture. As Donald Richie has observed, Ozu's films, in a strictly technical sense, are probably the most restrained ever made. He employs only one kind of shot; it is always a shot taken from the level of someone seated on the traditional Japanese mat. The camera, which in his films never moves, is always about three feet from floor level. He never uses pan shots, and only very rarely dolly shots. These decisions of his tie in very nicely with the basic dictates of traditional Japanese culture. As Richie (1971, 63) remarks:

> This traditional view is the view in repose, commanding a very limited field of vision but commanding it entirely. It is the attitude for watching, for listening: it is the position from which one sees the Noh, from which one partakes of the tea ceremony. It is the aesthetic passive attitude of the haiku master who sits in silence and with painful accuracy observes cause and effect, reaching essence through an extreme simplification. Inextricable from Buddhist precepts, it puts the world at a distance and leaves the spectator uninvolved, a recorder of impressions which he may register but which do not personally involve him.

This observation makes it abundantly clear how Ozu's cinematic style is reflective of the deeper currents of Japanese culture.

Let us now consider the third exponent that I have enumerated: the vision of the filmmaker. It need hardly be said that one does not have to be a staunch adherent of the *auteur* theory of film criticism to appreciate the fact that all good film directors project a vision of the world and society that they inhabit. This vision often reflects a sense of cultural identity. Let us, for example, consider the films of Satyajit Ray. In his films, one rarely finds villains; one finds only victims. He seems to be saying that the oppressor and the oppressed are both prey to larger social and metaphysical forces operating in the world. Even the most despicable characters appear to carry within them certain possibilities for redemption. As Chidananda Das Gupta (1980, x) comments:

> Ray's work has more than a trace of traditional Indian "fatalism." It has a sense of detachment, a distance from the event. It is imbued with a sense that no man chooses the time or place of his birth or the circumstances that surround it. It is within the circle predetermined by these that he struggles to exist, to make something of his opportunities. The nobility of man lies in the effort itself. This knowledge does not take away from man's effort, but gives it a serenity denied to those who think they have the power to change the world, and hence hold the end to be above the means that finally corrupt them. The philosophical outlook underlying Ray's work is Indian and traditional in the best sense of that overused word.

Another key concept that we need to examine, in order to understand the full implications of the term "cultural identity" in relation to films, is that of the internationalization of cinema. In order to discuss more meaningfully its full import, I should like to contrast it with an equally relevant concept in cinema, and indeed in all art in general, that of universality. By "universality" I mean the quality of drawing out the common humanity, the timeless human essence of a human experience that transcends territorial boundaries. In my judgment, the quality of universality is present in all good artistic films. At one level, the experience bears all of the inevitable marks of its cultural milieu: the topography, the weight of tradition, the force of convention, the overpowering presence of myth and ritual—in short, the symbolic universe that is associated with a given cultural milieu. On the other hand, a deep and sensitive exploration of this culture-specific experience results in the manifestation of a common humanity, a sense of universality.

Let us examine briefly two Asian films that have won the highest plaudits the world over. The first is *Ikuru,* directed by Akira Kurosawa. The second is *Charulata,* directed by Satyajit Ray. In *Ikuru,* the protagonist of the film, a middle-aged government official, is confronted with the fact that he is dying of cancer. It suddenly dawns on him with brutal force that in point of fact he has neither achieved anything of significance in life nor enjoyed the many good things that life offers. He decides to spend in a wild extravagance the money that he has saved. However, that yields no satisfaction. He then goes back to his office and decides to act on a petition that has been sitting on his desk for a long time—a petition requesting the creation of a public park. He pursues his objective with a firm resolve and steadfastness despite the unconcealed bureaucratic hostilities that he encounters. Finally, he achieves his goal. Watanabe, the protagonist, dies on the night his project is complete, as he sits on a swing in the park with the snow slowly falling on him.

At one level, this is a very Japanese film. Its portrayal of Japanese bureaucracy, customs, and rituals reinforces this impression. Indeed, it can be regarded as a restrained indictment of Japanese bureaucracy. At another, and perhaps deeper, level of appreciation, this film is a sensitive portrayal of a good and honest man who is seeking to make sense of the ineluctable givens of life. In that sense, it is a portrayal of a universal man. Kurosawa's spectacular success in bringing out this general human essence has no doubt contributed significantly to the wide critical acclaim that this film has received.

The story of Satyajit Ray's *Charulata* takes place during the height of the Bengal renaissance around 1879. This was a period in which the

CULTURAL IDENTITY AND ASIAN CINEMA 7

Western notions of individual freedom, the liberation of women, and the like were beginning to have an impact on the thought and imagination of the educated classes. The heroine of this film emblematizes the social and psychological conflicts generated by this clash of the forces of tradition and modernity. Charulata's husband, Bhupati, influenced by the liberal ideas of the West, devotes his time to their propagation. He spends his inherited wealth in running a newspaper designed to gain a wider following for these ideals. His wife, childless, is lonely and bored at home. Into this situation walks Bhupati's cousin, Amal. Charulata delights in his company. Amal gives her everything. His seductive behavior results in transforming Charulata's affection into sexual desire. He then suddenly decamps for a faraway city and decides to get married. Charulata is shattered by this news. Her unsuspecting husband now realizes the full import of the events that have taken place in his household. The film ends on an uncertain note. Charulata and Bhupati come together once again, but one is never certain what the outcome will be.

This film bears all of the cultural marks of Bengali society around 1879. Indeed, the human interactions take on a depth of emotional meaning only in relation to that cultural milieu. However, Satyajit Ray has explored the plight of the heroine caught in that situation in such a way as to project an image of a woman captured in a conflict between individuality and social mores. Once again, the element of universality imbues the film with its undeniable artistic force. The question of universality, then, is supremely important. The concept of internationalization is very different from that of universality. By "internationalization" is meant the process by which a kind of international cinema, in terms of both style and substance, is emerging, largely as a result of the impact of Hollywood. Internationalization has its positive and negative aspects. Jeremy Tunstall, in a book which is significantly entitled *The Media Are American,* points out how the worldwide spread of mass media is increasingly coming under the influence of America. What does this trend portend? What are its beneficial and harmful effects? These certainly are questions that demand close analysis.

Many filmmakers in Asia are understandably concerned about this trend. Lester James Peries, the leading filmmaker from Sri Lanka, remarks (Gunawardana 1977, 184):

> I think you would find that in practically every country struggling to establish an identity through film, the progress of a national industry has

been crippled or adversely affected by foreign companies operating in these countries for many years. When a cinema is saddled with the problem of national identity, you will find that the resulting products are unacceptable to the audience for which they were made. The audience has been brainwashed—practically computerised—into accepting another form of entertainment. I think this is a pattern found in most Third World countries that I know of. In some territories, Western companies are so dominant in terms of exhibition and distribution that local films are condemned as unworthy of screening.

Satyajit Ray makes the interesting point that rather than compete with Hollywood filmmakers, who have immeasurably more financial and technical resources, Asian filmmakers should make a virtue of the undeniable constraints with which they have to contend and thus create a different kind of cinema. Some thirty-five years ago, discussing the defects of Indian films, Ray (1976, 21–22) made the following observations:

> Often by a queer process of reasoning, movement was equated with action and action with melodrama. The analogy with music failed in our case because Indian music is largely improvisational.
> This elementary confusion, plus the influence of the American cinema are the two main factors responsible for the present state of Indian films. The superficial aspects of the American style, no matter how outlandish the content, were imitated with reverence. Almost every passing phase of the American cinema has had its repercussion on the Indian film. Stories have been written based on Hollywood successes and the clichés preserved with care. Even where the story has been a genuinely Indian one, the background music has revealed an irrepressible penchant for the jazz idiom.
> In the adaptations of novels, one of two courses has been followed: either the story has been distorted to conform to the Hollywood formula, or it has been produced with such devout faithfulness to the original that the purpose of a filmic interpretation has been defeated.
> It should be realised that the average American film is a bad model, if only because it depicts a way of life so utterly at variance with our own. Moreover, the high technical polish which is the hallmark of the standard Hollywood product would be impossible to achieve under existing Indian conditions. What the Indian cinema needs today is not more gloss, but more imagination, more integrity, and a more intelligent appreciation of the limitations of the medium.

These observations are equally valid today in most parts of the Indian subcontinent.

On another occasion, talking about the problems that Indian filmmakers have to face, Ray (1976, 57) observed:

CULTURAL IDENTITY AND ASIAN CINEMA 9

Here in India, and more particularly in Bengal, we dare not plunge into epics as vast as these [*Spartacus*]. For one thing, we do not have the money. Even if we did have the money, we would not have the market, and certainly not the know-how to compete with Hollywood. That is why—and not because we do not have the predilection—we have chosen for ourselves the field of the intimate cinema: the cinema of mood and atmosphere rather than of grandeur and spectacle.

This situation is not confined to Asian countries. The English commentator, John Russell Taylor (1974, 80), commenting on the problems faced by the British cinema, made the following observation some years ago:

> Indeed it is possible, oversimplifying a little but not really that much, to see the whole history of the British cinema in terms of its fluctuating relations with America and the American market. Even in silent days foreign films, particularly American, were the menace from which the home product supposedly had to be protected—hence the various quota acts with their results good and bad. Possibly one of the worst things that ever happened to British films was the surprise success of *The Private Life of Henry VIII*, which was the most important single factor in concentrating Korda's mind on the international super-production. Thereby hung a string of disasters—though undeniably among them some surprisingly durable films—and the haunting suspicion that the answer for the problems of the British cinema would be to break into the American market, be accepted on a par with the Hollywood product, if only the way to do this could be found.

Many Asian film commentators see the harmful impact of Hollywood on Asian cinema. The intrusion of alien values, the glamorization of violence, the cheapening of sex relations are usually cited as unwholesome outcomes of Hollywood movies. Some argue that through the visual media a kind of Americanization of the world is taking place. Tunstall (1977, 273) remarks that

> there may be an increasing tendency for films and television and media generally around the world to be put into primarily American packages. The more media each country has the more each bit of the media must compete, the more each country must either import or imitate competitive American practices. Whatever else current and future communication revolutions produce they will produce the increased internationalization of consumption, leisure patterns, youth culture, education, language and consciousness generally.

It is indeed true that Hollywood films are largely guilty of many of the charges levelled against them. However, one must also bear in mind the fact that there is a good side to Hollywood and that it can exercise a profoundly healthy influence. For example, many of the films of John Ford display the creative vitality of Hollywood. Satyajit Ray (1976, 209) has said that "for those who look for art, for poetry, for a clean, healthy, robust attitude to life and human relationships, John Ford is among the most rewarding of directors." Ford fashioned the western into a wonderful medium of creative expression.

The influence of Hollywood is somehow associated in the imagination of many moviegoers in Asia with what is trivial and meretricious in the cinema. Romantic love, nightclubs, mansions, cars, dream worlds constitute the essence of many popular movies in Asia, certainly in South Asia. These popular movies in varying degrees reflect the influence of the old Hollywood. While these popular and artistically poor movies generally draw vast crowds and have the backing of financiers, a handful of directors in Asia seek against severe odds to make artistic films while sensitively analyzing both interpersonal and social issues.

Regarding cinema in many regions of India—for example, the Malayalam cinema—film commentators talk of three broad categories of film: "Commercial Cinema," "Other Cinema," and "Ideological Cinema." In the category of commercial cinema are included all of those popular films that are consciously designed for the box office, adhering as they do to a tried and tested formula. The term "other cinema" refers to the artistic movies that seek to explore serious human issues of significance using the inherent strengths of the medium. The terms "parallel cinema" and "personal cinema" are also used in referring to this body of film. Self-evidently, "ideological cinema" refers to those films that portray social issues from a definite social standpoint with a view to raising the social consciousness of the people. Hollywood is almost always associated with the popular and cheap commercial movies.

The internationalization of cinema and the Americanization of the movie entertainment industries have had another harmful effect on the movie industries of Asia. That is the increasing enticement of the public by television and videotapes. The following observation by a commentator on the Thai scene is equally true of most other Asian countries (Buruma 1983, 53):

> Like Thailand's capital city, the Thai cinema is sinking fast. Within the next three years, it is said, the film industry will be pushed out of busi-

ness by TV and videotapes, which are fast becoming the main forms of mass entertainment. And the speed with which this process is taking place could cripple film-making in Thailand forever.

This is indeed a serious issue that demands the closest attention of policymakers as well as citizens concerned about cinema in general.

So far we have been talking mainly about the inimical influence of Hollywood and the perils of an internationalization of cinema. However, not all subscribe to this line of thinking. There are those who argue—interpreting the term "internationalization" in a way clearly at variance with the way I have interpreted it—that the internationalization of cinema affords a wonderful opportunity for Asian filmmakers, particularly those living in smaller countries, to break into the international scene and that there is no inherent conflict between cultural identity and the internationalization of cinema. For example, the following observations by a Hong Kong filmmaker are very revealing in this regard. She (Hui 1983, 74) says that

> an international market doesn't mean that the film will have to be nondescript in terms of cultural identity. A very distinct cultural identity, in fact, would help to make it more international, because what people are interested in is cultures different from their own.

The question of cultural identity and the internationalization of cinema is, then, not a question that is peripheral to filmmaking in Asia but one that is of paramount importance. It is, in many ways, linked not only with the elevation of standards but also to the very survival of films. As with all complex issues, answers do not readily present themselves. A careful delineation and discussion of some of the issues surrounding this question will enable us to attain a deeper understanding of just how complex the issues are. This book is committed to the task of examining various facets of cultural identity as they manifest themselves in Japanese, Indian, and Chinese cinema.

References

Buruma, Ian
  1983 "Thailand's Film-Makers Sink in a Morass of Money vs Artistry," *Far Eastern Economic Review*, 122, 43:53–54.
Das Gupta, Chidananda
  1980 *The Cinema of Satyajit Ray.* New Delhi: Vikas Publishing House.

Dening, Greg
    1980 *Islands and Beaches: Discourse on a Silent Land: Marquesas 1774–1880.* Honolulu: University Press of Hawaii.

Geertz, Clifford
    1973 *The Interpretation of Cultures.* New York: Basic Books.

Gunawardana, A. J.
    1977 "Third World Film-maker: An Interview with Lester James Peries," *Sight and Sound,* 46, 3:182–185.

Hui, Ann
    1983 Interview in *Asiaweek,* 9, 35:74.

Ray, Satyajit
    1976 *Our Films, Their Films.* Bombay: Orient Longman Limited.

Richie, Donald
    1971 *Japanese Cinema.* New York: Anchor Books.

Taylor, John Russell
    1974 "Tomorrow the World: Some Reflections on the un-Englishness of English Films," *Sight and Sound,* 43, 2:80–83.

Tunstall, Jeremy
    1977 *The Media Are American: Anglo-American Media in the World.* London: Constable.

PART 1
Japan

Japanese Cinema

THAT JAPAN has created some of the finest and most memorable films in the world is a statement with which few would want to disagree. The works of such indisputedly outstanding directors as Kenji Mizoguchi, Yasujiro Ozu, Mikio Naruse, Akira Kurosawa, Keisuke Kinoshita, Kon Ichikawa, Masaki Kobayashi, Shohei Imamura, Nagisa Oshima, and Masahiro Shinoda have enriched world cinema in interesting and unforgettable ways. One of the primary reasons for this indubitable artistic success is the skill and imagination with which the art of cinema—which originated in the West—has been employed to portray and examine various facets of Japanese cultural identity.

Thirty years after the Meiji restoration in 1868, which opened the door to Western influences, Japan's film industry began. As in most other countries, cinema in Japan was originally conceived of as a form of mass entertainment. From the beginning, there was to be seen an interesting interplay between tradition and modernity, the inherited art forms and this newly introduced form of entertainment. While the art of cinema was obviously new, the early filmmakers drew heavily on traditional literature and drama. Similarly, while the younger generation evinced a great interest in cinema, and some of them began to join the film industry as directors, camera operators, and so forth, the older generation viewed this with great displeasure.

From the outset, Japanese cinema presented two dominant genres: period drama and modern social drama. The period drama was largely influenced by the traditional Kabuki theater. For example, the earliest print of a Japanese film that is available at present is *Maple Viewing*, made in 1898. It is actually a filmed version of a Kabuki play with the identical title. During the forty years from 1910 to 1950, with the exception of the period of the Second World War, more than one hundred period dramas were made. These dealt with powerful and basic emotions and inherited social institutions and codes of behavior.

Modern social dramas vied with period dramas for the attention of the audience. This genre took root after 1910 with the filming of Shimpa stories. These dealt with sentimental and tragic love stories in contemporary settings. The staple theme of the Shimpa stories is the misery and sadness of young heroines who are abandoned by their lovers.

In the meantime, Western films were making a deep impression on the thought and imagination of the cinema-going public of Japan. These films afforded Japanese audiences the opportunity to enter into the culture, civilization, and life-styles of the West. Although German, French, and Italian films exerted an influence on Japanese filmmakers, by far the most palpable influence was that of American films. Some of the American filmmakers who attracted the attention of Japanese film directors in the early stages were Ernst Lubitsch, Frank Borzage, Frank Capra, D. W. Griffith, and Josef von Sternberg. Two aspects of prewar American films seem to have appealed to the Japanese mind: the new affluence and the sense of freedom that pervaded society.

While many discerning critics have quite rightly commented admiringly on the films produced in Japan in the 1930s and early 1940s, the golden age of Japanese cinema, in my judgment, was the 1950s, when such filmmakers as Ozu, Mizoguchi, Kurosawa, Kinoshita, and Ichikawa were making their wonderfully sensitive and artistic films, representing a truly imaginative combination of indigenous culture and Western influence. The climate at the time was propitious for the flowering of the artistic cinema. This was mainly due to the fact that film was then the most popular and powerful medium of public entertainment, and the industry was netting substantial amounts of money. Consequently, it was in a position to tolerate, and at times even encourage, daringly innovative and artistic efforts.

By the middle of the 1960s, the situation had changed considerably. The spread of television had a devastating impact on the film industry. Television usurped cinema as the major form of mass entertainment. This trend has continued unabated up until today, and the chances of it being very different in the near future are fairly remote. It is indeed saddening to note that the number of cinema tickets sold in 1985 added up to only a sixth of the number twenty-five years ago. For a short period, however, this trend seemed to create a more favorable climate for the growth of the artistic cinema as the industry, which was losing substantial sums of money consequent upon the severe threat from television, realized that it needed to attract an increasing number of young filmgoers back to the cinema. Working from this premise, the industry decided, as a matter of conscious policy, to afford more opportunities to the younger directors. What is sometimes referred to as the "New Wave" in Japanese cinema was a direct outcome of this decision. A number of remarkably gifted filmmakers—among them, Nagisa Oshima and Masahiro Shinoda—were able to capture instantly the imagination of the public. For a short period, it looked as though a new and exciting era in the development of Japanese cinema had dawned. However, this was not to be. As these young directors became more daring and innovative, and as they began to challenge and test the accepted tenets of the industry in both theme and technique, the industry did not waste much time in putting an end to this surge of creativity.

In the face of the strong threat from television, Japanese film producers had the opportunity to adopt a different strategy—that of catering to a younger and more discriminating audience. This was the strategy followed by Hollywood producers. Instead, Japanese filmmakers sought to win back their former audiences with remakes as well as by putting out films that closely followed those of the past. This proved to be unfruitful, and filmgoers began to forsake the cinema in ever larger numbers. Today we see that a more depressing strategy has been set in motion. Many filmmakers are turning toward soft-porn films, which apparently are enjoying a large measure of success. These films are not very costly to make and some of the most accomplished technicians in the industry are associated with them. Hence, it comes as no surprise that these are impressive in terms of their technical finish. It is believed that of the 500-odd films made in Japan in 1983, nearly 35 percent fall into the category of soft pornography.

Some film directors, in order to free themselves from the constricting demands of the system, have sought foreign funding for their films. Kurosawa's films, *Derzu Uzala, Kagemusha,* and *Ran* were made with Russian, American, and French financial backing, respectively. Similarly, Nagisa Oshima's *Merry Christmas Mr. Lawrence* and *Max Mon Amour* were made with foreign financial support.

However, the situation is not totally gloomy. One has to take note of some positive and encouraging signs as well. During the past few years, there have been indications of some brighter things to come. In this regard, I would like to call attention to a new kind of film that is gaining ground—films that rely on satire born of self-reflection and, at times, even unconcealed cynicism. Kenji Fukasaki, Yoshimitsu Morita, and Juzō Itami are three of the best examples of directors who represent this newer sensibility. They seem to have injected a refreshingly novel mode of perception and tonality into contemporary Japanese cinema. They evince a great interest in the exploration of various time-honored social institutions, traditions, and rituals with sardonic humor. Their films have not only won critical acclaim both inside and outside Japan but have also attained considerable popularity among certain segments of the cinema-going public. *Fall Guy, Family Game, Welcome to Shanghai,* and *Funeral* are four films that represent this trend.

The cinema industry in Japan may have had its ups and downs, but as far as the public is concerned, a feature that repeatedly attracts attention is the interplay between tradition and modernity, cultural identity and change. Consider, for example, the two Japanese film directors who are the most widely known outside Japan: Ozu and Kurosawa. Ozu has been referred to as the "most Japanese" film director, while Kurosawa has been called the "least Japanese." However, what is interesting to observe about their work is that both are centrally concerned with cultural identity and change. While Ozu seeks to preserve tradition and the values and aesthetic that it endorses, he is constantly aware of the intrusion of modernity. On the other hand, while Kurosawa is concerned with freeing himself from the hold of the past, he is constantly aware of its deep pull. In both cases, then, we see the interplay of tradition and modernity.

This interplay becomes even more complex when we begin to take note of the fact that both Ozu and Kurosawa, in their own ways, have sought to draw on the reservoirs of indigenous sensibility and artistic forms. Ozu's central theme, the nature of the Japanese family, his vision of wistful sadness, and his technique of filmmaking—distinguished by stationary and low-level camera set-ups, frontality of image, arrangement of characters, tempo, and the constant focus on empty rooms, shadows of bamboo, falling rain, river banks, and pathways—can most easily and illuminatingly be related to the traditional Japanese artistic sensibility. Similarly, the way Kurosawa—for example, in *The Throne of Blood*—draws on Noh drama in terms of vision, cinematic technique, and acting points out to us how much his artistic imagination is imbued with the essence of traditional culture.

1
Viewing Japanese Film: Some Considerations

DONALD RICHIE

> If there is a painting which is lifelike and which is good for that reason, the work has followed the laws of life. If there is a painting which is not lifelike and which is good for that reason, that work has followed the laws of painting.
> Tosa Mitsuoki (1617–1691)[1]

VIEWING a film means interpreting it, seeing beyond the story and its assumptions to the director and his assumptions and to the culture behind both film and director and the assumptions that it holds.

When a culture is markedly different from our own, we can and often do misinterpret the film. Our viewing is partial or incorrect because we are not aware of common meanings given what we are seeing.[2]

This paper is about some of the assumptions and premises of the Japanese film. Though the directors themselves have often been unaware of these, the foreign viewer cannot afford to be. These notes are intended to help him properly view and consequently more fully comprehend.

A Western premise is that what is empty holds no interest—only what is full is interesting. We are not, consequently, encouraged to contemplate what we find blank. Eastern aesthetics, however, hold that the empty has its own weight, carries it own interest. It does this by contrast to the full, the occupied space.[3] Indeed, as Chinese and Japanese painting manuals insist, emptiness does not actually occur until the first mark is put on the paper. Only then does the surface become empty.[4]

The Asian scene (scroll, screen, movie frame) is divided into two areas of space: positive, which is filled, and negative, which is not.

One is familiar with this: the landscape scrolls in which the upper two-thirds is left blank; the page of Japanese type with half the page empty at the top;[5] the many scenes in Japanese film where space is used (to our eyes) in a singular fashion.[6]

The same assumption (full/empty—their balance) informs many of the traditional and modern arts in Japan. In *ikebana* flower arrangement, for example, the spaces between the stems or branches define the space just as much as does the space that the stems or branches fill. It is the combination of the empty and the full which creates the aesthetic experience.[7]

In film, a temporal and usually chronological art, this emptiness plays a double role. Not only is the scene itself divided into the full and empty, but the collection of scenes which makes up the sequence is sometimes equally empty in that narrative information (in the Western sense) is missing—"nothing" occurs, though this nothing may be filled with another kind of information or something other than information.

The difference from the West is that we do not often tolerate the idea of the dynamic empty[8] and that Japan very often does. The empty is assumed to be "showing" something. Emptiness can be positive—it is always dynamic.

The dynamic depends also upon how we read what we are shown—the temporal sequence or the spatial image. The latter is pictorially structured—a balance of empty and full. So, to be sure, are most images everywhere. The difference comes in how we read them.

Reading habits, to a degree, determine viewing habits. Thus, in the West, our habit of reading from left to right has developed an entire composition theory which is based upon and justifies the way in which language insists that we read.

However, when the language leads the eye in the opposite direction, from right to left, as it does in Japan (and from up to down occasionally, as well) then the composition is likewise read in an opposite manner. Opposite, that is, to ours. They find us backward. We find them backward as well. It is not surprising then that the Japanese misread Western pictorial compositions and that we misread Japanese pictorial compositions.[9]

As an example of different readings there is the opposite way in which the same line, the diagonal line, is interpreted in the two cultures. The West assumes that a line beginning in the lower left-hand corner and rising across to the upper right is expressing certain qualities: endeavor, difficulty, progress, etc. This line is consequently itself often expressly used to suggest these qualities.[10]

In Japan, however, the same line is read from right to left. It is so common, this line, that its use even has a name, *nagari bigaku*—the line is thought to flow (*nagareru*) in a distinctly graceful fashion. As seen in many Japanese works of art[11] it implies something natural, a river or a stream, flowing as it must. Certainly "progress" and "striving" are not suggested, but neither are their opposites. This reading of the diagonal line insists upon the naturalness of its movement.

Thus if the Western reading suggests man against nature (society, fate, etc.), then the Japanese reading suggests man in accord with nature. And this reading of the line supports many other qualities to be observed in Japanese life and in Japanese film.[12]

Opposite ways of reading (left to right, right to left) ought interfere with understanding more than they do. That they do not is perhaps because the eye scans just as much as it reads. Also the Japanese are deft at alternate modes of reading. The West, however, is not and so is quite often misled by what it sees as empty and cannot properly follow a right-to-left composition.

There is also a further consideration occasioned by the Japanese (and Chinese) right-to-left reading pattern. This is that the right-hand side of almost anything is higher, more important, "better" than the left.

On the Japanese classical stage the right-hand side is upper, and the left-hand side is lower. This is seen in names given these areas. The right-hand side is called *kami* (upper) *te,* and the left-hand, *shimo* (lower) *te.* In the Noh, Kyogen, Kabuki, etc., the left is used for arrivals and departures. The right is where the important action most often takes place.

Another example of this left-right dichotomy is in the popular art of Rakugo (dramatized and usually humorous storytelling). When the performer is speaking about or impersonating important people he turns his head to our right (his left), but when impersonating inferior folk he turns his head to our left. This is a convention perfectly understood in Japan. The right-hand head gesture is always seen as referring to the *oya-san* (the landlord), for example, and the left-hand gesture refers to the *tanake* (tenants). This is so well-known that the performer need give no other indication as to who is talking and the audience follows with no difficulty.[13]

Once a scene is filled, or emptied, once a composition, balanced or asymmetrical, is constructed or discovered, there is still the fact that all views are partial in that all views are framed. The position of the frame, what it shows, what it does not, has long been considered important in the cultures of both East and West.

One of the reasons is that the frame presupposes a viewing position, and this position (from where to view the scene) is of crucial importance in all the arts, including certainly film. So much so that one of Japan's finest directors, Sadao Yamanaka, had but one main theoretical reference. This was "to establish the position of the camera." After that "it was easy."[14]

One chooses to frame one's view, and in that space we compose our information, or lack of it. There are two ways in which to think of this operation. One is that the space is filled and we cut out the scene we show. The other is that the space is empty and we fill in the scene we show. We might say that the first is what documentary filmmakers often indicate—the scene is there, we show its relevant part. And in so doing we suggest that it continues on outside our frame. The second, we might generalize, is the way of many film directors making fiction movies. There the suggestion is that the scene is reasonably complete as it is. There may be some suggestion that the scene continues outside the frame or there may not be.

Western cinema is remarkable for the number of directors who combine these two ways of thinking about the frame. Renoir, Ray, Rossellini, many, many more, seek to suggest life beyond the frame. The supposition is that what is shown is real and so it continues on.

Japanese cinema is remarkable for the number of directors who see the frame as something to be filled. It is empty before the director sees it. It is he who fills it. This is obviously true of such directors as Ozu and Mizoguchi and Kurosawa. But it is also true of many less artful directors (Naruse) whose ideas on composition are not so strong, as of others (Ichikawa, whose ideas are almost schematic) but who nonetheless compose their frames by adding things until it is full.

This way of thinking about frame has a number of effects. The first is that "actuality" and "spontaneity" play small part in the Japanese film. It is telling that there is even now nothing in Japan like the English or American documentary.[15] There is small suggestion in the feature film that real life continues outside the frame; there are many indications, however, that studio life continues.

Another effect is that we are being shown a self-contained world, one that is animated not by natural forces but by the mind of man. In short, the view is anthropomorphic. And this is what one might expect from the mind which finds that emptiness has no quality until man has made his mark, that nature is not natural until, again, man has intervened to make it so.

The temporal equivalent of empty space is silence. And, indeed, there are many silent scenes in the Japanese cinema.[16] But, much more common is the scene which is silent only in the sense that information is not forthcoming, the scene which seems not to add to our informational store.

Of stillness, that other temporal equivalent of emptiness, however, the Japanese film displays many examples. Nothing happening is an ordinary occurrence, and not only in the films of Ozu. What is not happening is not happening, however, only on the level of basic plot information. Much is happening on other levels—emotional, intuitive, etc.

One of the indications of this stillness in the Japanese film is the length of the shot. It tends to be longer than a similar shot would be in a Western film. Thus the Western viewer finds that he has (he thinks) exhausted its informational possibilities long before it ends.

The Japanese often has not because one of the reasons for the length is the speed at which Japanese read—both read the Japanese language and "read" a scene. Different cultures have different reading/"reading" speeds. If the Americans tend to be fast readers (and the cutting in American films and on the American TV would seem to indicate that they are), then the Japanese tend to be slow readers. Perhaps this has something to do with the admitted difficulty of the written Japanese language.[17] Certainly the image tends to stay longer on screen and tube.

There are other reasons, however. Among them is that there is an assumption of wholeness in all the Japanese arts. Things shown in their entirety is one of the aspects of art in the East (with, of course, many a telling exception). In film, too, the view is shown as complete, whole. It is often constructed to show just this aspect. Temporally wholeness is indicated by length. The more time we have the more we are able to see. And a sequence made, say, of three long shots gives us more time to view the *wholeness* of the scene than would a sequence of the same length made up of, say, thirty shots.

This inclination toward the presentation of wholeness is particularly noticeable in the ways in which Japanese directors edit their films, or have them edited.[18]

There are two major ways to think about editing. One is that it is an additive process: the montage is built. Eisenstein, for example, shot scenes which would be later used to add to the montage, to create it. The other kind of editing is a reductive process: editing as elimination. Kurosawa, for example, cuts—taking out one detail after another.

The assumptions behind these two methods are different. Eisenstein believes that he is *creating* the essence of his subject; Kurosawa believes that he is *revealing* the essence of his.

Behind this pair of assumptions is another pair. The European would seem to believe that the essential nature of the subject is to be captured only through the simulacrum that his montage has created; the Asian, that the essential nature is there already, in essence, and it is this quality which his pruning will reveal.[19]

Behind these two suppositions lies yet another pair. The Russian might be said to view reality as a quality not apparent in the object since it is he who (in this literal sense) creates it. The Japanese, on the other hand, could be said to view reality as inherent, since it is he who reveals it.

The ramifications of these diametrically opposed views could be further pursued, but here it should be noted only that this pair of assumptions has extensions into fields far from film. Kurosawa's suppositions are very similar to those of the Japanese landscape gardener who believes that nature must be "revealed" (made into nature) and by removing a tree here or taking out a rock there this nature can be made visible. The assumptions are also those of the Japanese flower master as well. Stems, leaves, blossoms are removed to display the essential nature (there perhaps but hitherto invisible) of the flowers. (In contrast, the Eisenstein-like European formal garden which starts from nothing and is created: the Western bouquet which starts with an empty vase.)

One further assumption here to be traced is that the additive process (Western) is based upon an apparent supposition that nature is prodigal, made up of many things, all diverse—with the accompanying assumption that nature is something which is burgeoning.

The reductive assumption indicates just the opposite. It presumes that nature is somehow frugal, made up of only one thing at a time; also that it is singular, with the assumption that, fecund though it be, nature—the rock, the flower—contains within the single example we have revealed (and also isolated) its dissolution.

One might then venture that the Eastern mind tends to dissolve the general into the particular and that the Western mind tends to build the particular into the general. In ordinary Western editing the sequence usually begins with an establishing shot, which is followed by shots of details (for dialogue scenes, reverse angles, etc.). This always constitutes a move from the general to the particular. The reason often given for this kind of backward movement (general to particular) is that this allows one to concentrate upon the all-important element of the shot (often its entire point), which is the action that occurs within it. Space is articulated for action. After the master-plan shot, we always know where we are and can follow the action freely.

Very different are the ingrained assumptions of Asia, which often (and in Japan usually) insist upon a progression in the opposite direction. A general statement is reached only through a particular example. This is the path taken, for example, by the haiku and other poetic forms such as the *waka* and the *senryu* where a single example is made to stand for the whole. Many examples come to mind: in Ozu the long still shot of the single detail; in Mizoguchi, the pan or dolly which moves from particular to general; in Kurosawa, the particular (knife practice with leaves, then knife fight with men in *Yojimbo*) structured into the general.[20]

The uses of the general-plan, the long shot which shows everything, are quite different in the West and in Japan. How often, for example, the general-plan occurs at the end of the sequence in Japan and how often it is used to reveal more than actually seems to show. From its earliest days Japan used the long shot in this particularly Japanese fashion.

An example would be a scene in the 1917 Tolstoy adaptation of Eijo Tanaka, *Ikiteru Shikabane*. A certain sequence *ends* with the long shot, the so called establishing shot. The heroine has received some bad news in a letter and may be presumed to be feeling sad. The establishing shot establishes just that. It is not concerned with action; all action has in fact ceased. Instead, it shows us (for the first time in the sequence) that the heroine is alone, that she is standing near a solitary tree (lonely as she is), that the sky is lowering and it will soon rain (and she will soon weep). In other words, what is established, and through that most unashamedly anthropomorphic means, the pathetic fallacy, is the feelings of the heroine. All of the particulars (downward glances, sighs, letter openings) have led to this *emotional* general scene—the establishment of emotional content.[21]

The process of editing in the two film cultures reveals likewise an amount of information concerning basic assumptions.

In the West there is an assumption of disunity. Hence dichotomies, polarities, and a movement from the general to the (broken up) particular. In film hence too a method of construction which breaks the scene into small units, each often at odds with the other.[22] Montage theory purposely pits one unit against another. This then is said to form a dialectic. That is, it is presumed that they will disagree. It is through this disagreement, this disunity, this drama, if you will, that Western film works itself out.

In Japan, and in other parts of Asia as well, there is an assumption of unity. Hence an overall, though often asymmetric, balance of parts. Thus everything is given an equal emphasis. Thus too a movement from the perhaps dissident particular to the usually unified general. In film hence a method of construction which rarely breaks the scene into small units. Editing often connects (merely) one long scene to another. And each scene has the same general tone and purport. There is little disagreement. One scene supports what went before and what will follow. In this sense, there is no "drama," if drama means dialectic, opposition, confrontation, etc.

Most Japanese films (including many the content of which is very violent—films of the *yakuza* genre, for example) are constructed (edited) in a manner that avoids conflict, avoids dialectic, avoids "drama" in this constructed sense of the word. Thus those Western critics who find that Japanese films "lack drama" are quite correct. The construction is nondramatic in any Western sense. And this is because the assumptions governing the construction are non-Western.

There are many other considerations to be taken into account when viewing a Japanese film, cultural considerations without some consideration of which the film becomes opaque.[23] But among those which have been briefly treated in this paper it will perhaps be seen that cultural differences can be radically apart. These differences and the assumptions behind them create an attitude which is important. Thus, Japan's anthropomorphic interpretation of the relations between man and nature, its assumptions—always working toward a harmonious whole—regulating an interpretation of life, inform artistic presentation to an extent that knowledge of these workings is necessary for a full appreciation.

Notes

1. From *Honchō gahō taiden* [The authoritative summary of the rules of Japanese painting], quoted in Ueda (1967).

2. "Imagine we are interested in the basic 'language' elements through which a film communicates. . . . To facilitate our analysis we make certain assumptions about the characteristic response to any particular configuration of 'terms' in this language. . . . This in turn depends upon a set of psychological assumptions about the ways in which we emotionally respond to particular perceptual situations, and such assumptions are themselves grounded in a body of psychological theory and knowledge. . . . [In] our society people respond to certain perceptual situations in the expected way. But in another society different patterns . . . alter the particular psychological response. . . ." Tudor (1973, 60–61).

3. "In all types of painting . . . it is always undesirable to draw things in the middle. Leave the foreground blank and draw toward the back." Ueda (1967).

4. This is an important aesthetic precept—without the initial mark no emptiness. Its ramifications extend throughout Japanese culture. For example, the idea that there is no nature until man has arranged it. The Japanese garden is not "natural" until the rock is moved, the bamboo shifted. Before then nature was not present; just as, before the mark, emptiness was not present. Space is not reticulated until it can be contrasted.

5. The West, on the other hand, assumes that the bottom is always heavier than the top. Thus Western layout has space at the bottom of the page to counteract this supposed heaviness.

6. Among many possible examples: the balance of full/empty in the Mizoguchi long shot; screen divided top/bottom, full/empty, in many Kon Ichikawa shots; the empty sides of the Naruse shots, etc. The Ozu shot is famous for its occasional emptiness: the scene empty of information, the space unarticulated and hence "empty" but full, of course, of another kind of information: the long shot of the empty vase in *Late Spring* is emotionally full in its nominal emptiness.

7. This aesthetic of the empty has a (Buddhist) term which is often attached to it. This is *mu,* the nothingness which has meaning, the emptiness which has weight. It is this character that Ozu chose to be carved on his tombstone.

8. But we certainly do have a theory of negative space, and it has influenced painters from Poussin on. However, the theory is not nearly so radical as in Japan, where emptiness is given its own entity. Recent Western art, however, that which is influenced by the East, now regularly incorporates this radical emptiness.

9. There is the case of a Japanese publisher bringing out an edition of Constable's prints. He found that one of them looked odd. So he reversed the negative. This meant that the composition was read right to left, and this satisfied both publisher and patron. When we find Mizoguchi's composition "piquant" or when we are struck by the oddities of Kurosawa's compositions (i.e., *Yojimbo*) we are misreading because we are reading left to right what has been

(albeit unconsciously) right to left. Just as we in the West are not even aware that we have a left-to-right bias, so the Japanese are not aware that their bias is from right to left. Yet, the entire culture informs us. *Emaki* scrolls are always unrolled from right to left; bolts of cloth are wound clockwise and so unrolled from the left; most books and magazines (regardless of the direction of the type face) read from the right; cartoons and sequential ads are all read from the right.

10. "Movements running from lower left to upper right are commonly sensed as ascending, while the opposite direction connotes a fall" (Lanners 1977, 104). Western cinema is filled with use of the diagonal, which is taken to "mean" ascension, for example, the celebrated shot of the men pulling the cannon in Eisenstein's *October.*

11. Among the many examples one could choose are the Kano iris and plum screens. In films there are many examples—the flowering grasses scene from *Sansho the Bailiff* of Mizoguchi, for example.

12. In a paper this brief and yet at the same time this wide-ranging, one cannot give the necessary connections. Like any culture, Japan is a whole. More so than most since wholeness is one of the aims of Japanese culture. It is possible to account for much, to see many a parallel—but only if one has the time and the space.

13. These separate attributes of left and right are often to be observed on the screen and the tube. During television newscasts, the "important" announcer is on the right, and his "assistant" is on the left. On educational programs, the professor is on the right, the interviewer on the left. In feature films, there are endless examples—mostly usually in film by minor directors who did not allow any other compositional ideas to cloud their unthinking assumptions. An interesting theory of the origin of right-to-left progression is that in addition to this being the direction adopted by the written language, it was also the direction adopted by the physical printing of the first books. These, called *kan,* were simple bamboo slats vertically arranged and connected with string. The slats were held in the left hand and the right was used for pulling the slats, one by one, for reading or for writing. It is further said that this "page" order was the origin of the top-bottom, right-left order, rather than the other way about. Communication from Joseph R. de Roo, Institute of Japanese Studies, Tokyo.

14. Quoted in Sato (1977). Excerpt translated by Peter B. High. The same source also quotes a remark made by Tadashi Imai to his pupil Kozaburo Yoshimura, in which the older director says that in making his first film he had no idea of how to begin. Then he realized that if he pointed his camera in a single direction, composed his shot, and established his frame, everything would be all right.

15. The "actual" film in Japan followed the pattern of the German *kunstfilm,* a genre the assumptions of which are far different from the Anglo-Ameri-

can documentary. Even now on Japanese TV, the so-called TV documentaries all carry voice-over, all insist upon the primacy of instruction, all use pictures of "nature" in a pictorial manner, etc. The American heightening of the rawness of a presumed nature in the raw is never seen. Nature is, in all forms, always processed.

16. Many, that is, compared to other film cultures. Nonetheless, the Japanese feeling about sound is that silence, like space, is something which ought to be filled. Hence explaining voice-overs in films even as realistic as *Ikiru*, hence ubiquitous music, hence, historically, the *benshi*, etc. Modern life in Japan is notable for its noisiness, and public silence is rare indeed.

17. One indication, Japanese subtitles in Western films. These contain fewer "words" per second of time than do, say, English subtitles for Japanese films. In addition, when Japanese subtitle their films (English, French, etc.) their ratio of words per second is very low. This ratio is invariably too slow for the Western reader. He usually has time to read the sentence twice. This is an indication that the Japanese read twice as slowly.

18. Naturally, Japanese are also and at the same time just as occasionally arbitrary in cutting methods as Westerners are. For example, the old Japanese studio rule that in the initial seven cuts you must establish the whole house (or other location). Or, the ancient *gyaku sandan kaishi* principle—the "harking back" rule, i.e., if you have a joke you must repeat it three times. Both these examples are from Sato (1977). Yoshikata Yoda has spoken of early (ca. 1930) editing methods. "At that time there seems to have been two methods. One was to consider each cut a 'unit' in the overall construction. The other was to think of it as a unit in the dramatic construction. . . . So, around that time, we were all instructed by [Director] Minoru Murata to go and see films as often as possible and take notes on the construction of foreign films. . . . I worked up a list of categories of my own making: Introduction, Interest-Pulling Scene, Sudden Unexpected Event Scene, Development of Uncertainty Factor Scene, Climactic Scene, Anti-Climactic Scene, etc." Yoda (1970), translated here by Peter High.

19. One need not stress but ought notice the parallels here with other aspects of Japanese creation and creativity noted above.

20. This use of the particular in Japanese cinema has often been noticed. Indeed, much has been read into it. Noel Burch, for example, finds the close-up detail a "dramatic signifier, comparable to the *signs* used in Japanese theatre to displace the gestures of emotion (the *oyama* tugging with her teeth at the sleeve of her kimono to signify weeping). . . ." (Burch 1979, 82). All of which may well be true. However, the role of the particular in Japanese film construction is much wider than this and always to be defined in terms of its opposite, the general.

21. To choose a more modern example, the final scene from Kon Ichikawa's *An Actor's Revenge* (*Yukinojo Hengei*, 1963)—a series of dissolves, show-

ing the unhappy heroine, Yukinojo, successively further and further away (or the camera backing further and further away), revealing the solitary emptiness, the loneliness, the cloudy (tear-filled) sky, etc.

22. Eisenstein's use of Japanese *kanji* to support his montage theory (characters for "eye" and "water" combine to make character for "to weep") is based upon a mistaken assumption which no matter how fruitful to his theory was not true for Japan nor for proper *kanji* reading. This kind of logical deduction is quite invisible to most Japanese. Signified and signifier are (*pace* Barthes) not identical in Japan, no more identical than they are anyplace.

23. A list of such considerations would be quite lengthy, but among those others worthy of consideration would be:

A. Genre in Japanese film. It has been stated that *everything* in Japanese cinema is a genre (Anderson and Richie 1960). While this is perhaps too emphatic, it is generally true. Not only are film varieties made into genres (*haha-mono, tsuma-mono*, etc.), but the structure of each film may often be viewed generically (in the *yakuza* film, the "homecoming scene," the "meeting with the boss scene," etc.). And within the scene itself, the acting proceeds through generic means—the "disdain" gesture, the "welcoming" smile, etc. One's point would not be that other film cultures do not have this (they all do) but that they do not think well of it and attempt to hide it. The Japanese do no such thing.

B. Structure—its division in Japanese films. How a narrative is cut up tells something about the culture that does the cutting. Most film everywhere takes from the stage the "opening scene," "the climax," "the final scene," etc. But in between these narrative blocks the Western director usually attempts to avoid stereotype scenes. Not the Japanese. Also, the role that dramatic narrative structure (i.e., the stage) plays in film has been much underrated (by myself, among others). The Noh play has just two scenes; the Kabuki has a number strung out. The way that Japanese film edits into scenes and the influence of theater would be a most fruitful topic.

C. The actor as indicator in Japanese film. Japanese drama is by and large actor's theater, more so than in many countries, certainly so in the Kabuki. How the actor/actress and considerations for his role and his performance affect Japanese film art is worthy of discussion.

These and other topics would indicate ways in which this paper and its interests might be continued.

References

Anderson, Joseph, and Donald Richie
1960 *The Japanese Film: Art and Industry.* New York: Grove Press.

Burch, Noel
1979 *To the Distant Observer: Form and Meaning in the Japanese Cinema.* Berkeley: University of California Press.

Lanners, Edward, ed.
1977 *Illusions.* London: Thames and Hudson.

Sato, Tadao
1977 *Nihon eiga rironshi* [A history of Japanese film theory]. Tokyo: Hyoronsha.

Tudor, Andrew
1973 *Theories of Film.* New York: Viking Press.

Ueda, Makoto
1967 *Literary and Art Theories of Japan.* Cleveland: Western Reserve Press.

Yoda, Yoshitaka
1970 *Mizoguchi Kenji no hito to geijutsu* [Kenji Mizoguchi: The man and his art]. Tokyo: Tabata Shoten.

2
The Destiny of Samurai Films

MICHITARO TADA

THE SAMURAI can be seen as pioneers with swords. Their dominance began in eleventh-century Japan. At this time the Kanto Plain, in eastern Japan near present-day Tokyo, was an untamed land, and this was the pioneer territory that the samurai opened up to rice agriculture. From this time on, the armed forces in Japan came to be mainly concentrated in the Kanto area. The Kanto Plain is the wellspring of the samurai class, which ruled over Japan until it was disarmed in 1867.

The samurai movies that I will discuss were important elements of Japanese popular (mass) culture for approximately fifty years, from the 1920s to the 1970s. While the samurai culture had faded into obscurity during the fifty years after the Meiji Restoration, with the coming of filmmaking technology to Japan in the 1920s the romantic image of the samurai world was recreated on film.

For the first half-century of Japanese cinematic history, the samurai movie would be the dominant form, comprising more than half of all movies made during this span of time. It was only toward the end of this period that Akira Kurosawa emerged into filmmaking prominence. His rise to fame, as we shall see, coincided with the downfall of the samurai movie genre.

The popular subjects of interest to twentieth-century society are action and violence. This is the case with the American westerns, with their derivative Hong Kong karate movies, and of course with our present subject, the samurai films of Japan. In the Hong Kong movies, violence is transformed into acrobatics, while in the samurai films, the violence is clearly patterned after traditional forms, such as Noh and Kabuki. The violence, then, underwent a refinement process.

When I was young, children in Japan would imitate this "refined" violent style of fighting, and we would describe the sound of two swords clashing together as *chan-chan, bara-bara*. Thus, such activities came to be known as "playing *chan-bara*," and eventually the movies themselves came to be referred to as *chanbara* movies. The filmmakers, together with the children who saw the films, created many heroes. One of them was known as Miyamoto Musashi. He is one of the classic Japanese heroes who has become known worldwide.

Miyamoto Musashi was the "fast-draw" of Japan, although he drew his sword and not a six-shooter. His strength was not gained through violence but through his fearless posture, which, in the form of a martial-arts stance, reflected an attitude based in Zen Buddhism. So, as children we were not so much interested in imitating the violence—it was the style of life that impressed us. And, perhaps when American children play "cowboys and Indians" they are doing more than merely copying the violence they see in the movies; perhaps they also feel drawn to the "pioneer spirit" image, and even deeper still there may be traces of a lingering Puritan ethic at work.

Following this train of thought leads us to find deeper parallels between American westerns and Japanese samurai movies. The samurai were the pioneers of Japan. They fought the Ainu and drove them off of the main island as far as Hokkaido. Thus, the samurai were the conquerors of the Kanto Plain. At the same time, they were rebels against the old central authority in Kyoto. The reason behind their rebellion was clearly to protect the immigrant rice farmers in the Kanto area from the unfair policies of the central government. This theme, of the samurai as protectors of the peasantry, is central to Kurosawa's masterpiece, *The Seven Samurai*.

The Japanese culture is a rice-based culture. I am inclined to use the word *civilization* here in reference to the idea of enlightenment. While in the Western context civilization and enlightenment carry the connotations of urban centralization and development, in Japan civilization can be measured according to the progressive development and extent of wet-rice agriculture. The civilization of the Japanese archipelago, then, spread from the West to the East. In the case of America, the path of enlightenment ran from the East to the West, and finally over the waters of the Pacific to the Hawaiian Islands. The West is therefore America's pioneer territory, while in Japan it is the East. America's West was an ideal area for livestock, and eastern Japan is perfect for intensive wet-rice agriculture. Unlike the already exploited lands of

Europe, these areas of America and Japan became important spawning grounds for new and innovative enterprises.

I do not make such a statement in order to boast about my own country; rather, I speak as a man from the Kansai area, in the West of Japan, with the same sense of regret and chagrin as does a New Yorker when pondering the rise of California culture in America. I believe that the American westerns anticipate and reflect the progression of civilization from east to west in America; while the Japanese *chanbara* movies anticipate and reflect the flow of civilization in the opposite direction—they are, therefore, "easterns."

The movie theater is a world of darkness. Light is enveloped within this darkness. And again, the darkness of the theater is itself encompassed within the flood of light which is Downtown. Finally, the lights of Downtown themselves are surrounded by the sleeping darkness of the good citizens of the country. A Japanese poet once wrote: "In the deep deep darkness, one sees an eye open." Whenever I am sitting in the darkness of a movie theater I remember these words. The movie screen is the sensitive eye which combines the light and the darkness together, and the flickering of the light on the screen is homologous to the floating anxiety found in a fast-changing world. This anxiety can be seen as clearly in Japanese *chanbara* movies as in the "sensitive" works of Federico Fellini.

It is interesting that the setting of most *chanbara* movies is sometime during the Bakumatsu period, the final half-century of the samurai system in Japan. The pioneer period in which eastern Japan was conquered and its heroes, such as Minamoto Yoritomo and Tokugawa Ieyasu, had only a small audience by comparison with more popular sword-wielding heroes such as Kondo Isamu. This antirevolutionary hero Kondo was clearly a man of action, but importantly, he lived in an era of cultural stability, especially in the realm of everyday life.

Even today, Japanese people are thought of as a people who sit on tatami mats and eat sashimi. But, in reality, it was only in the last fifty years of the Bakumatsu period that such habits became widespread. Tatami mats, for example, have been around since about 1,000 years ago, when noblemen would sit upon a sole tatami mat. Three hundred years ago, they were used extensively by high-class samurai to cover entire rooms. It was only 150 years ago, during the Bakumatsu period (historically speaking, it was actually during the period of *bunka-bunsei*, or civilization and enlightenment, directly prior to the Bakumatsu period), that urban dwellers came to use them in their humble homes.

The 1920s were the beginning of a period of growth and expansion in Japan; this expansion was accompanied by great turmoil and unrest. The new pioneers of the twenties were the industrialists. Japan became an information-saturated society in which radio, weekly magazines *(shukan-zasshi),* comics, and movies were all essential. The movies were a flood of light reflecting the floating anxieties of modern Japanese society—while at the same time, their audience, sitting in the darkness of the theater, looked to the movie screen for the sense of security and stability they felt was missing in their lives. The *chanbara* movies were a nostalgic look back at a time that was seen as a stable and ideal period. It is for this reason that the *chanbara* movies were always set in the Bakumatsu period throughout their fifty-year dominance of the Japanese film industry.

From out of the conflict between the Light and the Darkness many good movies were produced, and among them were also some very artistic works, such as those of Akira Kurosawa and Sadao Yamanaka. The latter of these two men has largely been ignored in the past. Only recently some French critics have come to recognize the samurai movies of Yamanaka as being perhaps even superior to those of the much-lauded Kurosawa.

It must be pointed out that there are two distinct lineages in the Japanese *chanbara* film tradition: Yamanaka belongs to the line founded by Mansaku Itami, while Kurosawa originated the tradition carried on by Masaki Kobayashi. While in foreign countries Kurosawa and occasionally Yamanaka are seen as isolated stellar figures at the zenith of the *chanbara* genre, in reality they are situated firmly within the two streams of *chanbara* movie history. To continue our metaphor, the realistic, action-filled, and violently inclined movies of Kurosawa and Kobayashi belong to the realism of Light, while Itami and Yamanaka's down-to-earth and enervated films were dropouts, so to speak, from the positive, aggressive, "pioneer" tradition of the mainstream *chanbara* movies.

Chronologically, Itami and Yamanaka were prewar figures, while Kurosawa and Kobayashi both gained their reputations in the postwar period. The prewar films of Itami and Yamanaka maintained an aesthetic distance from reality—they were intellectual creations that did not go along with the aggressive, expansion-oriented mood in Japan at the time. As dropouts from such social currents, the movies of these masters were seen as snobbish and were not, therefore, sufficiently appreciated at that time. They could be seen as films of resistance to the rise of fascism in Japan. Itami's resistance was based in the use of humor and irony when looking at the aggressive side of human nature, that aspect which is the root of fascism. Yamanaka's films portrayed the abandonment of the expansion-minded society at large by characters intent upon only settling into the common, down-to-earth world of the little man. In this way, the most nonpolitical themes came to take on great political meaning. Thus, while *chanbara* or samurai films were banned by the Occupation after the military disaster called World War II on the grounds that they had fueled the aggressive, expansion-oriented fascism in prewar Japan, it is important to make it clear that there was this one "resistance" movement within the *chanbara* movie tradition.

Mansaku Itami, the pioneer of the antifascist movement in Japanese film, was finally censored by the Japanese militarists and banned from making more films. Thus a director who focused on dropouts was himself kicked out and made able at last to experience the very environment that he had so often portrayed in his films. With this, Itami took up his pen instead of the camera and left us with a monument of critical works, including biting critiques of prewar and wartime Japanese films. His works have recently been published in five volumes and are enjoying great popularity among young intellectuals in Japan.

Itami's films are few in number. Perhaps the best among them all is his 1936 classic, *Akanishi Kakita*. In this film, one actor plays two central roles: one as the straightforward, serious Harada Kai, a deft, sword-wielding samurai who lives and dies according to the rules of *bushido;* the other character is our protagonist, Akanishi Kakita, who first strikes us as a lackluster, spineless lowlife and the complete opposite of the upstanding Harada Kai. He is a comic figure; but he is also more than that. Akanishi, although seeming to be a coward and a do-nothing, is not just the subaverage employee in a powerful house that he appears to be. In reality, he is spying on his employers on behalf of another powerful house to which he owes loyalty. Akanishi, then, is doubly ambiguous in that first he is seen as an ordinary employee while also being a spy, and secondly, while on the surface he obeys the code of *bushido,* deeper still he has chosen the worldview of the common folk. Harada Kai, meanwhile, is ambiguous in a simpler way. He is on the one hand a strict follower of the *bushido* code, while on the other hand he is a conspirator in a plot to take power from his own superiors.

While Harada Kai at first appears to be the leading figure in the story, as the title reveals, Akanishi gradually supplants him as the film progresses and endears himself to the audience as being somehow more human than the gung-ho Harada. Harada exerts himself to the utmost in his attempt for glory, only to be cut down and killed. On the other hand, Akanishi, with virtually no effort of his own, meets with one success after another. Itami's message to us is clear: The passive Darkness will triumph over the Light.

That the depiction of this battle between the Light and the Darkness is portrayed by a single actor, namely Kataoka Chiezo, reveals Itami's genius in the expression of two fundamentally opposite sides of human nature. These two sides competed inside the mind of Itami, and this movie reveals that for him it was the quiet, restrained, and humorous Dark aspect which won out. Itami, then, took the *chanbara* movies back "down to earth."

Like those of his predecessor Itami, Sadao Yamanaka's films are low key, and they maintain a restrained tone throughout. This, by the way, is also the case with the films of the modern moviemaker, Ozu. In Yamanaka's samurai movies violent outbursts are exceedingly rare.

In Yamanaka's movie *Ninjō Kami-Fusen* (1937), the main character is a dismissed samurai who earns a miserable living by making paper balloons. He is living in a *nagaya* (literally, "long house," this is a low, long structure composed of many small adjacent apartments gathered under the same roof; residents in the *nagaya* are said to be "leaning upon one another's shoulders," implying that the residents of the *nagaya* were very interdependent, unlike the ideal independent house of the "good" samurai). The scene inside the miserable *nagaya* represents the social attitude of the lowest members in society, those who are forced to rely upon each other for mutual aid and some sense of community. Although the protagonist attempts to become a "good" samurai again, in the long run he fails and sinks back down to earth: to the low social stratum of the *nagaya*.

The camera angles throughout the scenes in the *nagaya* are not arrogant views from above. Instead, as if in sympathy with the plight of the characters, the camera views the action from below. Outside the *nagaya*, like a murmur of consolation, the rain falls softly throughout the night.

Ninjō Kami-Fusen is a movie about darkness—not the darkness of evil and danger as imagined in the minds of many Westerners, but a darkness that symbolizes inconspicuousness and the abandonment of effort to sink slowly into a state incognito with one's lowly peers. Correspondingly we find that at the very bottom of Japanese society Jodo-Shinshū is the popular religion. This "Pure Land" sect stands in direct contrast to Zen Buddhism.

Where in Zen one attempts to achieve transcendence by one's own efforts to rise to nirvana, in Jodo-Shinshū belief it is thought that transcendence is achieved by the abandonment of effort and by deviating towards the "horizontal." Thus, while from a Western point of view Japan may appear to be vertically arranged, in my opinion this framework (popularized by Chie Nakane, among others) ignores the importance of the horizontal dimension in Japanese thought and society.

Kurosawa's world stands in opposition to that of Yamanaka. To continue our metaphor, Kurosawa's world comes from the Light—not the light of hope and justice we find in the West, but that of hard effort and perseverance to escape from the Darkness. Kurosawa's films differ from earlier *chanbara* films in that this effort came to be *individual* effort. So I believe it is significant that the hero in Kurosawa's first movie, *Sugata Sanshiro* (1943), was a young judo master. Unlike kendō, or Japanese fencing, judo uses no sticks or props and instead transforms the body itself into a weapon. Karate does this as well, but significantly, in its original form karate was nonaggressive and centered on making the body into a shield that could withstand any attack. Modern judo, however, is different in that the emphasis is, from an originally defensive position, to use the attacker's own strength against him in a sudden reversal of offense and defense. In this manner, the weaker man may sometimes defeat the stronger. While the loser may feel that it was unfair and tricky, still, it is the only way for the weaker party to win. It is the competitive spirit that creates such devices. In Kurosawa's movie I was deeply impressed by the violent, relentless struggle Sugata Sanshiro fought against the judo masters above him, never giving up, no matter how many times he was thrown to the ground. The final judo match was fought on a bleak riverbank, and when the struggle began black clouds filled the sky, and the wind raged across the land.

As in Yamanaka's films, in Kurosawa's movies the rain would fall, but as you remember from his movie *Rashomon,* Kurosawa's rain is a violent downpour that threatens to pound everything down into the mud, and in *Yojimbo* Kurosawa had the wind blow at gale force through the dusty streets whenever a conflict erupted. The struggles and efforts of Kurosawa's characters are not only directed outward, toward the enemy, but inward as well, as if to destroy a certain small-scale area of stability deep inside. (The process of casting away one's own inner stability and finding a larger one, and then of destroying this new stability in pursuit of yet a larger one, and finally of the largest and most final stability, *mu*, or nothingness—this is the core of Zen Buddhist philosophy. This is, I believe, the spiritual wellspring of Kurosawa's world.) Kurosawa himself, in opposition to the stable pattern of *chanbara* movies of his day, destroyed all residues of traditional clichés such as the Kabuki- and Noh-influenced staging of fight scenes and replaced them with a brutally realistic view of the fighting spirit.

What, then, is the purpose or cause of this fighting spirit? Originally, it was pointed out, the efforts of the samurai were made to protect the farmers. This was motivated by the recognition of the right of the farmers to survive. In Kurosawa's final masterpiece, *The Seven Samurai*, he returns to this historical origin of the samurai spirit. In *The Seven Samurai* the enemy is defeated and the village is saved, but the leader of the samurai is found saying to himself, "It is not we who have won, but the farmers. We will just fade away." I felt that the nihilism of the samurai was not that of Zen Buddhism, but rather a nihilism of desperation.

This desperate nihilism is again found in the works of Masaki Kobayashi, especially so in his classic tragedy, *Seppuku* (also read *hara-kiri*), released in 1962. This was six years after the release of *The Seven Samurai*, and in my opinion *Seppuku* was the "last skyrocket" in the *chanbara* movie universe.

Seppuku is the act of suicide by self-disembowelment, and I believe that Kobayashi's film can be seen as the honorable death of the *chanbara* tradition. Before we go on to analyze the movie, let us consider the place and the meaning of *seppuku* in Japanese literature and history.

Seppuku is perhaps the most painful of all ways to die; it involves prolonged suffering and unbelievable agony, and while the uninformed observer may see it as a cruelly imposed punishment, it is important to note that it was the method *chosen* by the samurai as a last proof of their individual honor. The Japanese, who ignored the science of anatomy until at least the nineteenth century, believed that the stomach or the bowels were the deepest areas of the human body.

Thus, the act of *seppuku* exposed his most inner self to the outer world in order to prove his ultimate purity and innocence. It was a paradoxical demonstration of how the exposure of one's most dirty or revolting insides could be interpreted as an expression of purity, and this paradox can only be comprehended by considering the spiritual view of the human body that was prevalent in the traditional Japanese context.

By the act of *seppuku*, the samurai, no matter how much condemned and disgraced by society at large, could demonstrate his unshakable resolve by cutting deeply into his own body and revealing the uncontaminated nature of his deepest self. In this way, a samurai could regain his honor no matter how disparaged he may have been. The act of *seppuku* can be seen as a form of radical individualism of the highest order, a form wherein a man chooses to die an excruciating death by his own hand, without the support of any religion and solely motivated by individual honor. It is a final protest against the society that condemned him.

The beginnings of *seppuku* can be traced back to the rise of the samurai class in the eleventh century. At that time *seppuku* occurred only sporadically and completely as a product of the individual samurai's will to prove his ultimate innocence. As the *seppuku* tradition grew stronger, it came to be ritualized by the samurai to a greater extent. Finally, in the seventeenth century, it was officially incorporated into the samurai code of ethics and was systemized to the point that all individualistic aspects of the ritual suicide were erased. It was no longer an act of protest; it had become merely another element of the honor system of samurai society at large. The act of *seppuku* itself was watered down as the ritual was co-opted by the whole of samurai society. Where originally *seppuku* meant a slow, lingering death by loss of blood from the wound in one's gut, the mainstream samurai introduced the use of a second who would cut off the dying man's head from behind as soon as he thrust the blade into his abdomen. Later still, the liberating cut was made as soon as the convicted samurai moved to pick up his sword. The change of the place of *seppuku* in samurai society is indicative of the fundamental transformation from warrior to bureaucratic class which occurred in premodern Japan.

The Edo era saw the development of a social structure that is perhaps unique in world history. On the one hand, the various clans, or *han,* all had their bureaucratic headquarters in the city of Edo, while their true support was to be found out in the countryside, where they had established distinct territories. Although this system brought stability to Japanese society, it was not without its casualties. Like bureaucracies anywhere, the Japanese *han* had no qualms about firing unnecessary or unwanted employees, and in the Japanese case these men became the leaderless samurai, the *ronin*. These *ronin* massed in Edo and made their livings by working odd jobs in the city, where they mingled with their more fortunate samurai/businessmen counterparts.

It is in this world that Kobayashi's *Seppuku* takes place. In the opening scene we find a young *ronin* at the gate of a powerful *han* headquarters in Edo. He requests that he be allowed to use the entranceway, "a place of honor," in order to commit *seppuku*. He goes on to explain that he cannot continue living a life without honor and so he would prefer to die an honorable samurai death at their gate instead.

This confounded the bureaucratic, business-minded samurai, who were torn between feelings of empathy for a fellow samurai fallen on hard times, on the one hand, and by their reluctance to allow a messy suicide at their gate—no matter how honorable it might be—on the other. But the truth is that at this time in Edo this technique was being widely used by desperate *ronin* as a way to blackmail the powerful *han*. The vexed businessmen (samurai) could only resolve such cases by giving the *ronin* money and asking them to leave.

This trend had gone on for some time before the samurai/businessmen decided that to continue to compromise with such *ronin* would only taint the honor of the clan. Therefore, it was decided that no matter how messy and unpleasant it may be, they would make this *ronin* actually commit *seppuku* at their gate.

The Japanese personality can be analyzed at two levels: the level of *tatemae* (the ceremonial or ideal) and that of *honne* (roughly, the "real"). These two are usually kept in balance in everyday life, but when a critical situation arises, the *tatemae* is abandoned in favor of the *honne*. In this case, the crisis was brought about by the *ronin*'s blackmailing practices. When his bluff is called and he is told to commit suicide, the *honne* of the desperate *ronin*, as well as that of his tormentors, is revealed. The *han* samurai's *honne* is that of a butcher, while that of the *ronin* is dominated by the simple want of money. When the situation is bared so blatantly, the powerful side crushes its victim.

The tragedy of Kobayashi's *Seppuku*, then, is that of the butchering of a lone individual by the immense strength of a big organization.

The culminating point of the tragedy comes when it is revealed that the *ronin*'s sword, the very symbol of a samurai's honor, while appearing on the surface (the level of *tatemae*) to be intact, is in reality only equipped with a bamboo blade befitting a child's toy—it is a symbolic relic of the *ronin*'s lost honor.

The situation having come to this, the poor *ronin* had no choice but to disembowel himself with the symbol of his ruined honor and to die like a miserable mouse in the clutches of a miserable torturer. Instead of allowing the *ronin* to die a graceful and quick death, the cruel samurai/businessmen force him to commit archaic *seppuku:* the style involving two perpendicular slashes, one horizontally across the waist and one vertically cut down from the abdomen. This style results in a gaping cross-shaped wound without any honor for the suffering *ronin*. It was the cross of a pathetic death.

The movie *Seppuku,* and the miserable death of the *ronin* it depicted so graphically and realistically, strangely enough also symbolizes the suicidal end of the *chanbara* movie tradition. This realism is clearly a product of Kurosawa's influence. Kobayashi's *Seppuku* was released in 1962. Kurosawa's *Seven Samurai* was released in 1954. This period of eight years was the denouement of the *chanbara* tradition.

The fading away referred to at the end of *The Seven Samurai* was doubly tragic in that it marked not only the end of Kurosawa's brilliant genius, but also the end of the samurai movie genre itself. Kobayashi's *Seppuku* was the final period capping the long *chanbara* narrative. It is interesting to note that from this time on samurai movies in general declined and finally faded away entirely from the movie screens of Japan. It was the end of an era in Japanese film history. Japanese society had arrived at a point where the nostalgic viewing of the Bakumatsu period, of the conflict between the Light and the Darkness, between stability and effort and aspiration, had become unnecessary.

3
The Multi-layered Nature of the Tradition of Acting in Japanese Cinema

Tadao Sato

ONE OF THE characteristics of contemporary Japanese culture is the maintenance of a certain balance between ancient Japanese tradition and the modern culture that has been transmitted from the West. Traditional culture and modern Western culture coexist in Japan. This can be seen in the various styles of acting in Japanese cinema.

Those who want to become actors in cinema often begin by being trained in the theater. If one were to make a broad generalization, one might say that while one class of actors was born out of the classical traditional theater, another class developed under the influence of Western theater. It should be recognized, however, that as far as traditional acting in Japan is concerned, there are several streams, such as, for example, Noh drama, the forms of which have evolved under the patronage of the warrior class from the fourteenth century onward, and Kabuki, the forms of which developed under the patronage of the city or merchant class during the seventeenth century. The differences between these two schools of acting are as great as the differences between, for example, Greek theater and Shakespeare. In addition, one should mention that there are numerous actors who, while influenced by the acting techniques of the West, can be divided into those who practice modern European techniques and those who imitate Hollywood models. At the same time, both approaches are woven into traditionally Japanese modes of acting, thereby creating a variety of streams of acting. All of these can be seen in various acting groups, each of which is quite different in nature from the other. It must be noted that in Japan no one school of acting has ever dominated all others. Therefore, the cinema studios have been able to choose their actors from among these various approaches according to popularity and specific aesthetic criteria. Consequently, several styles could be present in one production at the same time.

One actor of Noh drama who often appears on the screen is Sakao Kanze. It must be said that, in general, the techniques of Noh have had little influence on Japanese cinema. However, this is not to say that its influence has not sometimes been strongly felt. For example, when Akira Kurosawa made *Throne of Blood (Tsuchigumo)* in 1957, he required his actors, Toshiro Mifune and Isuzu Yamada, to perform in a style that is close to the style of performance in Noh drama. In the same way, when Kenji Mizoguchi made his *Ugetsu* in 1953, he required the actress Machiko Kyo to perform according to the acting style of Noh drama. Even though Machiko Kyo had no background in Noh, she was eventually successful in creating an atmosphere that resembles that to be found in Noh drama. When Yasujiro Ozu first approached his favorite actor, Chisu Kasa, about an important role, he said to him: "You are always expressing too much with your face. I would like you to stop that and try to show me a face that is like a mask of Noh drama." Even though it is not clear to what degree Ozu intended to introduce Noh into his preferred acting technique, it is quite clear that he generally requested from his actors a definite calm and slow pace of acting, and this is easy to explain if one considers that he may have learned from Noh to ask his actors every so often to act in a state of motionlessness. In fact, in his film *Late Spring (Banshun)*, made in 1949, he depicts a performance in a Noh theater. Thus, even though the examples are few, one sees that the performing style of Noh drama has had some influence on Japanese cinema.

The movie actors who were trained in Kabuki are numerous. They include such great stars of period film as Matsunosuke Ogami, Chiekura Kataoka, Utaemon Ichikawa, Kanjuro Arashi, Kazuo Hasegawa, Nishikinosuke Yorozuya, and Kaizo Ichikawa. In order to become an actor in the Kabuki theater, one had to become the disciple of a particular star. The same custom was followed in the studios where period films were produced. As a consequence, those who trained as film actors as disciples of some of these great masters received in an indirect manner a strong influence from Kabuki.

Kabuki is a form of theater in which acting is highly formalized. This particular style of performance seems to be far removed from what we would call realism. However, in cinema, those actors who came from the Kabuki tradition somehow watered down the highly formalized aspects of acting to the point that they were able to perform in a manner close to what could be called realism. In spite of this, it is still quite possible to see the kind of influence that Kabuki had on their acting. This is especially evident in the case of status consciousness. For example, when someone of high status talks to someone of low status, or vice versa, the status relationship is clearly expressed in the facial expression, in the way the actor carries himself, and in the tone of voice. When the actors of period film who were trained in the Kabuki tradition appeared on the screen as samurai, they had an attitude of extreme dignity. They were able, through a specific movement of the eyes, to look at others in a condescending manner, or to express forgiveness with a particular smile indicating generosity. In the same manner, it was possible to reprove other characters from an elevated position on a podium. They were thus able to express in strong terms their position of high authority. Even though many of the theatrical forms of Kabuki were adapted in order to create a stronger sense of realism in films, it is clear that if actors were to use the same techniques in a contemporary drama that worked so well in a period film, the effect would be anachronistic.

Toshiro Mifune has no connection with Kabuki. He made his film debut in 1947, after having received an extremely brief period of training at a studio from someone who had absolutely no experience in acting. In 1948, in Akira Kurosawa's *Drunken Angel (Yoidore Tenshi)*, he was able to depict extremely vividly the spirit of despair that prevailed among the youth of that time following Japan's defeat in World War II. His acting in this film made him famous. He was so convincing that audiences couldn't believe that he was acting, but rather felt that they were actually confronting someone who had gone absolutely mad. At this point, Kurosawa began to wonder whether he would be able to overcome the conservatism of period films, which until then had been under the strict influence of Kabuki, by using this type of actor, who was able to be vividly realistic in a historical drama. This line of thinking governed the creation of *Rashomon* in 1950 and *The Seven Samurai* in 1954. These two films are remarkable and revolutionary historical dramas because in them the mannerisms of Kabuki, which were responsible for the expression of a very strong consciousness of feudal social order, were completely absent. Toshiro Mifune also came to play in a large number of totally traditional period films, and he finally assimilated into his style all of the mannerisms that characterized the stars who were born into the Kabuki tradition, as one can see in later films such as *Yojimbo* in 1961 and *Tsubaki Sanjuro* in 1962.

Akira Kurosawa had Toshiro Mifune act as a samurai, and it is quite clear that in this acting there are numerous mannerisms that are extremely close to those found in the formalism of the stars who were trained in the Kabuki style. Toshiro Mifune exemplifies the fact that even those who have successfully tried to break away from formal tradition have eventually been swallowed up by it again.

One more aspect of Kabuki that is worth noting is that it is a kind of musical show that is of a very energetic, and at the same time orderless, nature. In the 1960s, part of the young generation of Shingeki, or "new drama" (which will be discussed later), reacted against Shingeki's realism; they formed a group called "underground theater." The new form of acting that they created had something of the feeling of Kabuki. It used lines from ordinary speech, which were often quite poetic. Also, rather than emphasizing the lines, this form of acting emphasized extraordinary actions or decoration and costume. Such elements came directly from Kabuki. All of those who started this underground form of theater were people who had had absolutely no training in Kabuki. They were, rather, people who were completely in love with the cinema and theater of the West. One of the leaders of this movement in Japanese acting was Shuji Terayama, who also made movies. The influence of Western films on his work is extremely clear. For example, in his 1974 movie, *Pastoral Hide and Seek (Den'en Shinsu)*, the clown scene shows Fellini's influence. However, one can also see in the type of acting and in the actors' costumes something of the presence of Kabuki in his films. It is impossible to think that Shuji Terayama had a particular liking for Kabuki, for it is quite evident that both he and all of the other members of the underground theater movement had nothing but scorn for the kind of feudalistic social order that one finds expressed in Kabuki. However, in contrast to the Noh drama, a form of art that belonged to the warrior class, Kabuki belonged to the townspeople. The tendency of the townspeople toward the nonrepression of the pleasure principle and toward decadence is expressed in Kabuki. Also, part of the spectacle that is prominent in Kabuki derives from popular rural forms of acting and from popular urban entertainments. Thus, the members of the underground group found in Kabuki a vigor that they felt had been lost by the school of realism, and they attempted to recreate that feeling in contemporary society. Shuji Terayama, even though he had no orthodox relationship with Kabuki, knew from his early experiences in the countryside that this was where he could pick up the elements of spectacle that appear in his work. Thus, one can say that his movies are Kabuki and that the actors who have come out of the underground group often portray attitudes and demonstrate forms of acting that are typical of the conventions of Kabuki and that find ways of manifesting themselves even in the art of people who have no conscious intention at all of transmitting that tradition. What is interesting to observe is that one of the most important concepts of Kabuki, an awareness of social order, is completely absent from the acting style of the underground group.

From the end of the nineteenth century to the 1920s, the dramatic form called Shimpa, or "new wave," was popular. It was strongly affected by the acting style of Kabuki. Film dramas of that general period used actors mainly from within the Shimpa school. Shimpa provided a popular style of film acting, particularly in melodramas dealing with the theme of lovers who cannot marry because of differences in social status, until the 1950s, when the representation of love scenes greatly changed. In the theater, the Shimpa dramatic form has become almost a thing of the past. However, in the same way that both Noh and Kabuki are still being performed, there is one theater that continues to present performances in the Shimpa style. Therefore, it is possible that a form of Shimpa could be adapted to cinema again. Furthermore, even though as a form of theater it has become virtually a thing of the past, the mood of resignation and melancholy that is its main characteristic still survives clearly in one of the two forms of popular song. Therefore, one can say that Shimpa is still present in contemporary cinema through the medium of popular songs.

Shingeki, or "new drama," incorporates a style of acting that is completely realistic and that fundamentally differs from the highly formalized modes of acting that one finds in both Kabuki and Shimpa. Shingeki arose due to the introduction of Western theater to Japan at the beginning of the twentieth century, and it has become today the most widespread single style of acting in Japan. It incorporates acting techniques and theories proposed by Stanislavsky and the Actors' Studio and has absorbed aspects of modern European theater, especially from Russia, France, Germany, and Scandinavia. At first, to see Japanese actors in Western clothing was regarded as very strange, and Shingeki was regarded as a kind of performance to be appreciated by a small group of intellectuals who were enamored of Western culture. However, from about 1910 on, Japanese authors began to write many comedies for Shingeki, and to it was applied a technique of acting that expressed in a realistic manner the life of contemporary Japanese. In the 1920s, a large number of theatrical groups of the Shingeki movement were influenced by left-wing ideology. For this reason, Shingeki actors were able to have discussions of an ideological and intellectual nature that one would not expect from cinema stars. Furthermore, they were able to perform roles representing modern individualistic people very different from the type of popular representations characteristic of the aforementioned Shimpa or "new wave" acting style.

During the 1930s, after the left-wing theatrical movement had been the object of suppression on the part of the police, a large number of actors from the Shingeki movement went into cinema, where they reinforced the realism that was characteristic of Japanese films at the time. They played an important role in making possible the expression of intellectual content. The type of role that they performed in cinema belonged mostly to supporting actors, since depicting beautiful men and women and entertaining the audience were not strong priorities within the Shingeki movement.

Many of the stars of the so-called contemporary drama cinema arose out of nowhere and often took American cinema as their model of acting. A great star of the 1920s, one who became the main actor in several movies made by Yasujiro Ozu in the 1930s, was Tokihiko Okada. He was one of the first actors who became popular because of their Americanized manner. It was thought then that a certain way of smoking, a certain way of wearing a soft hat, and—first and foremost —a certain gentleness with women were typically American. However, at the time, these ways of behaving were negatively viewed by conservatives as adolescent.

In the 1930s, actors such as Kamibara Ken and Toshinobu Sawake sometimes appeared to be figures directly from American cinema. Yet at other times, they seemed like actors who had come straight out of the Shimpa movement. The period during which they were popular— the middle 1930s—was the time when American cinema was at its most popular in Japan. Their Americanized manner was thought to be smart and modern. It was, therefore, highly appreciated. Their gentleness and openness with women and the way they spoke to women were particularly appreciated by young people, who were living in a society where free social interaction between men and women was still regarded negatively. However, at the time of World War II, the government decided that love scenes in film belonged to the enemy—the United States or England—and therefore these scenes were strongly repressed. As a result, these Americanized stars became unable to present a positive attitude toward women. Consequently, their style of acting at that time became much closer to that of the Shimpa style.

In the period after World War II, the top star of the 1960s, Yujiro Ishihara, typified the performers who became popular because of their Americanized manner on the screen. At first, he was perceived as a Japanese James Dean; later he performed in jazz dramas and boxing movies. Finally, his image became like that of John Wayne and Steve McQueen: a tough fighter who could also be involved in romantic love scenes. At the same time, however, he was distinctly non-American. For example, whereas in American cinema, we expect the hero to have a sense of humor and to use that humor to solve the problems that he faces, Yujiro Ishihara displayed an extraordinary seriousness. He also had the ability—which was connected to the Shimpa movement—to represent a certain type of sentimentality like that found in the melancholic songs. In Japan, displaying an "American" manner on screen meant behaving in a jolly and open manner like an American youth. In order for a middle-aged actor to resemble a Westerner, he had to behave in a polished manner, like the Japanese perception of an English gentleman. This, in fact, is what Yujiro Ishihara did as he entered middle age.

During the same period—the 1960s—*yakuza* movies came into fashion. The style of performance in *yakuza* films was derived from the esthetics of Kabuki. Until the 1950s, stars who were considered Americanized and stars who were expected to perform according to the models of Kabuki were thought to be two entirely different types of actor. However, by the 1960s, it did not seem surprising to replace one with the other. An Americanized actor like Yujiro Ishihara could also perform in *yakuza* films. After the period when *yakuza* films were in such demand, the most famous of the *yakuza* stars, Ken Takakura, began playing roles that depicted him as a perfectly good citizen. His image became close to that of the American "tough guy."

Thus it is clear that Japanese film actors come from diverse backgrounds. Their techniques are grounded in art forms that are extremely different from one another. Until the 1950s, the cinema studios tended to rely on specialized actors, with different studios representing different acting styles. For example, studios that specialized in period films tended to be organized around a number of stars who came from the Kabuki tradition. However, from the 1960s onward, especially since television began to use actors coming from different acting backgrounds, the codes governing the techniques came to be completely blurred.

It is not that we have a single, unified tradition, but rather that we are the bearers of multifarious traditions and that as we attempt to have them coexist, we may decide to emphasize selective aspects of this multilayered tradition. For example, at the time of nationalism, the courageous and self-sacrificing attitude of the samurai was widely represented on screen, and male actors were seen to wear expressions of stoic courage. The stars of period film, whose models of acting were born from the tradition of Kabuki, were widely popular. After the defeat of World War II, the period was one of self-reflection, melancholy, and sentimentality, moods that were repeatedly depicted on the screen. I think that this type of acting was a result of an improvement brought about through the realism of Shingeki and applied to the style of acting that came out of the Shimpa school. Finally, in the 1950s, after the great upheaval following World War II, the great film masters, Mizoguchi, Ozu, and Kurosawa, attempted to borrow the formalism of acting that one finds in Noh drama. This particular technique used the tradition of the spirit of the warrior class but approached it from a completely different avenue from that of the nationalists. It may be said that this came from a desire to focus on the Japanese sense of pride, which had not been destroyed by the temporary experience of defeat.

In these pages, I have attempted to trace the traditional currents of acting represented by Japanese cinema actors. My treatment of this subject has been necessarily broad and brief. However, even with such a broadly sketched picture, it is possible to understand that if one chooses to use the term "traditional" to describe Japanese acting, one has to recognize that this tradition is made up of extremely complex layers. It is impossible to say that any one of these truly represents *the* tradition. It is also quite impossible to discount a particular tradition because it has been borrowed from a foreign source. The Shingeki style, for example, which started as a copy from the West, has had an eighty-year history in Japan, and, as it has given birth to a number of actors who have supported an extremely Japanese type of cinema (for example, Kenji Mizoguchi, Yasujiro Ozu, and Akira Kurosawa), one may say that it has become a part of the Japanese tradition.

4
Japanese Film Genres

AUDIE BOCK

WEDNESDAY EVENING, 5:45 P.M., autumn. In a central metropolitan office building, Suzuki rises from his desk, crammed in closely with the desks of three colleagues. He stretches and jokes with them while putting on the jacket of his dark blue suit over his white shirt and dark tie. He tops this with a dark, beltless raincoat and gathers up his black Naugahyde attaché case.

Suzuki walks with upright posture and wastes no movements. He wears his hair moderately close-cropped and makes no attempt to disguise his mid-thirties crows' feet and clean-shaven, sagging jawline. A postwar baby-boom product, Suzuki now has a wife and family of his own to return home to. His radical student days in the late 1960s are an episode he'd rather forget, and he's grateful to have found a good stepladder position in a major corporation in spite of his hotheaded youth.

Out on the congested sidewalk, thronging with men dressed exactly as Suzuki is dressed, rather than drinking with them for an hour or so, he bids goodbye to his colleagues in the dusk. But instead of proceeding into the cavernous din of the subway station, to squeeze into a steaming train car with hundreds of his millions of co-workers heading home to the suburbs, he follows along a side street, skirting the overhead train tracks. The space under the tracks is crammed with tiny shops cosmetic stores, noodle shops, tobacconists. Suzuki continues alone, until he comes to an unprepossessing door set back from the street. Beside the door is a "one sheet" poster showing a woman in braids and a schoolgirl's sailor blouse. The air brushing disguises her age; she looks about fifteen. Her tongue pokes coyly from her mouth, and her white middy blouse is pulled down over her shoulder. Emblaz-

53

oned over her breasts are large, splashy red characters proclaiming: "Wayward schoolgirls of Aoyama." Suzuki glances up and down the street, then gives the cashier his money and ducks into the theater.

In 1983 the most popular Japanese film was a tear-jerker about sled dogs abandoned in Antarctica, *The South Pole Story (Nankyoku Monogatari)*. But this was because the sponsoring giant conglomerates made all their employees attend by simply docking the ticket price from their pay. In terms of production, the greatest number of films made in Japan were pornographic movies, so Suzuki-san's taste does not represent an isolated or abnormal phenomenon. In a country where the average person sees only slightly more than one movie per year, if the average in question is a male attending a domestically produced film, that film is most likely to be a porno film. How can this be going on in the country that gave us films like *Seven Samurai, Ugetsu, Floating Clouds,* and *Tokyo Story* and directors like Akira Kurosawa, who is indisputably the greatest living, next to Ingmar Bergman and Federico Fellini? Japan in the 1950s was a nation of moviegoers. Television had yet to make deep inroads into Japanese life, and other diversions were still too expensive for the average Japanese. A flourishing studio system consisting of five major organs of production, distribution, and exhibition supported thousands of contract employees. Among these were superior talents in acting, such as Toshiro Mifune and Hideko Takamine, playing a wide variety of challenging roles, and directors such as Kenji Mizoguchi, Akira Kurosawa, Mikio Naruse, and Yasujiro Ozu, all of whom were in their prime.

Japan was still in its true postwar era of reconstruction and spiritual revitalization, following its 1945 defeat in the Pacific War. The new values of freedom, equality, and the emancipation of women were being taken seriously and were finding expression in the arts. But it was not until Kurosawa's 1950 film *Rashomon,* a story of four different, conflicting, and self-serving eyewitness accounts of a rape/murder incident, was presented at the Venice International Film Festival and took the top prize that the Japanese film industry achieved world rank. *Rashomon* was not, as many still believe, the first Japanese film ever made; it was merely the first Japanese film permitted to compete internationally in the postwar era. Kurosawa was still a young man, though already established as a top director with his star, Mifune, who had already played a tough gangster, a stoical physician, and an idealistic police inspector prior to his appearance in *Rashomon* as a bragging bandit.

Far better established were directors like Mizoguchi, Naruse, and Ozu, who had acquired devoted followings and won top prizes in Japan in the 1930s. After *Rashomon*'s international award, Mizoguchi's 1952 story of the decline of a court lady, *The Life of Oharu*, and his 1953 tale of the potter and the ghost princess, *Ugetsu*, won the top prizes at Venice. A glittering film, called *Gate of Hell*, by an old established director, Teinosuke Kinugasa, who had made his best films in the 1920s, went on to win the U.S. Academy Award in 1954. In short, the fifties were a time of a wealthy, self-confident film industry that could allow artists to make what they wanted the way they wanted to in Japan. Bolstered by international awards, audience support was at its peak. It was Japan's golden age of movies.

But the numerous Japanese films creating sensations abroad did not all express Japanese popular taste. *Rashomon,* the film that sparked the foreign interest in Japan, was so unsuccessful on first release at home that it was pulled from distribution. Apparently no one could understand the story because the ending did not reveal who, in fact, was in the right. It was not until after "Grand Prix" became a household word in Japan that the audience made a second attempt to comprehend a story that was not linear and whose point was that truth is relative to self-interest. This phenomenon of quality in the arts requiring foreign endorsement in order to succeed at home remains a prevalent current of Japanese taste.

Some of the most solid successes at home were films by directors whose work was not shown outside Japan. Yasujiro Ozu's 1953 masterpiece, *Tokyo Story,* a modest study of aging parents visiting their busy grown-up children in Tokyo, only to be shunted aside by all but their widowed daughter-in-law, was not seen in Europe and the United States until the 1970s. Mikio Naruse's *Floating Clouds,* the story of a young woman's obsession with an irretrievable love affair she had with a Japanese forestry official in southeast Asia during the war, was the most acclaimed film of 1955, yet its introduction abroad has had to wait until the 1980s. Even Kurosawa's most imitated work, *Seven Samurai* (1954), was not released in its uncut three-and-a-half-hour version until the 1980s in the United States.

Does this mean Japanese taste and Western taste in movies are irreconcilably different? Not really. People everywhere recognize a masterpiece when they see one. *Tokyo Story, Floating Clouds,* and the uncut *Seven Samurai* all have their staunch devotees in the United States today. But there are certain tendencies that can be distinguished.

It remains an incontrovertible fact that the domestic dramas of Ozu and Naruse will never gain the Western audience of the opulent period films of Mizoguchi and Kurosawa, and none will ever come close to the cult for the samurai duel films like Kurosawa's *Yojimbo,* Masaki Kobayashi's *Harakiri,* or Hideo Gosha's *Goyokin,* without which Western directors like Sergio Leone and Clint Eastwood would never have gotten started. Nor it is accidental that Kurosawa's *Seven Samurai* and *Hidden Fortress* (1958) were cut for their first U.S. theatrical releases. The average Japanese has always had a great capacity to relish dramatic detail over a period of many hours—the classical theater forms of Noh and Kabuki still take a whole day to be seen properly.

The Japanese have always enjoyed seeing movies that are about people like themselves: middle-class, struggling with the eternal difficulties of marriage, family relationships, illnesses, and death. Moreover, mundane complications, which are the dramatic meat of the Ozu and Naruse films, need not, for the Japanese mentality, end in happiness forever after. Not one of the films cited here has a happy ending. Even Ozu's *Late Spring* (1949), about a girl who finally makes up her mind to get married, leaves the viewer with the sad image of her widowed father peeling a pear-apple at home alone, followed by wavelets breaking on the shoreline. There is no Japanese equivalent of *The Graduate,* which shows the elopement of a girl with her mother's gigolo as a victorious happy ending, the final shot showing the grinning couple on a public bus. Japanese dramatic sensibilities recognize that the aberrant situation precludes happiness, but this does not mean that sad stories can't be enjoyed. The best indicator of fifties' popular taste appears in the 1952 Naruse film *Mother,* where two young women enthuse about going to the movies in order to have a good cry.

Obviously, the situation in the Japanese film industry is quite different today from what it was in the fifties, when there were no porno films and the movies were the premiere family entertainment. There has been a serious, even devastating, decline in the popularity of the domestic product. The record-breaking box-office success of *The Godfather* in 1971 heralded an age when the Japanese movie would permanently take a back seat to the Hollywood product, a reversal of the relationship in the fifties.

In 1970, with *Dodeskaden,* Kurosawa had his first box-office failure. He fled Japan and would never be able to work again without foreign financing. Daiei, the studio that had produced *Rashomon* and

JAPANESE FILM GENRES 57

Ugetsu, among many other masterpieces, went bankrupt in 1971. Ozu, Mizoguchi, and Naruse were all dead, but even if they had lived, they would not have had the freedom to work the way they wanted to. Of the four remaining studios, most were surviving not on their film grosses, but on their income from real estate, department stores, and railroads. One of the oldest names in Japanese cinema history, however, the Nikkatsu Studios, was on the verge of devoting itself exclusively to porno films.

In 1983 a Japan that once made hundreds of films per year for new weekly double features in thousands of theaters, produced barely more than a hundred movies. By far the greatest volume production was the Nikkatsu porno contribution, totalling fifty-five pictures, but when the term porno (*poruno*) is used in Japan, it describes a genre that only vaguely resembles the standard fare at Pussycat Theaters in the United States. When Suzuki-san ducks into the dark recesses of a cramped sidestreet porno house in Tokyo or Osaka, or Sapporo or Fukuoka, he will indeed see a low-budget "skin" picture, but there the resemblance to Western hard core porno ends. Japanese porno is all soft-core, showing breasts and bottoms but no pubic hair and no sex organs in action. The dramatic rhythm relies not on the number of "come" scenes, as in American porno, but largely on the intricacy of the violence being perpetrated against the female sex objects (whipping, hanging, and cigarette burns are popular methods; the brutal rape of young virgins is a standard). All in all, Japanese porno films are pretty ridiculous, hardly deserving to be classed in the genre at all. Shohei Imamura portrayed their absurdity to perfection with his 1968 film adaptation of Akiyaki Nozaka's novel, *The Pornographers*.

It is all a grand convention. The iconoclastic director Nagisa Oshima sought to overthrow the sham by making *In the Realm of the Senses* (1976) a true hard-core film. It had to be developed, printed, and edited in France and reimported to Japan as a foreign film, with French subtitles over the Japanese dialogue. All the sex scenes disappeared in a white haze of censors' air-brushings. Oshima was taken to court, not for the film, which had been fully censored, but for the pornographic content of the published screenplay. Pushing his case to the National Supreme Court, over an agonizing four years of trials, he was found innocent, but he did not succeed in overturning the legal attitude toward pornography in Japan. His great success lay in the fact that he made a disturbing movie that made him a worldwide sensation (thirteen screenings at the Cannes International Film Festival) and because he made the first porno film to be shown at "women's film" theaters in Japan (as a prestigious French import) and hence the first "women's porno" film. Most of the Japanese response to the film came from women.

In fact there is no legal definition of pornography, Oshima found. The notion that the Japanese nation may not be permitted to see pubic hair—hence the elaborate blacking out of the privates of every imported *Playboy* magazine's "Playmate of the Month" photo—is nowhere written down in Japanese law. Any hard-core pornographic film produced in Japan would be seized at the developing lab (only one major laboratory handles motion-picture film) by the police, without any need of a warrant. This explains why Oshima had to go to France for the financing and development of his film, and it also explains why busloads of Japanese male tourists in San Francisco head straight for the Mitchell Brothers' porno theaters.

So what is Suzuki-san doing in that silly soft-core theater? Exercising his imagination, no doubt. As a typical breadwinner, he gets virtually no sexual stimulation from his wife, whose vital interests lie in her children and strictly female pursuits such as flower-arrangement, knitting, or classical dance. The Suzukis' social life is entirely separate, so there is no room for romance in their busy schedules. In fact, an office worker who is known to spend time alone with his wife would be thought a little strange, while regular attendance at porno movies would be accepted as a healthy male pastime—a source of relaxation, as a Japanese economics professor (who makes it a practice) recently explained.

And Mrs. Suzuki? Does she go to movies? Most assuredly not, with one possible exception. In the fifties it was the women who provided the bulk of the support for the film industry. Directors like Naruse and Ozu made their "home dramas" for a loyal female clientele who came regularly to see how Hideko Takamine, Setsuko Hara, or Kuniko Miyake would handle her next domestic crisis. In Naruse's case, his films were sometimes double-billed with a "men's film" or an action drama by a director like Kurosawa to ensure that both sexes would attend the theaters that week. The "home drama" form, developed by Ozu, in which several generations appeared in the same story, usually in the same household, was one that particularly well reflected the everyday concerns of the average Japanese. *Tokyo Story*, for example, shows the relationship among the three generations crumbling as ambitious children leave their provincial birthplace to make their lives in larger cities. But the home drama made a quick departure from the big screen with the advent of television. By the mid-sixties the housewife no longer needed to go downtown to see her favorite stars in her favorite quandaries. Stories of love, marriage, in-laws, accidents, disease, and death fill the daytime television hours to a saturation paralleling that in the West.

But there is one remaining representative of the "women's film" genre today. For a "Tora-san" movie Mrs. Suzuki just might bestir herself to the movie theater, particularly if it means an occasion to visit with an elderly mother or aunt. The twice-yearly phenomenon of this series called *Otoko wa tsuraiyo* ("It's tough being a man") features a bumbling but lovable bachelor uncle, Torajiro, who has an indulgent family in the working-class Shibamata section of Tokyo. He makes a haphazard living as a travelling salesman and always manages to fall in love with a damsel in distress who is far above his station in life. Never failing to involve his reliable if reluctant family, he always rescues the girl, who goes off with someone else. Tora-san is both romantic and ridiculous, squeaky clean and harmless. The formula provides an opportunity to raise contemporary social issues such as divorce, wife-beating and rape in a gentle, nonpolemical way. But no one has ever had his traditional values challenged by Tora-san: it firmly upholds the cohesive family system, women waiting on their husbands, in-laws, male siblings, and male children. Tora-san, who has now gone through more than twenty-five films since his first appearance in the late 1960s, is the last vestige of the woman's film and the last commercial movie support for the once-mighty Shochiku Studios, where Ozu and Naruse worked in the 1930s. Tora-san's popularity is an expression of nostalgia for old familial values that are very much threatened, if they exist at all, today. If Mrs. Suzuki goes to see any Japanese movies, it more than likely is a Tora-san movie she will see.

Poor Suzuki-san. Must we leave him to his cruel soft-core and cold wife? Surely he must have some fantasy heroes other than the greasy fellows in the porno films? Isn't Japan the source of the almighty samurai film and the enigmatic, noble *yakuza* gangster who subscribes to a similar code? True enough, the samurai was always there in Japanese film from the very first filmed Kabuki performances just after the turn of the century. Throughout the twenties, thirties, and forties, the samurai with his code of loyalty to his lord, and finally his emperor and country, was the most popular good guy in the men's action swordplay movie genre known as *chanbara*. But after the proscription of sword movies, and all period films under the Allied occupation of Japan until 1950, the reentry of the samurai into the popular film medium was accompanied by new values of humanism and individualism. Loyalty in the blind, unquestioning sense of the forty-seven loyal retainers who waited years in hiding to avenge their lord's death and then, to a man, committed suicide, had to be rejected as "feudalistic."

Kurosawa initiated a new samurai hero in *Seven Samurai* who had a selfless devotion not to a feudal lord but to humanity, the common folk, even if they weren't worth the effort. This humanistic value was in keeping with European, particularly Italian Neorealist themes, at the time. In Japan the critics took him to task for making the peasants, who are defended by the idealistic samurai, less attractive than Marxist doctrine would want them to be. The audience, however, does not seem to have been bothered by the portrayal of the peasants, finding the film most impressive due to its immense budget and two-year-long shooting schedule—an emphasis that still works in Japanese film promotion today.

By 1961, however, Kurosawa's samurai hero had become quite cynical. The unshaven *ronin* (masterless samurai) of *Yojimbo,* a scruffy, hard-drinking Toshiro Mifune, who gives a false name when questioned, helps the underdog only as part of a game in which he is the director of the show. Mifune is no longer the buffoon, as in *Seven Samurai,* but the superhero. Tadao Sato, in his book *Currents in Japanese Cinema,* suggests that the superhero "lone wolf" samurai became the leading figure in the downtown movie theaters along with the porno starlet because of demographics; families moved out to the suburbs and left the young bachelors alone in the city with the bar-hostesses. This of course would leave nothing for the young "office lady" but to patronize the foreign cinema, which she has done.

In the 1970s, however, the samurai disappears from the big screen altogether. Part of the reason, the production companies say, is the cost of doing period films. Kihachi Okamoto, director of such "lone samurai" classics as *Sword of Doom* and *Kill!* has a better explanation: "It's exactly like what director John Milius says happened to the Western. It went to television early on, and became overexposed on television." By the end of the 1960s there was nothing special about the idea of a samurai film, and the television production values were so bad, no one would think of going to the movie theater and paying money for what he could see at home for free.

Now in the 1980s we have the last samurai, Akira Kurosawa, trying

JAPANESE FILM GENRES   61

to buck the trend. By bringing the production values back to the samurai film, as in his *Kagemusha* (1980) and *Ran* (1985), he hopes to inspire the audience with the opulence of a historical authenticity that is totally lacking in the TV samurai dramas. With budgets that break the backs of the studios—*Kagemusha* cost six million dollars to make and broke all the box-office records in Japan, but that meant it brought in only thirteen million dollars—Kurosawa is going back to the oldest concerns of the samurai film. *Kagemusha* was a film about the nature of loyalty, or fealty to an individual lord. It had nothing to do with superheroes or humanism. *Ran* is about internal familial loyalties in a similar sixteenth-century wartime setting. People in Japan went to see *Kagemusha* out of curiosity: Who is this director, whose name is better known abroad than that of the emperor or the prime minister? But very few understood the film. The visual aspect of it has had to satisfy audiences both at home and abroad. It is doubtful that Kurosawa will be able to win back a permanent audience for the samurai film.

The reality of the Japanese cinema today is economic. The production values of the 1950s cannot be duplicated without budgets that are too large to be covered in the domestic market. The best filmmakers flee Japan—Kurosawa's financing for his last three films has been secured only by foreign involvement. Nagisa Oshima has completely abandoned Japan. *Merry Christmas Mr. Lawrence* (1983) was technically a New Zealand production, though it dealt with Japanese-Western relations in World War II. His next film will be written, produced, and filmed in France with no Japanese involved in it but himself.

The 1960s saw a brief sputter of independent production when Suzuki-san's generation were students and believed in film as a revolutionary medium. Now his generation doesn't go to the movies any more, so we cannot expect anything like a Mizoguchi film, or I'd venture to say, a Kurosawa film, to come from Japan in future.

What there may be in the future is a totally new genre: self-parody. There is a new sense of cynicism in Japan with its new wealth, loss of spiritual values, and criticism from abroad. A new group of young directors working independently from the old major studios, and scraping together the meagerest of budgets, is making films that laugh at Japanese manners and customs in the last few years. A film called *I am You, You are Me* or *Turnabout (Tenkosei)* pokes fun at sex differences, particularly in language, through the story of junior high school kids who accidentally switch identities, but not bodies. *Family Game*

(Kazoku Geemu) is a parody of the examination society, the Japanese need to achieve through school test scores, through the character of a tutor who acts like a gangster, but gets results, so the whole family allow themselves to be terrorized by him. *The Funeral (Osōshiki)* shows a Japanese family dealing with the overwhelming tradition of the funeral, one of the two most important ceremonies of Japanese life, as Nagisa Oshima showed in his 1970 film, *The Ceremony.* But this family in *The Funeral* doesn't know the procedures—they can't even sit on the floor. The movie laughs, gently, at the fact that these contemporary people are cut off from their traditional roots. All these films are intellectual films, wry in spirit, and not for the masses. There *is* no popular Japanese cinema anymore. Suzuki-san does not go to the movies, but his children, who are teenagers now, may soon, when they have outgrown *Star Wars,* start going to films like the new parodies.

5
Change in the Image of Mother in Japanese Cinema and Television

Tadao Sato

UNTIL THE mid-1950s, one of the popular genres in Japanese cinema was the *surechigai* melodrama. This genre is called *surechigai* (literally, "to pass by each other") because the following kind of incident occurs: Two lovers who are not allowed to marry meet and then separate. In order to stretch the story, there are many scenes in which the two separated lovers coincidentally appear near each other but, not realizing the other's presence, pass each other by. These kinds of emotional scenes keep the audience in suspense and help make the melodrama a commercial success (thus allowing for a sequel). In these kinds of movies, the main reason that the two lovers cannot marry is that they come from different societal classes and their families oppose their marriage. The biggest commercial success in Japanese film history was a *surechigai* melodrama entitled *Aizen Katsura*, which appeared in 1938. After Japan's defeat in World War II, however, it became difficult to produce movies that used this kind of plot. One reason was that, after the defeat and the subsequent occupation, Japanese people stopped considering status differences a reason for not allowing a marriage to occur. This was one indication of progress in the democratization of Japanese society. From 1945 to 1952, the American occupation forces transformed Japan from a militaristic society to a democratic one. Naturally, this changed Japanese patterns of behavior and therefore it also changed the way characters in Japanese films reacted to events. One example of this was the fact that love between persons from different social classes no longer could be considered a subject for tragedy.

During the 1930s a new genre, the salaryman movie, became popular. This kind of movie is about rather pitiful white-collar office workers who behave in extremely ingratiating ways toward their bosses.

In the 1950s, however, a new kind of salaryman drama, in which employees were shown as being able to control their good-natured employers, began to evolve. A comedy genre called "irresponsible series" appeared in which low-level employees ignore their supervisors and act in any manner they please.

Despite these new tendencies, many sentimental love stories were produced during the first seven or eight years after World War II. In 1953, however, there was a hit movie entitled *Kimi no Nawa* in which two lovers could not be united, not because of status differences, but because the woman was already married to another man. After *Kimi no Nawa,* sentimental love stories rapidly disappeared.

During the 1960s, the audience for Japanese film suddenly decreased. For that reason, Japanese film companies began to put more emphasis on eroticism and violence, thus driving away much of their female audience. Women turned instead to foreign films and television, and many Japanese actresses moved over to television.

The home drama, a television genre that depicts family life, became popular. Home drama as a genre actually developed first in the cinema. The 1950s was the golden age for cinematic home dramas, and television had only a minor influence on Japanese life.

Many great Japanese films were created by such directors as Yasujiro Ozu, Keisuke Kinoshita, and Mikio Naruse. The finest works of Ozu have a story line in which the family worries about the daughter's marriage. These stories begin with the marriage proposal and end with the marriage itself. Many other movies also end with the daughter's marriage. Compared with the movies, many television home dramas deal with the long years of a woman's life after her marriage.

Consequently, these television home dramas feature a middle-aged housewife as the heroine. The mother, who is the center of the drama, is of an age to have the supporting actor and actress as her children. In the 1970s, leading actresses aged forty to sixty became popular on television. Like the young melodrama film stars of that period, these older television actresses were shown as charming women in fancy clothing who enjoyed a carefree life-style. The houses these women lived in tended to be lively, with many rooms for the large family and for neighbors and relatives who visited frequently. The housewife-heroine assumed the role of managing this lively family. She was so busy that she had no time to be bored. Her impressive strength of character could be seen in her ability to ensure a caring and harmonious environment around her. Home dramas dealing with self-employed families were particularly frequent in the 1970s; in these dramas, the heroine is able to show her ability to supervise others skillfully.

From the end of the 1940s to the end of the 1950s, this kind of popular middle-aged heroine appeared in the "mother drama," such as the ones which featured Aiko Mimasu. About thirty such mother dramas featuring this actress were produced during this period. Some examples of these films based on the theme of motherly love are: *Haha* (1948), *Haha Sannin* (1949), and *Haha Kōbai* (1949). One could also mention films starring Yuko Mochizuki that appeared from 1950 to 1960 and could be called realistic mother dramas. Some examples of Mochizuki's films are: *Nihon no Higeki* (1953), *Ofukuro* (1955), and *Niguruma no Uta* (1959).

Both Yuko Mochizuki and Aiko Mimasu were popular actresses who showed the misery of middle-aged mothers. Although it may be rude to say so, neither of these actresses was a great beauty, and both of them lacked charm. They left an impression of women who had struggled. Their appeal was in their tragic visage, which showed that they had been sacrificing all of their lives in order to rear their children. If the children forget about their mothers' struggles and instead do whatever they please, the mothers show an intense feeling of resentment and discouragement. Actually, these melodramatic mother dramas draw sympathy from the typical Japanese mothers in the audience who share the same feelings, and they make Japanese young people appreciate their own mothers' struggles.

The basis of morality for the Japanese is filial piety. Although this hasn't changed since the Edo period, "moral teaching" lessons *(shushin)* were discontinued in the public schools after World War II. Because of this, Japanese parents still regret that their children have lost the feeling of filial piety. Some people think that what enforces Japanese feelings of filial piety is not the *shushin* but the complaining Japanese mother. Japanese mothers often remind their children how much they've suffered for them. Children who hear those kinds of statements grow up feeling guilty towards their mothers, and they fear causing their mothers sadness. The image of a complaining mother became a typical one, an image of almost mythic proportions, through its frequent use in stories, plays, and films. Even if their own mother is not a complaining type, Japanese children have this image of a complaining mother set in their mind, and they tend to empathize more with the suffering type. Yuko Mochizuki and Aiko Mimasu portrayed this kind of suffering, resentful mother.

Until 1960, it was necessary for a middle-aged movie actress to give this impression of having suffered. Home drama movies generally ended with the daughter's marriage, and the main attraction of the mother drama was the suffering, complaining mother. Therefore, the basic assumption in Japanese movies of that time was that a woman could be attractive until she was married, but after marriage, she had no choice but to pursue a life of incessant suffering.

In this sense, in the latter part of the 1960s, the portrayal of beautiful and happy middle-aged women in television home dramas was a truly revolutionary phenomenon in the history of Japanese popular culture. This new kind of story emphasized the idea that women could enjoy their life after marriage. While mothers in movies lived only for their children, mothers in television began to assert the fact that there were other sources of happiness in their lives. Hit television shows of self-employed families, like *Arigato* (1972) and *Terauchi Kantaro Ikka* (1974) featured housewives who occupied such interesting positions in the family that they had no time to complain.

Sorezore no Aki (1975) is the story of a family undergoing a period of so many problems that it seemed as if the family would be torn apart. It could be held together only by the strength and caring of the housewife. In earlier films, Japanese housewives were shown as sacrificing themselves for their families; in the more modern examples, such as *Sorezore no Aki*, the housewife was required to display leadership.

Another example of a story in which the family is about to split up is *Kishibe no Album*. One of the reasons for the family's situation was the mother's extramarital love affair. The fact that this television housewife had an affair rather than complaining about rearing children meant that she could no longer carry out her leadership role in the family.

In 1976, a television drama entitled *Kumo no Jutan* appeared. This story was noteworthy in that it created a new type of woman. *Kumo no Jutan* was the true story of the first female Japanese pilot. The heroine, played by Yoko Asaji, won the trust and help of others, not by suffering and struggling, but by her lively and positive nature. With these attributes, she was able to overcome various difficulties. This kind of positive image of a woman had not appeared in movies but rather was the inspiration of television.

Viewers' surveys revealed that a surprisingly large number of people watched the television program *Fufu* (1978), which dealt with the old theme of the conflict between mothers-in-law and daughters-in-law. This theme had appeared previously in family tragedies like *Kimi no Nawa* (1953) and in stories of traditional merchant families like the ones in *Onna no Issho* (1953), directed by Kanehito Shindo, and *Bonchi* (1960), directed by Kon Ichikawa. All of these films had the theme of the bride's ability or inability to endure her mother-in-law's bad temper. All mothers-in-law at that time were shown as having this bad image. Japanese mothers-in-law at that time still tended to be tyrannical toward their daughters-in-law. The only kinds of films that would be popular were those that fit the convention of the younger actress taking the role of the suffering wife and the older actress taking the role of the irrational, ill-tempered mother-in-law.

If a young actress and a middle-aged actress were featured together, and if one had to be given a villain's role, that role invariably fell to the middle-aged actress. In television home drama this convention fell apart because the middle-aged women were often more popular than the younger actresses. In the home drama *Fufu*, the mother-in-law, played by Hisano Yamaoka (age fifty-two) was more of a star than the bride, played by Mikiko Otonashi (age twenty-nine). There was, therefore, no convention for making Hisano Yamaoka more of a villain in the story. The mother-in-law in the story was so strong-tempered that the wife could not endure it, but the mother-in-law was not just blindly following a convention of nagging the daughter-in-law for no reason. Indeed, she had her own reasons for doing so, and she said freely what she wanted to say. This kind of behavior on the part of the mother-in-law had a cathartic effect on the audience. The appeal of this home drama was that Hisano Yamaoka was able to maintain a charming and attractive presence while playing the role of the nagging mother-in-law. Even though the mother-in-law was quite strong-tempered, the viewer felt sympathy with her because the character was so persuasive. (Of course, the fact that Ms. Yamaoka was a star was not the reason the character was so persuasive.)

In Japanese tradition, it was assumed that the oldest son would take care of the elderly parents, but after World War II, the Japanese family system fell apart, along with this assumption. In addition, the population became more dispersed, and the housing situation worsened. There were more and more Japanese households in which it was unclear who would care for elderly parents. It was up to each individual wife to decide whether she would care for her mother-in-law. This gave relatively more strength to the wife, and the mother-in-law began to be more obsequious to her as wives began to consider mothers-in-law a burden. Because of this change in conditions, Hisano Yamaoka's nonobsequious assertiveness drew sympathy from the audience.

In 1983, the hit of the year was a television drama entitled *Oshin*, in which the mother-in-law was a more empathetic character than the wife. The story, based on a script by Sugako Hashide, is about the life of a woman who was born during the Meiji period (1866–1912) in a poor village in the Tohoku (northern) region. From a young age, she could not go to school, and she suffered many hardships. Finally, she became the owner of a store. This story was a revival of the theme of the suffering mother.

Oshin was so popular because it aroused a feeling of nostalgia even among members of the younger generation who had not experienced such mother dramas. Nevertheless, *Oshin* was, in some ways, completely different from the older mother dramas. Although Oshin endured the typical kinds of conservative pressures, she also opened the way for new possibilities in life, as had the female characters in *Kumo no Jutan*. Contemporary audiences did not feel the sense of guilt toward this mother heroine that they had felt toward the older mother dramas. Oshin struggled, but she never gave up her pursuit of happiness. Aiko Mimasu, in the older mother dramas, had a miserable, resentful appearance as a result of her suffering. Nobuko Otowa, who played the older Oshin, impressed the young people in the audience with her ability to achieve dignity, social status, and fortune as the result of her suffering. The younger generation may feel envious toward Oshin because they themselves are part of such an organized social system that they do not know how to endure suffering.

Because of the dramatic differences in these two eras, Japanese parents cannot explain their younger days to their own children. The grandchild cannot imagine the grandparents' childhood memories, and the grandparents cannot use their lives as a lesson for their grandchildren. The result is that the grandparents are ignored and silenced. One reason for *Oshin*'s popularity is that the heroine of the drama may have been able to communicate what contemporary grandparents could not.

Critical reviews of *Oshin* were not favorable, especially among the critics who value high artistic quality in television dramas. However, *Oshin* was a popular success not only in Japan but also in other Asian countries. This was probably the first time that a drama that was not based on heroic tales of samurai or male karate experts but instead focused on the life of a Japanese woman had reached this level of popularity in Asian countries.

Unfortunately, in the Japanese cinema of the past ten years, no comparable heroines have been created.

PART 2
India

Indian Cinema

INDIA IS by far the largest film-producing country in the world. In 1985 alone it produced more than nine hundred films. The influence that Indian films continue to exert over the thought and imagination of the vast masses is both pervasive and profound. As is true in most other countries, India has a tradition of high art and popular art in the domain of cinema. If the names of Satyajit Ray, Mrinal Sen, Adoor Gopalakrishnan, G. Aravindan, Nirad Mohapatra, and Kumar Shahani are closely connected with the artistic cinema, a whole galaxy of other names—Raj Kapoor, Dilip Kumar, Dev Anand, Guru Dutt, V. Shantaram, B. R. Chopra, Manmohan Desai—are intimately linked to the tradition of popular cinema. In any discussion of cultural identity and Indian cinema, both of these traditions need to be examined.

Whenever we talk of popular Indian films, our attention is immediately drawn toward the Bombay Hindi film. This is because it is in Bombay that the popular Indian film took on its characteristic shape and style and began to exercise a hold on the cinema-going public both inside and outside India. Although we should not lose sight of the fact that popular Indian films are also produced in large numbers in Tamil Nadu and Andhra Pradesh, I will confine myself here to the popular Bombay Hindi film.

Film critics, both in India and outside, have sometimes accused Bombay Hindi films of being puerile, melodramatic, sentimental, meretricious, and formulaic. All of these charges, artistically speaking, have much substance to them; however, it must also be conceded that these films offer a wonderful window onto the world of contemporary Indian culture. Nobody who is seriously interested in the study of contemporary Indian culture can afford to ignore the manifold riches of popular Hindi films.

The first Indian feature film, *Raja Harishchandra,* was produced in 1913. It was directed by D. G. Phalke, who is generally considered to be the father of Indian cinema. This film is based on the celebrated Hindu epic *The Mahabharata,* and it gave rise to a genre of mythological films, a genre that continues vigorously up to the present day. In 1931 the first Indian talkie, *Alam Ara,* was produced. It was in Hindi and contained many songs. This musical form took instant root in the consciousness of the people and has become a distinguishing feature of popular Indian movies produced both in the North and in the South. As in the classical Sanskrit theater, drama, music, spectacle, and dance were combined in a lavish production. In 1935 *Devadas,* which sought to explore a specific moral problem—the rationality and legitimacy of arranged marriages—inaugurated a new genre of social drama. Films such as *Achut Kanya* (1936) and *Duniya Na Mane* (1937) quickly followed. These films dealt with such social themes as untouchability and the emancipation of women. However, these social dramas never allowed the simmering social discontent to boil over into open rebellion; this discontent was held in check by a pervasive and overwhelming romanticism. These three films, which in many ways are landmark productions in the evolution of popular Indian movies, contain within them most of the vital ingredients that have imparted so inescapable a flavor to the popular Indian cinema.

Examined from a sociocultural viewpoint, popular Bombay films present us with an interesting harmony of divergent discourses. This harmony of discourses can be analyzed at a number of different levels of scholarly apprehension. First, we observe the harmonization of the twin discourses of tradition and modernity. The last seven or eight decades have witnessed the progressive intensification of the conflict between the forces of tradition and those of modernity in the Indian subcontinent. As a consequence of the unprecedented spread of technology, of mass communication, of Western influences, and so on, forces of modernization began to sweep through the country with increasing vigor. This phenomenon, naturally, began to threaten traditional values, belief systems, and patterns of living. On the one hand, the forces of modernization had much to offer by way of improving the standards of day-to-day living; on the other hand, the homogenizing and totalizing tendencies associated with them held out the bleak specter of the obliteration of the cultural identity and stability of the people. The conflict that has been engendered has profound consequences for the emotional and psychological lives of the people.

The artistic cinema presents us with a different aspect of the Indian cultural sensibility. Satyajit Ray's *The Song of the Road (Pather Panchali)*, produced in 1955, won for Indian cinema the international artistic recognition that it so badly needed. This film deals with the problems and hardships encountered by a Brahmin family living in a Bengali village in the opening years of the present century. This film, along with *The Unvanquished (Aparajito)* and *The World of Apu (Apu Sansar)*—generally referred to as the Apu trilogy—is considered to be a masterpiece of modern cinema. Since this trilogy, Ray has gone on to produce such films as *Charulata, The Goddess (Devi),* and *Music Room (Jalsaghar),* which clearly display the creative originality and deep humanism that characterize his work. Next to Ray, Mrinal Sen is perhaps the most internationally well-known Indian filmmaker. Mrinal Sen is primarily interested in social modernization and its human consequences. He is a more socially committed filmmaker than Satyajit Ray and is invariably drawn toward social themes. Apart from these two, a number of other extremely talented directors are also closely associated with the artistic cinema of India. Of them, I find Adoor Gopalakrishnan, G. Aravindan, Kumar Shahani, Mani Kaul, Ketan Mehta, Buddhadeb Dasgupta, Goutam Ghose, and Nirad Mohapatra particularly significant in terms of their technique and vision.

The division between popular cinema and artistic cinema has been acutely felt in the Indian cinema for the last twenty-five years or so. Many eminent Indian film critics have lamented this situation. The government, on the other hand, through its loan schemes, film institutes, film festivals, film awards, and National Film Archives, has encouraged the growth of the artistic film. Some filmmakers like Shyam Benegal and Govind Nihalani have sought to pursue a *via media* between the artistic and popular styles. However, it needs to be said that this division between the artistic and the popular cinema is a continuing problem for the serious filmgoer. In addition, the spread of television in recent times is beginning to have an adverse impact on the film industry of India. Cinema attendance is falling visibly, and there has been a series of major box office failures lately. All of these trends naturally give cause for concern to Indian film producers.

On the other hand, there are some positive signs as well. It has been generally contended by the popular film producers that the mass of

Indian people prefer not to see anything that deviates significantly from the well-tried formula of the popular film. However, the phenomenal popularity of television serial dramas has given the lie to this contention. These dramas contain none of the familiar ingredients of the popular cinema, and they deal realistically with the everyday lives of ordinary people. It is also interesting to observe that some film artists associated with the artistic cinema, for example, Kundan Shah, Sai Paranjpye, and Basu Chatterji, are playing a significant role in the making of these television dramas. It may be that in time to come we will see a fruitful interaction between television and film, leading to the elevation of standards in both media.

6
Innovation and Imitation in the Contemporary Indian Cinema

MIRA REYM BINFORD

THE ANCIENT CULTURE of India is one of the primary "seed cultures" of the world, a source of unique, widely disseminated concepts and images and a culture that has continued to maintain its own basic identity in the face of repeated incursions from abroad. The technology of cinema was imported into India at the end of the nineteenth century. The first Indian feature film, *Rajah Harishchandra*, premiered in 1913, was based on a myth from the epic *Mahabharata*, a text central to Indian culture. Its director, Dadasaheb Phalke, stated that he was impelled by a desire to project "Indian images" onto the screens of India. Some forty years later—and four decades ago—Satyajit Ray (1976, 2) wrote, "What our cinema needs above everything else is a style, an idiom, a sort of iconography of cinema, which would be uniquely and recognisably Indian." But cultural identity is not a simple issue, and in cinema as elsewhere, the question of "What is Indian?" cannot be answered by merely pointing to theme or form or intention. It is, however, a question that has frequently figured in the history of Indian cinema and one that underlies much of the following discussion.

Despite recent threats from the rapidly accelerating spread of television and of video cassette technology, the Indian film industry is still the earth's most productive, making approximately one-fifth of the world's annual output of feature films. Its mainstream popular cinema has become a staple of entertainment in many other countries as well as in India itself, but outside this mainstream there are currents that define themselves by their rejection of the conventions of commercial cinema. The inception of the Indian art cinema goes back to the midfifties with the internationally acclaimed films of Satyajit Ray, as well as those of two other major filmmakers from Bengal, Mrinal Sen and Ritwik Ghatak. As a movement, it began to spread across the country only after 1969 and is now often referred to as the "New Indian Cinema," an overarching term which includes many different approaches to the handling of socially relevant themes and, for some directors, issues of formal experimentation. A "Middle Cinema" can also now be distinguished, a term applied to certain "well-made" films that avoid the excesses of escapist formula films and appeal to a middle-class audience interested in relatively sophisticated entertainment rather than experimental or thematically unsettling cinema. Another significant, though still small cinematic current consists of independent documentary filmmakers whose films investigate abuses of established power as well as other political or social problems of contemporary India.

India consists of a number of culturally and linguistically diverse regions. Films are produced in some twenty languages in half a dozen film production centers, but when I refer to India's commercial cinema in this article, I mean primarily the contemporary Hindi-language cinema, generally considered the archetypal commercial cinema of India. The Hindi language is spoken by the largest proportion of India's population, about 30 percent, and is understood by a larger number, partly due to the popularity of Hindi films. Produced both in Bombay and Madras, Hindi films have long been the dominant force in Indian cinema and are seen by many as a major factor unifying people across India's complex cultural barriers. Although they now represent a shrinking proportion of total Indian production, they are distributed all over the country and are heavily imitated by regional filmmakers.

When we look closely at the commercial and art cinemas of India, many interesting contrasts in their stylistic and thematic approaches emerge. The present-day Indian commercial film is the end result of a lengthy process of imitation, adaptation, and indigenization. Confronted with challenges from abroad, Indian society has often responded by indigenizing invasive foreign cultural elements and creating a new synthesis that is fundamentally Indian. The development of the commercial film industry has largely followed this traditional pattern; and the New Cinema, with its much shorter history, is going through a similar process as its filmmakers, though with greater self-consciousness and differing purpose, struggle to evolve their own indigenized forms of Indian cinema.

Hollywood provided the Indian film industry with a variety of

INNOVATION AND IMITATION IN INDIAN CINEMA 79

important patterns. The industry adopted Hollywood's studio and star systems, and it has adapted plots and cinematic techniques to its own needs. But instead of being overwhelmed by competition from Hollywood films, India's producers assimilated and altered successful elements from those films and, when sound technology became available, developed a film form that enabled them to resist foreign domination of their nation's screens. Their success in doing so is strikingly demonstrated by statistics. During the silent film era, imported films, primarily from the United States, had occupied 87 percent of India's screen time. Within a decade of the coming of sound, the ratio of imported to domestic films diminished to less than one-tenth (Dharap 1979, p 1).

Spurred by the availability of sound technology, the Indian film industry developed an indigenous narrative form, the "all-talking, -singing, -dancing" Bombay film, based on the interpolation of songs and dances, comedy and romance in highly ritualized, theatrically mounted melodrama. It is a cinema produced by hybridization and, like many hybrids, has proved extremely hardy. Although the Indian commercial cinema has often taken its inspirations from Hollywood and, to a much lesser degree, from other foreign commercial film centers, many of its stylistic and narrative traditions are derived from aspects of Indian theater, both folk and urban, some of these in turn stemming from classical Sanskrit drama. Such influences have been especially evident in the tradition of highly stylized acting, the extended, elaborate depictions of emotion, and the obligatory inclusion of songs, dances, and sequences of broad comic relief—elements that can be found as far back as A.D. 400 in the Sanskrit dramas of Kālidāsa. It has often been said (although television is now beginning to alter the terms of this truism) that for the culturally displaced peasants in India's towns and cities, movies are the only available form of entertainment, and their "variety show" character is familiar to audiences accustomed to the conventions of rural folk drama.

The obligatory song-and-dance sequences of the Indian mainstream film are a striking example of indigenously based aesthetic principles shaping the use of imported technology. The use of song and stylized movement has remote antecedents in the traditional Sanskrit drama. With minor exceptions, these plays were constructed of prose sections interspersed with short poems, which were sung or melodically chanted. Although the high period of Sanskrit drama ended around A.D. 1000, the classical form influenced the popular theater, first the regional folk theaters and subsequently the urban "Parsi" theater of the nineteenth and early twentieth century, which incorporated already indigenized Persian-Muslim rhetorical and musical practices and most directly influenced the narrative conventions of Indian cinema. In the West, the separate genre of the musical developed to accommodate extensive use of music and dance in film. Indian dramatic traditions did not isolate song from spoken rhetoric, and music plays a vital role in ritual and daily living. When song and dance were incorporated into film in India, they powerfully molded the medium.

A genuine national cinema evolved, its films pervaded by song and dance. In its contemporary form, this cinema is rooted in the history of India after World War II and especially after independence, a period when social and economic transformations of considerable magnitude occurred. The Indian film industry, which had grown and changed greatly in response to an influx of illegal war profits, reached beyond its primarily middle-class audience of prewar days to a new, larger audience of uprooted peasants confronting the unsettling realities of urban and industrial life. This cinema thrived in a symbiotic relationship with its "seminal audience," to use the suggestive phrase of Australian film critic John Hinde. Hinde (1981, 40–41) describes a seminal audience as "a very large group in some state of communal anxiety, looking for new social directions, extended social maps, which a cinema of its own can display for it with an unrivaled efficiency. . . . With the conjunction of filmmaking and a seminal audience, an enormously powerful system of social feedback is under way," which is the source of a national cinema's great vitality. This description seems especially applicable to the situation in India after World War II. For this new mass audience, the Indian film industry developed narratives that papered over conflicts between the traditional and the modern and seemingly reconciled the tensions brought by wrenching social and personal change through fundamentally conservative and reassuring fictions.

Within the overarching musical-comedy-romance-melodrama form, the genres of the Indian commercial film have tended to become increasingly blurred, especially in the contemporary era of the *masala* (or "spice-mix") film. In earlier periods of the Indian sound film, genres such as the "mythological," the "historical," or the "social" (dealing with contemporary themes) were still distinguishable from each other. The contemporary *masala* film, which I have characterized as a permeable portmanteau form, has been continually expanded to accommodate elements from various imported genres such as *kung fu* and disaster movies, westerns and spy films—as well as from domestic sources, since the socially conscious themes of the New Cinema have begun to figure in commercial films, though in bizarre, co-opted fashion.

The contemporary *masala,* or formula, film has developed a distinctive aesthetic of its own. Its narrative structure does not depend on psychologically consistent characters, plausible plots, coherence, or unity of composition. Realism, in the sense of visual or psychological authenticity, has not been valued. The mandatory song-and-dance sequences, like operatic arias, tend to serve as both narrative and emotional points of culmination or punctuation. Baroque and sometimes highly dramatic camera movement is complemented by flamboyant use of color and sound effects and flashy editing, which can be very rapid despite the films' customary three-hour length. Sound and visuals of song-and-dance sequences are often edited in blithe defiance of conventional laws of space and time, whisking a pair of young lovers from a Himalayan mountaintop to a Parisian boulevard to some impossibly elegant hideaway, without missing a beat. Or, as in the film *Justice (Inquilaab,* 1984), a heightened emotional state, like that of superstar Amitabh Bachchan's honest cop blackmailed into silence, is represented by a doubled Amitabh Bachchan, one singing a song that compares the hero to the encircled Abhimanyu in the epic *Mahabharata,* the other suffering through a kaleidoscopic series of entrapment images, some of which are effective, some clumsily melodramatic. At their most successful, such song-and-dance sequences may be expressive and genuinely moving, but often they are vulgarized portrayals of feelings, especially sexual desire, that cannot be forthrightly represented on film because of the puritanical values embodied in censorship restrictions. In general, these film songs are only lip-synched by the actors and actually performed by a small number of "playback singers," who are heard in film after film, becoming unseen stars in their own right, and whose voices are, like much else in the commercial cinema, reassuringly familiar.

Stock situations, characters, and plots are repeated over and over and often tend to run in cycles of fashion. Revenge themes, for instance, have become quite common in the eighties and are frequently combined with other recurrent themes, such as the redemptive power of a mother's love or the loss and reunion of siblings. The popularity of specific subjects at particular periods is often a feedback reflection of sociopsychological conditions caught in an idealizing mirror. The repressed anger of contemporary Indian urban youth finds a comforting echo in stories of revenge, and the perennial subject of separated and reunited families strikes a constant chord of memory in a traditional society where many families were fragmented historically through India's partition and perennially through continuing internal migration.

The freewheeling variety show of contemporary commercial cinema moves its spectators through extravagant worlds of myth, fantasy, and desire, often powered by great energy and entertaining spectacle but rarely confronting the complexities of contemporary India, which it exploits rather than honestly explores. Hollywood is one of its parents, but this effectively indigenized hybrid form functions on its own terms, continuing to absorb and transform the foreign fertilizer fed to it.

India's New or Parallel Cinema encompasses a wide variety of filmmakers linked primarily by their rejection of the values, both aesthetic and thematic, of the commercial cinema. Through the 1950s and 1960s Satyajit Ray had been the only Indian filmmaker with major international recognition. The critical appreciation that Ray received internationally helped to legitimate cinema within India as a respectable art form, worthy of official patronage and the involvement of artists and intellectuals. Mrinal Sen and Ritwik Ghatak are also important precursors of the New Cinema. Sen, an adventurous explorer of cinematic style, actively experimented with a number of European avant-garde approaches. Sen had been making films since 1956, but it was the popular as well as critical success of his playful satire of a petty bureaucrat, *Mr. Shome* (*Bhuvan Shome,* 1969) that marked the start of India's New Cinema as a movement. The film was financed by a low-interest government loan and helped inspire a new government policy of giving loans for low-budget, unconventional films. It is unlikely that the Indian art cinema would have come into existence without such central and state government funding and other forms of support.

The films of Ritwik Ghatak began to draw increasingly serious attention after his early death in 1976. In contrast to Ray and Sen, each of whom has been making about one film a year for many years, Ghatak was only able to complete eight features during his stormy life, but his work has been highly influential on some of the younger and politically oriented New Cinema directors. Ghatak imbued his films with passionate directness through an expressive use of sound and the wide-angle lens and, at his best, as in *Cloud Capped Star (Meghe Dhaka Tara,* 1960), he succeeded in transforming and energizing melodrama through an epic use of female characters and elements of nature as archetypal symbols.

Inspired in part by the examples of Ghatak, Sen, and Ray, as well as by the new waves in European cinema of the sixties, New Cinema directors from the very outset rejected the contemporary commercial cinema's theatrical artifices, its extravagance and wastefulness, its distortions of social reality, the stifling constraints of box-office formula, the dictates of distributors and stars, and the exploitation of sexuality and violence. In contrast to the limited, ever-repeated themes of the formula film, New Cinema directors turned to the discovery and exploration of the enormous variety of subject matter offered by a society as diverse and complex as India.

Discussing his response to India's commercial cinema, one of the New Cinema's most prominent directors, Shyam Benegal, stressed his concern with being true to the culture and social realities of India. He saw the New Cinema as a reaction against the "vulgarity, stylization and non-expressiveness of mainstream cinema." By "non-expressive," Benegal explained that he meant "alienated, unconnected with life . . . films that don't express the environment around them" (interview with author, November 1981). New Cinema director and theorist Kumar Shahani (1980, 51) has written of the need to counter what he sees as commercial cinema's destructive themes as well as their form:

> Gratuitous violence, a life dependent upon miracles (whether of Gods or super humans), change of heart in evil men, and the abuse of women as servile objects of sexual and social exploitation are the cultural products of a lumpen consciousness. Whatever the ostensible and overt themes of these films, their disorganised and anarchic form itself can subvert all hope and determination.

It is precisely through such "disorganized and anarchic form" that the commercial cinema speciously reconciles the many contradictory ingredients and innuendos included in its *masala* mix, but interestingly this same quality also allows the commercial cinema its freedom and sometimes exuberant power, while other varieties of "disorganized" form have certainly characterized such major Indian aesthetic accomplishments as the Sanskrit prose novel and the numerous folk epics of various language areas.

One of the major influences on the New Cinema, as on the early work of Satyajit Ray himself, has been Italian neorealism. It is easy to see the appeal of neorealism with its humanist values, its directness and simplicity, its stress on discovering the drama inherent in the lives of ordinary people, for artists disturbed by the poverty and inequities of their society and trying to oppose a dominant mainstream cinema extravagant in mise-en-scène as well as budget. Out of necessity—and in contrast to the commercial cinema—New Cinema films have generally been shot on small budgets, under conditions varying from modest to extremely spartan. Working within the constraints of a small budget has had its positive side by diminishing the pressures on the directors' creative choices exercised by investors lacking a film background. A central tenet in the New Cinema has been an auteurist emphasis on the director's artistic freedom, as opposed to the situation of the commercial cinema, in which films bearing a strong directorial stamp are now rare and producers, distributors, or financiers tend to dominate aesthetic decisions.

Unlike the synthetic and rootless "all-India" world created by the Hindi commercial cinema in order to appeal to the largest possible pan-Indian audience, many New Cinema films have striven to project a strong sense of place, creating recognizable environments with a high degree of social and cultural authenticity, grounded in what might be called an aesthetic of "rootedness." Such films have required extensive field research, and shooting on location has been common. A well-known example was Shyam Benegal's *The Churning* (*Manthan*, 1976), which was shot in a Gujerati village and grew out of the director's work on a documentary film about the organization of a successful dairy cooperative in Gujerat.

The treatment of actors also constitutes a critical difference between commercial film and New Cinema. In the national film culture of India, the star has taken on a unique and mythical weight, which equals or perhaps surpasses that accorded to the star in any other film culture. Much of the reverence traditionally offered to the Indian saint is accorded to the film star, and stars are so central to box-office success that films are often financed, without a script, on the basis of a producer's contract with a star or two, a few songs, and some ideas on the proper mix of *masala* ingredients. Shooting schedules in the mainstream film industry, dependent on the availability of stars who may be working as many as thirty films at a time, can be long and fragmented. Some of what Kumar Shahani calls the anarchic form of

INNOVATION AND IMITATION IN INDIAN CINEMA 85

masala films may be linked directly to this factor. When shooting is spread out over months and even years, plot lines can become even more tangled than intended and even the appearance of characters can change not through directorial choice but at the hands of time. On the other hand, New Cinema films have usually been shot on short, tightly planned schedules and have used new or nonprofessional actors who lack the conventionally glamorous attributes of "stars." Their naturalistic acting is in great contrast to the melodramatic stylizations of commercial cinema. Some of the actors introduced in New Cinema films (such as Naseeruddin Shah, Shabana Azmi, and the recently and tragically deceased Smita Patil) have now attained star status of their own and are employed in commercial films as well, retaining some of their more naturalistic acting style, an example of the impact that New Cinema has begun to exert on the formula film. The influence of the New Cinema can also be seen in the increased tendency by commercial filmmakers to shoot on location and give at least some appearance of material reality.

Once again in contrast to the commercial cinema, the participation of women in the New Cinema, filling various creative functions, is significant and is increasing. So far only a small proportion have been directors, but some significant films have been made by women. Noteworthy among female filmmakers are Aparna Sen, Prema Karanth, and Vijaya Mehta, a veteran stage actress and director who has recently made her first theatrical feature film, *Raosaheb* (1986). In handling its early twentieth-century story of an English-educated, reform-minded barrister's progressive ideas confronting the issue of widow remarriage among high castes, *Raosaheb,* though not formally experimental, is a real original, even among New Cinema films, for its blend of strong feeling and restraint through the elevation of melodramatic plot elements—hereditary insanity in a landed family, the sudden death of a young husband, the ritually imposed humiliation and isolation of widows, and the betrayal of a marriage promise—to the level of deeply affecting art. Mehta shows a similar quiet yet powerful restraint in her affectionate direction of the carefully drawn characters and the sure, measured rhythms of the editing.

In general, New Cinema directors have been concerned with examining the complexities of ordinary life, and even when using experimental forms, they have preferred to make workers or peasants or middle-class people their heroes and heroines, while *masala* films either move through a world of impossible wealth or glamorize their protagonists even when they are ostensibly working-class, as in the Amitabh Bachchan vehicle *Coolie* (1983), directed by Manmohan Desai, with its hale and handsome baggage-carriers dancing at the drop of a valise. Mainstream producer-director Yash Chopra, who has made popular hits such as *The Wall* (*Deewar,* 1975), expresses a point of view frequently heard in *masala* film circles (Subramaniam 1980, 39):

> I present beautiful things on screen. Is it bad to show good things? India is full of the poor, the sick, the workless. In a way it's lucky that people accept their sufferings as their *karma,* as the will of God, otherwise they would be up in arms and there would be killings and bloodshed. I don't want to make our people cry all over again when they come to the cinema.

In the process of showing "good things," however, the commercial cinema also conveys values. Within the limits of censorship, *masala* films tease their audiences with all sorts of "modern evils," fast cars and loose women and disco dancing, but their weight is overwhelmingly on the side of traditional values and authority—family, religion, the small idealized community; while in many New Cinema films that deal with problems of the oppressed and the dispossessed, a recurring theme is the crushing burden of tradition. Pattabhi Rama Reddy's courageous *Funeral Rites* (*Samskara,* 1970) shocked many in its time with its challenge to Hindu orthodoxy. The complex portrayal of an orthodox Brahmin, combined with the harsh imagery symbolically suggesting the doom of the traditional way of life, made *Funeral Rites* a powerful and seminal achievement. In the Kannada film *Phaniyamma* (1982), to cite one example among many, Prema Karanth deals with the theme of child widows, forced to lifelong loneliness and ritual penance through no fault of their own. The story is set in the late nineteenth and early twentieth century, and its theme is an indirect reflection not only on the largely superannuated practice of enforced child marriage and possible widowhood but on the still powerful prejudice, among more conservative members of India's higher castes, against divorce or remarriage of women.

The endemic violence in Indian society is a recurrent theme of New Cinema films. Violence is also a constant of the *masala* film, but the two cinemas handle violence in radically different ways. Violence in commercial films is cold-blooded, ritualistic, and staged entertainingly, with much use of acrobatics, stylized *kung fu*-tinged moves, and extravagant sound effects. "Fight masters" specialize in this type of choreography. No matter how overwhelming the hero's adversaries in number and firepower, the hero ultimately triumphs, without bruises or exhaustion. Lavishly expended gore at the death of villains has become a standard ingredient of the contemporary action film, but when the evil characters are finally dispatched, the triumph is that of a near-superhuman, usually invincible, "good" individual over other "bad" individuals, and all problems, no matter how socially complex and wide-ranging, are resolved through the physical combat of heroes and villains.

New Cinema films, on the other hand, attempt to show the consequences and causes of violence more honestly and to anchor it in the structure of social injustice rather than individual villainy. Many films have confronted the connections between entrenched feudal power, violence against the weak, and the subjugation and sexual exploitation of women. The inevitability of violence given the inequities of India's social order and system of justice is conveyed in such films as Girish Karnad's *The Forest* (*Kaadu*, 1973) and two films by Govind Nihalani, *Cry of the Wounded* (*Aakrosh*, 1980) and *Half-Truth* (*Ardh Satya*, 1983), both of which enjoyed successful commercial runs. Shyam Benegal's village trilogy—*The Seedling* (*Ankur*, 1974), *Night's End* (*Nishant*, 1975), and *The Churning* (*Manthan*, 1976)—depicts a whole range of violence inflicted by social superiors on their inferiors and particularly on women. In *The Seedling* and *The Churning*, the responses to injustice are small significant events—the servant woman's tongue-lashing of a village landowner, the flicker of hope and resolve to action in an oppressed untouchable community—and even in the less successful *Night's End*, which ends with a spontaneous village uprising against a family of vicious landowners, violence is portrayed not as a mere duel but as an endemic social weakness or a collective revulsion.

There have been directly political New Cinema films, though they usually do not suggest solutions or attempt to stir their audience toward action. Goutam Ghose's *Our Land* (*Maa Bhoomi*, 1979) deals with revolutionary action in its depiction of a peasant revolt in South India; and several filmmakers have dealt sympathetically with India's radical left underground movement, the Naxalites, who were especially active in the late 1960s. More recently, there have been left-wing films of greater ambiguity, dealing in part with the failures of the radical left. The Bengali director Buddhadeb Dasgupta, in such films as *The Distance* (*Dooratwa*, 1978) and *Blind Alley* (*Andhi Galli*, 1984), portrays characters who are former or inactive leftists dealing with personal traumas that are partially conditioned by the effects upon their lives of their lapsed activism. In Adoor Gopalakrishnan's Malayali film *Face to Face* (*Mukhamukham*, 1985), a charismatic political hero who has fled to avoid arrest returns years later to his followers as a melancholy drunk who does nothing but fall asleep before their adulation. Yet, struck down at night by thugs reacting perhaps to his past role, he takes a place once again in local revolutionary mythology under the red flags of his funeral procession. Gopalakrishnan and his fellow Malayali G. Aravindan represent a strain of humanist realism in New Cinema that is directly connected with the example of Satyajit Ray. It is a lyrical, poetic strain, drawing on patient, often silent observation of fine nuances of behavior and atmosphere. Another form of reflective lyricism, highly original in Indian cinema, appears in a first feature film by Nirad Mohapatra, *The Mirage* (*Maya Miriga*, 1983). The Oriya director owes much to the inspiration of Yasujiro Ozu for his quiet gaze at the gradual dissolution of an extended family without dramatic confrontations. Some of the emphasis on restraint in the New Cinema seems largely reactive, a rejection of the melodramatic excesses of the *masala* film, but Mohapatra's restraint is not imposed ideologically from outside his theme. It is an integral part of his narrative structure and of the sensibility informing it.

The central figures in New Cinema's formalist avant-garde have been Kumar Shahani and Mani Kaul. Rejecting linear narrative, they have experimented with alternative forms and explored the application of traditional Indian aesthetic theories to filmmaking. Shahani was at one time an assistant to Robert Bresson, and his work shows some influence of the French master's precisely controlled sense of order. Shahani's *The Wave* (*Tarang*, 1984) is a highly ambitious attempt to produce a modern epic form, linking a contemporary story of industrial turmoil and a liaison that crosses class lines with the ancient Indian legend of King Pururuvas and his lover Urvashi, courtesan of the gods. The film is rich in carefully textured sound, color, and brilliantly composed images, and the influence of Ritwik Ghatak is evident in its concern with archetypal symbolism, but the high degree of formalism often inhibits the epic intention. Films of such experimental nature have not found commercial distribution in India, but the vastly increased spread of television has now created new opportunities for such work. *The Wave*, for instance, was recently shown nationally on Sunday evening in prime time.

Beginning in the late 1970s, a number of New Cinema films dealing with issues such as governmental or police corruption have succeeded, sometimes against considerable resistance, in passing through censorship, though they probably would not have done so earlier. Govind Nihalani's *Half-Truth* was an especially controversial film and as a result highly successful commercially. The film bravely broke ground in its portrayal of connections between police, criminals, and government, though it was marred by a psychological reductionism which ascribes the brutality of an otherwise honest policeman essentially to his childhood family situation. Such New Cinema films have had their effects on the mainstream cinema, where political themes have been adopted though they have been reduced to caricature. In *Justice,* Amitabh Bachchan, the leading superstar of the commercial cinema, becomes innocently embroiled in a web of political corruption as he rises from poverty to become chief minister of a state government and at his first cabinet meeting, machine-guns his entire cabinet of corrupt politicians in a sequence of slow motion and spurting blood obviously suggested by the films of Sam Peckinpah.

Ketan Mehta's *Holi* (1984) is another New Cinema film dealing with controversial subject matter. Mehta addresses the highly charged issue of the tensions and frustrations on Indian college campuses, which often lead to outbursts of violence. Using long, continuously moving camera takes and a large group of nonprofessional actors who partially improvise their roles, Mehta creates a swirling sense of talk and time, analogous to the carnival festival of Holi, which we do not really see being celebrated until the tragic end of the film. Like the trails of colored powder flung into the air at Holi, the sound and visual lines of the film convey a sense of intoxication and distortion, a psychic world too tense for reflection or hesitation and out of which anything may erupt. Mehta's other two films are even more interesting for their ambitious formal experimentation. In his latest film, *Chili Bouquet* (*Mirch Masala,* 1986), Mehta returns to the highly original, indigenized Brechtian style that characterized his first film, *A Folk Tale* (*Bhavni Bhavai,* 1981). In *Chili Bouquet,* for his story of feudal oppression, about the attempt by a rural official in the 1940s to seize a married village woman for his pleasure, Mehta combines the use of song and dance based on folk theater with Brechtian distancing devices. In *A Folk Tale,* he had already produced a fresh and lively synthesis of indigenous and Western narrative elements, using and undermining a number of *masala* film conventions. He stated in an interview at the time that he had borrowed elements from commercial cinema, which it had itself "taken from folk art—speed, rhythm, color, flash. I've used these deliberately, at the same time taking care to short circuit them before they become benumbing" (Mohamed 1981, 35). This approach toward breaking down the barriers between the entertainment values of the commercial cinema (and its predecessors in the popular theater) and the artistic values of the New Cinema may point the way toward the creation of a new Indian cinematic hybrid. Other New Cinema directors as well, notably Saeed Mirza, have experimented with Brechtian subversions of commercial cinema styles. In Mirza's *A Summons for Mohan Joshi* (*Mohan Joshi Hazir Ho,* 1985), a retired office worker turns to the courts in order to obtain repairs from a corrupt landlord on behalf of himself and his fellow tenement dwellers. The film becomes a vehicle for songs, broad comedy, and stylized villainy but retains its serious focus on the details of bureaucratic and legal injustice, as Mohan Joshi, like an ultimately less fortunate Mother Courage, struggles against absurdist odds and refuses to buckle. This indigenized Brechtian vein in the New Cinema is especially interesting for its combination of political awareness and formal experimentation in the service of effective communication with a mass audience. In an interview discussing *Chili Bouquet,* Ketan Mehta recently supported this approach with the following rationale (Baghdadi and Rao 1987, 18):

> Somewhere along the line, the kind of naturalistic tradition that we have borrowed from the West became unnecessary. . . . it is not natural for us to use realism in the way it was used in Europe in the '50's. It is alien to us. We have much more in common with the Latin American tradition. . . . Brecht used this distancing technique to make people reflect, rather than to titillate their senses. It is basic to what he did and to what I'm trying to do. I want the people to carry the film home. . . . The film has to have the power to make people reflect.

Mehta is obviously concerned with overcoming the aesthetic limitations on the New Cinema's ability to reach a mass audience, a concern shared by others in the New Cinema. Yet even among those whose work seems geared toward an elite audience, the question of "what is Indian?" in film, the problem of developing a genuinely Indian cinematic aesthetic is a live issue. Clearly, there can be no single or definitive answer. It is, however, striking that despite the aesthetic of "rootedness" shared by many directors and New Cinema's preoccupation with problems of Indian society, most of the New Cinema, in rejecting commercial formulas, has turned toward Western narrative styles, ranging from the classic Hollywood narrative to influences from the international art cinema. The commercial cinema, for all its absorption of foreign influences, remains firmly grounded in traditional Indian musical-dramatic sources and therefore still speaks most directly to the mass audience. For New Cinema, the process of evolving indigenized forms, begun much more recently, is still open-ended, and its directions cannot be neatly predicted.

A key stimulus for the development of the New Cinema was state and central government support, ranging from finance to the sponsorship of film awards, festivals, and training, support to film societies, and the promotion of New Cinema films abroad. But government aid did not extend to helping New Cinema films break through the bottleneck of commercial distribution, which has been a severe problem for most directors. The tremendous growth of the television and video cassette media, as a result of government policy over the past five years, has added new complications as well as opportunities for film dissemination. After decades of hesitation regarding television development (which began on an experimental basis in 1959), the government recently shifted its television policy from an educational orientation to an emphasis on entertainment, including commercial sponsorship. A network of transmitters hooked up to a satellite rapidly brought more than half of the country within range of a television signal. Because of the immense popularity of films in India and the great expense of producing original television material, Doordarshan, the government monopoly television network, has come to rely heavily on feature films and film-related shows as a mainstay of its programming. Television, while it has apparently further damaged the viability of New Cinema films at the box office, now also offers a showcase for films that have been unable to obtain commercial release. More and more New Cinema directors are seeing their previously unreleased films broadcast to a potentially very large audience; and an increasing number are involved in making films or series specifically for television. New Cinema's dependence on government support therefore continues and is further complicated by both government television censorship and the aesthetic constraints of the small screen. But television has the potential to reach much deeper into India than New Cinema has as yet penetrated. We may soon see some interesting effects of new kinds of dissemination on New Cinema's development of more indigenized forms and on commercial cinema's responses, not only to the practical threat of television and video, but perhaps to an increasing familiarity, in wider sectors of Indian society, with the aesthetics and themes of New Cinema.

References

Baghdadi, Rafique, and Rajiv Rao
    1987   " 'There's No Point in Making a Film Which Will Not Be Seen,' Says Ketan Mehta," *Cinema India-International*, 1, 16–18.

Dharap, B. V.
    1979   *Indian Films 1977–1978*. Pune: Motion Picture Enterprises.

Hinde, John
    1981   *Other People's Pictures*. Sydney: Australian Broadcasting Commission.

Mohamed, Khalid
    1981   "Ketan Mehta—'To Be Esoteric Is to Be Ugly,' " *Filmfare*, May 1–15, 35.

Ray, Satyajit
    1976   *Our Films, Their Films*. New Delhi: Orient Longman.

Shahani, Kumar
    1980   "Cinema of Research and Relevance," *Film World*, October, 51.

Subramaniam, K. N.
    1980   "Yash Chopra—Putting It Across Romantically," *Filmfare*, March 16–31, 39.

7
Art, Vision, and Culture: Satyajit Ray's Apu Trilogy Revisited

WIMAL DISSANAYAKE

SATYAJIT RAY's Apu trilogy was a milestone in international cinema. It consists of *The Song of the Road (Pather Panchali)*, *The Unvanquished (Aparajito)*, and *The World of Apu (Apu Sansar)*, produced in 1955, 1956, and 1959, respectively. Based on a two-volume novel by the popular and critically acclaimed Bengali writer Bibhutibhushan Bannerji, the trilogy won wide international recognition for Ray and an honored place for Indian film in world cinema. Nearly twenty-five years have passed since the third film in the trilogy, and it is opportune now to take a retrospective look at all three.

A striking feature of the Apu trilogy is the way in which Satyajit Ray demonstrates the idea of film as cultural expression, in the deepest sense of the term. The objective of this paper is to examine how Ray was guided by, and gives creative expression to, some essential configurations and impulses of Indian (or, more precisely, Bengali) culture.

All films, in varying degrees of sensitivity and understanding, reflect the culture of their background: but the portrayal of the contours of a given culture is a means and not an end—the end being the creation of cinematographic art.

To make use of the unique richness of a given culture, a filmmaker needs not only a commitment to serious art, but also the vital ability to project a distinctively personal vision. Cinema does not reflect culture passively; it confronts, probes, and challenges its culture and in turn is shaped and guided by it. This dialectic between filmmaker and culture is argued graphically in Ray's Apu trilogy.

All cinema operates at two levels of artistic receptivity. On one level, it communicates and is an emblem for what is most distinct about the culture with which it is preoccupied. At another level, it transcends the specifics of culture in a timeless humanity, a universality of feeling and introspection. Aristotle said that the historian deals with the particular and the poet with the universal. This is equally applicable to the filmmaker. By delving deeply into the essences of a local habitation, within a temporal framework, filmmakers arrive at a universality of experience and emotion.

Their dialectic is between the parochialisms of a culture and an individual creative impulse that is both transcendent and universal. The personal vision of the filmmaker assumes a position of supreme importance in this encounter. A successful director like Satyajit Ray is able to make use of what is most characteristic and instinctive about Indian culture, through the instrument of controlled art, and to arrive at a global vocabulary of emotion and response.

Satyajit Ray's Apu trilogy had a profound impact on cinema audiences the world over because the dynamics between artistic commitment, personal vision, and cultural sensibility evoked a universally valid poetic metaphor of human struggle and suffering. The three films, taken together, give cinematographic expression to configurations of Bengali culture so that the artistic intentions of the director are fulfilled. He opened a poetic door to the human mansion in which we all dwell.

The idea of culture is central to this metaphor. Unfortunately the term defies simplistic formulation. In 1952 two well-known anthropologists, Kroeber and Kluckhohn, seeking to define the concept of culture, counted at least 154 definitions, and many more incomplete descriptions and statements. This underlines culture's elusive nature. It has been defined as social heritage, customs, and inherited tradition; its description encompasses the sum of all that is artificial and man-made. Thus culture consists of man-made systems for ordering social and natural environments into conceptual structures, which generate meaning out of the phenomena of human life.

There are three important characteristics associated with culture. First, culture has a memory that manifests itself in tradition, convention, custom, and belief systems. Second, culture constitutes an open system. Interactions within this system, and between it and the outside environment, act as stimuli for change. Third, culture seeks to maintain its integrity and exercises authority over its members by means of accepted values, norms, and established patterns of behavior. Clifford Geertz (1973, 46) says:

Undirected by culture patterns—organized systems of significant symbols—man's behavior would be ungovernable, a mere chaos of pointless acts and exploding emotions, his experience virtually shapeless. Culture, the accumulated totality of such patterns, is not just an ornament of human existence but—the principal basis of its specificity—an essential condition for it.

With these views of culture in mind, let us examine how the maker of the three films that compose the Apu trilogy seeks to delineate and define Bengali culture. He does so by bringing an unflinching artistic commitment to his task as well as a probing, creative mind and an instantly recognizable personal vision. The stories of the three films are as follows.

The Song of the Road, the first film in the trilogy, deals with the problems and privations of a Brahmin family living in a Bengali village in the opening years of the present century. The head of the household is the father (Harihar), who is a poor priest and a poet who does not earn enough to support his family. The life of the mother (Sarbojaya) is typical of that of an Indian peasant woman, an unending series of daily chores. The daughter (Durga) is playful and mischievous. In an adjoining house lives a feeble old aunt, and there is constant tension between her and Sarbojaya.

Into this family Apu is born, the protagonist of the trilogy. His father, somewhat optimistically, talks of securing a new job which will usher in a new and prosperous period for the family, but it does not materialize. When Apu is six years old he goes to an ill-equipped school run by the village grocer. Meanwhile the tensions between the mother and the old aunt deepen, and the latter decides to leave. The immediate cause of this flare-up is that the aunt has begged a shawl from a neighbor, an act that Sarbojaya finds distasteful. The aunt returns later and pleads to stay on with the family, but Sarbojaya refuses to consider the idea. The old woman leaves, and the two children, Durga and Apu, who are fond of her, go in search of her. On a dark and windy day, as they dart across the field to watch a train pass by, they discover her dead body by the roadside.

The father, Harihar, has gone away to a neighboring village to officiate at an initiation ceremony. He writes home that the ceremony has been cancelled and he intends to go to the city to earn money. Some months later, he returns with his small earnings and a new sari for his daughter, only to find that while he was away Durga was caught in a heavy downpour, went down with a fever, and has died. The family resolves to move away from their ancestral home to the holy city of Benares, and the film ends with the three of them leaving the village in a cart. In a wonderfully evocative shot we see a snake slowly coiling its way into the deserted house.

The Unvanquished is the second film of the trilogy. Apu is now ten years old and living with his parents in Benares. As he grows into adolescence, he confronts the marvels of city life. His father is preoccupied with priestly activities, while his mother is busy taking care of the house. One day they receive a letter from one of Sarbojaya's uncles, suggesting that Harihar and he change places, that Harihar take over from him as priest in their local village, while the uncle spends the remaining years of his life in Benares. Sarbojaya turns down the request, but during the day of the Diwali festival that year, Harihar catches a fever and dies a few days later.

In order to support herself and her son, Sarbojaya accepts a job as servant in the house of a landlord, for whom Apu also does odd jobs and thus manages to earn a little money. One day Sarbojaya's uncle appears and suggests they go back to the village. Realizing her son has no future in the city, finally she accepts. Back in the village, Apu learns the basics of priestcraft and attends the village school. He does well in his studies, wins a scholarship, and departs for Calcutta, leaving behind his lonely mother. At first, he is lost and bewildered in the city but soon adapts himself to its life-style. His mother longs for him, and when he returns during the vacation she is full of joy, but he now finds his native village dull and uninteresting.

While he is studying for his examinations in Calcutta, Apu receives a letter from home informing him that his mother is critically ill. He goes home but learns that his mother has died the previous day. His uncle tries to persuade him to stay and continue his father's vocation, but he is not interested and returns to Calcutta. The final shot of the film shows Apu walking away from the village.

The third film in the trilogy is *The World of Apu*. Apu, still a student, lives in a rundown apartment in Calcutta. In his spare time he is writing a novel and plays the flute. His most intimate friend is Pulu, who takes him to a small village to attend the wedding of Pulu's sister Aparna. However, the joyous atmosphere quickly turns sour when the bridegroom is discovered to be mentally defective. Aparna's mother refuses to allow her to go through with the ceremony; but if she is not given in marriage at the appointed time, according to tradition, she has to remain unmarried until she dies. A desperate search for a bridegroom begins, with the result that Apu, much against his will, is married to Aparna.

They return to Calcutta, where he finds employment as a clerk. They are poor but lead a happy and contented life in a beautiful relationship that strengthens day by day. Aparna becomes pregnant and goes home to her parents to await the birth. Apu remains in Calcutta, where the tender love letters of his wife help him to survive his loneliness; but Aparna dies in childbirth, and he is devastated. The beautiful world he has built around himself begins to crumble. His baby son was saved, but Apu refuses to see him, believing him to be the cause of his mother's death.

Apu tries to run away from the tragedy, and from himself, by going to work in a distant coal mine. Five years pass. Pulu, his friend and brother-in-law, returns from abroad and persuades him to go home and take care of his son. Apu agrees without enthusiasm but soon is attracted to the little boy; and so ends the story of *The World of Apu* and the trilogy.

Thus Satyajit Ray charts the growth of Apu from childhood to maturity with all his attendant emotional and psychological upheavals. In an interview, speaking about the theme of the trilogy, Ray said (Rangoonwalla 1980, 109):

> The theme is "growth"—of a person—from childhood to manhood. It is like the saga of a typical Bengali youth, going through some typical circumstances, being moulded by them and reaching certain crucial stages of life. The transition itself is the strongest link in all three films, represented by the train symbol.

The Apu trilogy is based on the two-volume novel by Bibhutibhushan Bannerji. Discussing his selection of this work of fiction for cinematic recreation, Ray (1976, 33) said:

> I chose *Pather Panchali* for the qualities that made it a great book: its humanism, its lyricism, and its ring of truth. I knew I would have to do a lot of pruning and reshaping—I certainly could not go [in the first film] beyond the first half, which ended with the family's departure for Banaras—but at the same time I felt that to cast the thing into a mould of cut-and-dried narrative would be wrong. The script had to retain some of the rambling quality of the novel because that in itself contained a clue to the feel of authenticity: life in a poor Bengali village does ramble.

Satyajit Ray's trilogy illustrates admirably the notion of film as cultural expression. The original work of Bannerji captures with beauty and sensitivity the life of rural Bengal and its contrasts with the faster pace of city life. As the translator and critic T. W. Clark (1975, 16) says:

> The merits of Bannerji's work rest on the ease with which it is written, with its naturally executed changes of style, and the vivid and sympathetic realism of its portrayal of the day-to-day life of the two children, their parents and the other members of the village community.

These novels struck a deep, sympathetic chord in Ray and stirred his cinematographic imagination to action. The result is not a simple translation of the novel into visual terms; while retaining the flavor and pastoral beauty of the original, he has shortened the narration, tightened it, reduced the number of characters, and imposed a sense of causality.

How does the Apu trilogy give creative expression to Indian culture? First of all, Ray as film director has spent much imaginative energy on his sensitive depiction of human relationships. The trilogy deals with three generations of a peasant Brahmin family in Bengal, and the dynamics between the generations, as well as within them, are portrayed in ways that bring out some crucial cultural determinants. The relationships between Sarbojaya and the old aunt, between Apu and his mother, and between Apu and Aparna, are etched with poignancy. They acquire definition and denotation from the frame of reference of Bengali and Indian culture in general, which pays great attention to children, their likes and dislikes, hopes and fears, work and play. Bannerji as a novelist and Ray as a filmmaker are deeply fascinated with the world of children and here is a meeting of kindred spirits, so that the trilogy reflects a sensibility imbued with the flavor of Indian culture.

Secondly, the centrality of the family as the most significant social unit is also deeply embedded in traditional Indian culture—the notion of the family as a background against which the strengths and weaknesses of personal relationships can be charted. This concept finds eloquent expression in the Apu trilogy. *The Song of the Road* deals with a peasant Brahmin family struggling against adversity and losing two of its members. *The World of Apu* ends with Apu and his son united and a family bond being strengthened. Central to the whole trilogy is the notion of family as both the means for self-fulfillment and a constraint on individual initiative. The Apu trilogy engages its audiences in a penetration of the complicities of intimacy and estrangement that derives its imaginative force only within the context of the Indian family. Marie Seton (1971, 117) says: "The prominence of the family in Satyajit Ray's work is reflective of life in Bengal, and in India, where few people's lives become divorced from a family setting."

Ray has not only sought to explain human relationships under the unmistakable imprint of traditional Indian culture. He also offers a distinctive personal vision that emerges from this culture and is illustrative of its deeper currents. In the ultimate analysis, Ray is concerned with affirming faith in the individual in his many struggles in the world. A prerequisite for facing these challenges is self-knowledge. Despite the numerous tragedies that befall his characters, what emerges in the end is Ray's unshakable faith in the ability of human beings to confront life's myriad problems with confidence and fortitude.

In the course of the trilogy, Apu traverses a path strewn with disasters and calamities; but in the end we see him, chastened by experience and sobered by self-knowledge, yet ready with assurance to confront life's complexities. Ray's deeply humanistic vision is reminiscent of the spirit of the Upanishads and the Gita.

Another aspect of his vision, also strongly reminiscent of the Hindu attitude, is a view of human existence as endlessly flowing. Human beings live and die, experience joys and sadness, triumphs and defeats; but life goes on. Human beings transcend their tragedies by acting them out. Apu's life and that of his mother illustrate this.

In this incessant flow of life, Ray cautions us that we should be sensitive not only to larger concerns, but also to little things: lilies blooming in a pond, raindrops dancing on leaves, grass swaying in the wind, waterbugs flitting across the pond's surface, a flock of birds taking flight—Ray's films capture these moments, reminding us to exult in simple joys. These simple scenes and episodes, characteristic of the Hindu tradition, are in Ray's hands metaphors of larger forces both powerful and mysterious. He remarked in an interview (Isaksson 1970, 120):

> This is Indian tradition. It's very, very important. The presence of the essential thing in a very small detail, which you must catch in order to express larger thing; and this is in Indian art, this is in Rajput miniatures, this is in Ajanta, this is in Ellora, this is in the classics, in Kalidasa, in Sakuntala, in folk-poetry, in folk-singing. . . .

The vital center of Ray's vision can be located in his profound compassion for human beings. Unlike the works of most other filmmakers (Eastern and Western), there are no villains in his work, only victims deserving our sympathy. As Chidananda Das Gupta has observed, Satyajit Ray's films mirror more than a trace of Indian fatalism, and Ray himself has admitted this openly.

One observes a sense of detachment, a distancing from the immediate unfolding of action, resulting in a mood of meditation. In the manner of traditional Hindu thinkers, Ray seems to be saying that nobody chooses the circumstances of his birth, and the struggle to exist is circumscribed and predetermined by this imperative. As Das Gupta (1980, x) points out:

> The nobility of man lies in the effort itself. This knowledge does not take away from man's effort, but gives it a serenity denied to those who think they have the power to change the world and hence hold the end to be above the means that finally corrupt them. The philosophical outlook underlying Ray's work is Indian and traditional in the best sense of that overused word.

Thus Satyajit Ray analyzes human relations and projects his vision of man and society in ways that display the imprint of Indian culture. So, too, does his cinematographic art gain meaning and depth as a consequence of its close affinity to the defining spirit of Indian culture. The word that seems to encapsulate the objective of Ray's art as a filmmaker is "wonder"—the wonder of nature, of small children seeing a train race by, of an old woman facing death, of an estranged father seeking to cement a relationship with his son. Ray's meditative and lyrical art of cinema serves to heighten this sense of wonder.

His camera, sound track, and the pace of his films, ruminative and explorative, reinforce this element of wonder, much in the manner of Vedic hymns. The word "wonder" *(chamathkara)* has deep implications for Indian aesthetics. One of the greatest contributions of classical Indian poets to world aesthetics is the conceit of "aesthetic emotion" *(rasa)*. According to this concept, the ultimate aim of any work of art is the creation of an aesthetic emotion in the mind of the connoisseur. This can happen only when the raw emotions *(bhava)*, extracted from life, are transformed and transmuted by the poetic imagination *(pratibha)* of the artist into aesthetic emotion.

Indian aestheticians, like Abhinavagupta and Bhatta Lollata, explicate at great length exactly how this process takes place. According to these classical theorists of literature, the essence *(sara)* of aesthetic emotion is the element of wonder. This quality permeates Ray's trilogy as well as his subsequent works, thereby investing his creations with an unmistakable "Indianness."

The theory of suggestion *(dhvani)* is another pivotal concept of Indian aesthetics. Formulated and developed by ninth-century aestheticians such as Anandavardhana and Abhinavagupta, it has exerted a profound influence on Indian creative and critical sensibilities.

The kernel of this concept is that in "good" literature suggestion takes precedence over explicit statements and depictions. Indian thinkers would have agreed with the observation of a Western writer who said that prose is heard, while poetry is overheard. Satyajit Ray, in making his films, pays great attention to the concept of suggestion. The subtlety in his portrayal of human relations, the muted musicality and unobtrusive grace characteristic of his trilogy and subsequent works, derive from his adherence to it.

In discussing *Charulata,* which is arguably the finest of Ray's films, the British film critic Penelope Houston (1965, 31) remarked:

> Beauty, tenderness, lyricism; but also a rigorous discipline. There is a characteristic Ray scene. . . . A shadowed interior, shuttered against the sun; rooms rather large and cluttered, with the sounds of birds or animals just penetrating the walls; two people, arriving at some moment of discovery about themselves, caught in an instant of absorbed silence.

In a scene like this, quintessentially Ray, one can detect what the ancient Indian aestheticians referred to as "suggestion." Ray composes every frame with utmost care, seeking to secure his impact through audio-visual nuances of perception. The Apu trilogy is full of such instances. One of the most memorable is at the end of *Song of the Road,* when the family leaves the ancestral village to go to the city.

Ray uses visual symbols with supreme artistry in order to evoke a mood, to create an atmosphere, and to bring out the deeper layers of meaning in human interaction—as with the symbol of the train, which appears in all three films. It is a realistic detail, but one charged with symbolic meaning: the antithetical but concomitant relationship between man and nature, the contrary pulls of tradition and modernity, the transition from village to city, and the notion of man's life being an unending journey. Ray comments (Isaksson 1970, 117): "Trains have something about them . . . it's a symbol of a journey, it's a symbol also of connections, between the rural India and metropolitan India."

Symbols such as these play a crucial role in his films, serving to create a complex world of emotion through compression and suggestion.

Classical Indian theorists considered the simile (*upama*) to be one of the most potent instruments of poetic enquiry. Aestheticians like Vishvanatha, in his treatise *Sahitya Darpana*, sought to taxonomize similes into scores of discrete categories, depending on their nature and function in poetic statement; and Kālidāsa, the finest Sanskrit poet and playwright, is generally regarded as the greatest exponent of the art of simile. In Ray's Apu trilogy, as well as in his later films, he makes skillful use of similes to vitalize the scenes and events he portrays, for example, in *The Unvanquished*.

In traditional Indian writing, both Hindu and Buddhist, the departure of the soul or the life-force is likened to a flock of birds flying off into the faraway sky. In *The Unvanquished*, Ray uses this otherwise fairly commonplace and traditional simile in a manner that infuses great poetic beauty and controlled dynamism into the scene depicting the death of Apu's father.

It is Ray's manner of cutting that brings his simile to life. Gerald Mast perceptively compares Ray's editing to that of Eisenstein: Ray cuts from the father's deathbed to an image of the birds, just as Eisenstein cut from images of workers on strike to those of oxen. As Mast points out, Ray's camera focuses on Harihar's face as it collapses suddenly on the pillow. At the same moment, there is a startling sound of a crack, and Ray cuts immediately to a close-up of a flock of birds, frightened and taking wing, apparently startled by the noise. About twenty-eight frames later, Ray cuts again to a long shot of the birds.

After this strategy of startling movement and sound, Ray alters the mood of the film as his camera languidly observes the birds flying off into an evening sky with grace and poetic tranquility, catching beautifully the way they fade into the distance. Mast (1977, 67) goes on to point out:

> he lets us watch this flight and dwell in this languidness only briefly, perhaps five seconds, before he jerks us back into the story, cutting short our pleasure in the gracefully flying birds as life has cut short the existence of the father. The flight of the birds on screen is like the man's life itself, so beautiful yet so ephemeral, so short. The moment is not only exquisite in itself; it is a startling and effective depiction of the moment of death, of loss, of departure from life.

There are many other instances from the Apu trilogy to show how Ray uses what would otherwise be commonplace similes to vivify his scenes through deft manipulation of sound and image by imaginative cutting.

The element of rhythm plays a significant role in classical Indian poetry, music, and art. Traditional Sanskrit aestheticians dwelt at length on this aspect. They sought to demonstrate how rhythm reveals emotions and meaning. Satyajit Ray also makes great use of rhythm in his films to dramatize their content, paying utmost attention to the juxtaposition of scenes and movement. The pastoral beauty of *The Song of the Road* and the pervasive lyricism of *The Unvanquished* derive in no small measure from the beautifully controlled and modulated rhythm of these films. Pauline Kael (1975, 142) says that:

> What is distinctive in Ray's work (and it may be linked to Bengali traditions in the arts, and perhaps to Sanskrit) is that sense of imminence—the suspension of the images in a larger context. The rhythm of his films seems not slow but, rather, meditative, as if the viewer could see the present as part of the past and could already reflect on what is going on.

Many critics have called Ray's trilogy a poetic exploration of life in Bengal, which seems an accurate characterization. Once again, this aspect of his films is connected to traditional Indian culture. Drama constituted a vital segment of classical Sanskrit literature, and one of the terms to denote drama in Sanskrit is *drishya kavya* (visual poetry). Poetry played such a crucial role in classical Indian drama that works of master dramatists like Kālidāsa and Sri Harsha can be regarded as extended poems. In Sanskrit dramas, as in Ray's films, poetic undertones and lyrical explorations take precedence over explicit human conflicts.

However, Ray does not merely translate the imperatives of his culture into film. If that were so, his films probably would be excruciatingly dull to watch and would be unlikely to have much impact on the international scene. What he tries to accomplish is something more complex and meaningful. As someone from the urban middle class, familiar with both Western and Indian culture, he seeks to explore the deepest layers of his consciousness and that of his society, which has led him to an invigorating creative encounter with the structures of Indian culture.

Ray is a modern who is turning to tradition to see how best his modernity can be enriched and given depth by the force of tradition. He was once asked in an interview who did he think was the greater man, Gandhi or Nehru? His reply (Isaksson 1970, 120) illuminates a vital aspect of his personality as well as his creative pursuit:

I was closer to Nehru, I think. I admired Nehru, I understood him better, because I am also in a way a kind of product of East and West. A certain liberalism, a certain awareness of Western values and a fusion of Eastern and Western values was in Nehru, which I didn't find in Gandhi. But of course as a man, as a symbol, in contact with India's multitude [Gandhi] was quite extraordinary. But as a man . . . I always understood what Nehru was doing. . . .

These comments reflect Ray's desire to create a cultural synthesis, to make use of his familiarity with Western culture to draw out the inner essence of his inherited culture, as is amply evidenced in the Apu trilogy.

As Ray has pointed out, film as a medium of artistic communication is an importation from the West. In order to understand the grammar of cinema, one has to have some acquaintance with Western culture. Ray says that a Bengali folk poet or primitive artist would not be able to understand the medium of film. Ray attempts to convert this imported and alien medium of artistic communication into a ductile medium capable of giving creative expression to the defining configurations of his own culture. He invests it with an indigenous flavor while promoting the highest goals of mature art. In short, he strives to indigenize the medium in the best sense of the term.

He learned his craft from such masters of Western cinema as Renoir, De Sica, and Rossellini. Speaking of Renoir, Ray says he liked his films because of "A feeling for nature; a deep humanism with a kind of preference for the shades of grey, a sort of Chekhovian quality; and his lyricism and the avoidance of clichés" (Isaksson 1970, 115).

These are the very qualities that can be discerned in Ray's films. The Western masters of cinema quickened his imagination and acted as catalysts in the awakening of his own creative faculties. In his films, cinema as cultural expression and cinema as cultural synthesis are at their finest; and they are one and the same.

It is important that Satyajit Ray, by his own account, is city-born and city-bred and had to learn the culture of rural Bengal as a conscious effort. This permitted him a certain distance from it, which has proved extremely advantageous in his creative explorations of village life. Ray's depiction of village life is more mature and pulsates with forebodings of change in a way that Bibhutibhushan Bannerji's novel does not. Bannerji was deeply immersed in rural culture, and it is arguable that creative detachment is needed for sublime art.

As reflected in the Apu trilogy, Ray presents a wonderful intermingling of tradition and modernity, or rural sensibility and urban consciousness, Indian and Western values. He makes use of the distance and detachment afforded by his Western education to probe more deeply into the springs of Indian cultural life and modes of feeling. This observation has important implications: film as cultural expression succeeds most when the artist is at once attached to and detached from the culture under scrutiny. In cinema the expression of a culture is the fruit of an active search and not of passive reception.

The Apu trilogy is not a flawless work of art. Revisiting it after twenty-five years, viewers may find many more deficiencies than they saw in it originally. For example, the first half of *The Song of the Road* is flawed in many ways, as Ray himself has admitted. It betrays an inadequate and uncertain grasp of the film medium: shots are held unwarrantedly for long periods, there are deficiencies in pace and thoughtless cuts, and the camera is sometimes held in inappropriate positions. There are also problems of social identification of the characters. Clearly the director was learning as he went along. These defects notwithstanding, the Apu trilogy, imbued with intimations of deep humanism and lyrical sensibility, stands as a just testimony to the creative fecundity of a burgeoning talent. The British film director Lindsay Anderson (quoted in Seton 1971, 114) said of *The Song of the Road:*

> With apparent ease and formlessness, *Pather Panchali* traces the great design of living. . . . You cannot make films like this in a studio, nor for money. . . . Satyajit Ray has worked with humanity and complete dedication; he has gone down on his knees in the dust and his picture has the quality of intimate unforgettable experience.

This quality of "intimate unforgettable experience" is engendered by the fruitful interaction between art, vision, and culture.

After completing the Apu trilogy, Satyajit Ray went on to make more complex and artistically mature films such as *Charulata, The Goddess (Devi),* and *Days and Nights in the Forest (Aranyer Din-Ratri).* Following Ray's pioneering efforts many other filmmakers, like Mrinal Sen, Aravindan, Karnad, Gopalakrishnan, and a whole host of younger directors, have sought to widen the scope of artistic cinema in India and give it a greater dynamism.

However, Ray's Apu trilogy will stand as a memorable work that ushered in a new phase in Indian cinema and won for it international recognition. The success of the trilogy is largely due to the skillful manner in which Ray sought to give expression to the culture of which he is a part. Clifford Geertz was quoted at the beginning of this paper, to the effect that undirected by cultural patterns, man's behavior would be ungovernable and would amount to mere chaos of pointless actions and shapeless experiences.

As we study the Apu trilogy, we become more and more persuaded of Geertz's perceptive observations. Both the substance of Ray's work and its form (being indissolubly linked at the deepest level of artistic receptivity) bear out Geertz's viewpoint. It is the shaping power of culture, when artistically and insightfully presented by a filmmaker like Satyajit Ray, that crystallizes film images into vivid metaphors of the human condition.

References

Clark, T. W.
    1975 *Song of the Road*, trans. T. W. Clark and T. Mukherji. Bloomington: Indiana University Press.
Das Gupta, Chidananda
    1980 *The Cinema of Satyajit Ray*. New Delhi: Vikas Publishing House.
Geertz, Clifford
    1973 *The Interpretation of Cultures*. New York: Basic Books.
Houston, Penelope
    1965 "Ray's Charulata," *Sight and Sound*, 35, 1:31–33.
Isaksson, Folke
    1970 "Conversation with Satyajit Ray," *Sight and Sound*, 39, 3:114–120.
Kael, Pauline
    1975 *Reeling*. Boston: Little Brown and Company.
Mast, Gerald
    1977 *Film/Cinema/Movie: A Theory of Experience*. New York: Harper and Row.
Rangoonwalla, Firoze
    1980 *Satyajit Ray's Art*. New Delhi: Clarion Books.
Ray, Satyajit
    1976 *Our Films, Their Films*. Bombay: Orient Longman Limited.
Seton, Marie
    1971 *Portrait of a Director: Satyajit Ray*. Bloomington: Indiana University Press.

8
The Woman:
Myth and Reality in
the Indian Cinema

ARUNA VASUDEV

IT IS NO COINCIDENCE that the first Indian film was a "mythological." The moral education of all but the thinnest layer of affluent, Westward-looking Indians is derived from the epics. These stories, despite liberal doses of miracles and fantasy, are no fairy tales easily told and easily forgotten. Nor are they irrelevant to real life, a part of the literary and artistic heritage of the past like Greek mythology for Western civilization. On the contrary, they have a living reality and a dominant say in the conduct of daily life still today.

Unfortunately for the women of India.

The example of Sita, the perfect woman, the perfect wife, acquiescing unquestioningly to her husband's rejection of her in what is nothing more than an abject surrender to the prejudice of male dominated society, has been held up as the ideal for all women to follow. In the epic *Ramayana* (Lal 1981), she says:

> A wife's god is her husband,
> He is her friend,
> He is her guru,
> Even her life is less
> Than her husband's happiness.

Bound by the Rules of Manu the Law-Giver, the average woman in India has had no opportunity to become anything more than the role to which she has been restricted as daughter, wife, mother. "In childhood a female must be subject to her father, in youth to her husband, when her lord is dead to her sons; a woman must never be independent," wrote the "great" Manu, following this with: "She must not seek to separate herself from her father, husband, sons. . . . She must always be cheerful, clear in the management of her household affairs, careful in cleaning her utensils, economical in expenditure. Him to whom her father may give her, or her brother with the father's permission, she shall obey as long as he lives and when he is dead, she must not insult his memory." With these few lines, women were condemned for two thousand years to a life of subjugation. Tradition required it, and the popular cinema enthusiastically upheld it. In film after film, one sees these popular values reiterated, underlined, reinforced.

To the weight of this tradition is added a Victorian hypocrisy that still dominates the thinking of Western-educated, urbanized Indians—a middle-class morality that makes a sharp distinction between woman as wife and mother and woman as mistress and lover. Love is by no means forbidden. A woman may love a man—Radha loved Krishna—but it has to be an all-consuming, pure, and eternal love. The prostitute, too, must subscribe to this convention. When she falls in love, she must give up her profession to devote herself to the object of her devotion—more frequently, to the memory of that unattainable love.

Subscribing to the predominantly orthodox views of the large majority of their audience, rather than acknowledging the reality of woman's growing influence and contribution to society, filmmakers generally prefer a portrayal of women that perpetuates male domination. As such, these images reflect not so much society as it is evolving as the way they would wish it to remain.

Within the Family: Wife and Mother

The pinnacle of ambition for a woman is marriage: of achievement the birth of a son. Within marriage, her role is clearly demarcated. If, for whatever reason, she deviates from it, it is seen as a betrayal of her biological and functional role, and she must pay a price in humiliation and defeat. In a film made in the late seventies, *Thodisi Bewafaii,* for instance, the talented actress Shabana Azmi is the personification of a modern young woman. The spoiled daughter of an indulgent father, she marries the man of her choice. When he loses his money, instead of putting her education to constructive use by working, as is happening more and more in real life, she simply picks up her son and goes home to her father. When he in turn loses his job, she trails aimlessly around the house, ending up a drudge in her brother's home. The wheel comes full circle. Her brother's wife resents her as much as she resented her own sisters-in-law. Eventually, crushed and defeated, she is pathetically eager to return to her husband. This pattern is endlessly repeated in the majority of "social" films, where the modern, educated woman is seen as a threat to the status quo, which has to be maintained.

Another seventies film, *Do Anjane,* is the tale of a wife determined to pursue her career as a classical dancer. She is shown as petulant and selfish, driving her loving, impecunious husband into debt and then leaving him. Inevitably he comes out on top, rich and successful, while she suffers all the humiliation due to a woman who dares to rebel against her role as wife and mother.

A film that is considered a landmark in the Indian cinema is Shantaram's *Duniya Na Mane,* made in both Hindi and Marathi in 1937. An orphaned young woman is duped by her money-grabbing uncle into marriage with an old man. Fearlessly unconventional, she refuses to fulfill any wifely duties. Her spirited revolt brings the husband round to recognize the iniquity of his action and the injustice to women practiced by society. He kills himself to leave her free. The ambivalence in the perception of the woman's role also comes through. Earlier, when the husband wipes away the *bindi* (the red mark that traditionally signifies marriage) from his wife's forehead and calls her *beti* (daughter), she is distraught. Fear of rejection? Fear of "what will people say"? Her courage seems to evaporate. Although this film has been hailed as the first blow for women's emancipation, it provides only limited answers, because the fate of a widow then, and to a small extent still today, is almost worse than servitude in marriage.

It is one of the paradoxes of the Indian film, as of Indian life, that the woman is, on the one hand, victimized as a wife and, on the other, venerated as a mother. The mother-figure has a prominent place in the cast of characters of most films, none of which ever treat of a relationship between mother and daughter. Even with sons, it is not so much a relationship that is explored or portrayed as the deification of the mother. Self-sacrificing, martyred, and ill-used by the husband, or by fate, she is shown as indestructible when it comes to protecting her sons. The strong mother-son tie is in the background of most films. It frequently manifests itself in the maltreatment of the young daughter-in-law, in real life as in the cinema. Thus the implication is that a woman's only hope of salvation lies in becoming the mother of sons.

Beyond the Family: The Courtesan

Obviously, in the circumstances, no real relationship can develop with a wife who is a potential mother/goddess and therefore must be a pure and sexless creature. With whom, then, can a man have a satisfying relationship, physical and emotional? The courtesan has always been a significant figure in classical Indian literature and, until the seventies, a staple of the Indian film. Since she is forever excluded from the pale of domesticity, she can answer his physical needs, cater to his fantasies (unlike the wife, who must be used only for procreation). Of course, he may not fall in love with her, but inevitably her heart is lost to him. She provides solace, a haven, and when he recovers sufficiently from his sorrows, he goes his way, leaving her to pine for the rest of her life, having lost all taste for her profession. This archetypal prostitute was created in the thirties in *Devdas*. Based on a story by the well-known Bengali writer, Sarat Chandra Chatterjee, it was made simultaneously in Bengali and Hindi. Later, a Tamil version appeared. It was a phenomenal success; a generation is said to have wept over it.

Bimal Roy, the cameraman of the original *Devdas,* moved to Bombay, became a highly regarded maker of "social" films, and twenty years later, made another Hindi version with the stars of that era. It had an almost equal success. Twenty years after that, the poet-filmmaker Gulzar, who had been Bimal Roy's assistant, launched a third, still-to-be-completed Hindi version. However, it seems unlikely that today's audiences, fed on a diet of sex, violence, and the rebel hero, would be moved by the *Devdas* neoromanticism.

In the sixties, *Chetna,* broke away from the pattern and made a big impact. It showed a young man falling in love with a girl he discovers to be a prostitute and marrying her. However, the film stopped short of allowing the marriage to be consummated by contriving an ending in which she kills herself. The premise is daring, the resolution once again conformist. Suicide, or a conveniently accidental death, has always been the solution for uncomfortable situations of all kinds, particularly for women.

Women at Work

The working woman has suffered a still more ignominious fate. In the thirties a few films had shown women with professions, but by the end of the film they were made to renounce them. In *Dr. Madhurika,*

THE WOMAN   111

adapted from a story by the celebrated Hindi novelist K. M. Munshi, the doctor has to end by becoming a submissive wife. In *President,* which was revolutionary in the sense that it showed a woman as the head of a company, the woman commits suicide when she discovers her sister is in love with the same man.

Despite the transformation in society that has taken place in the last two decades and the remarkable way in which women have emerged from the doubtful shelter of their homes into a wide variety of jobs at all levels, most films show even educated women with no occupation. When they do work, it is as a typist, a secretary or school teacher, very occasionally as a lawyer or doctor. The working woman is invariably a young girl doing a job while waiting to get married. This modern miss is almost always shown as the temptress, as man's evil genius. She dresses provocatively in Western clothes, smokes, and laces her vocabulary with English words.

In contrast, and in conflict with the working woman, is the traditional, barely literate, sari-clad damsel, a model of conservative virtue who always wins out. The "modern" girl is either defeated or made to reform, having been brought to see the error of her ways. Everything is idealized, romanticized, sentimentalized. Refuge and release are found in a song or in prayer. Confronted with situations she cannot handle, and there are many, this woman rushes off to the prayer room of the house to pour out her grief to the image of the God. Women are seldom shown as capable of rational, logical thought or action.

The result of this denigrating depiction of education and a career for women had serious consequences for Indian society. In the fifties, educators and social workers petitioned the government to take steps to counter the effect of films that showed educated women in a negative light. According to them, all efforts to introduce education for girls were being nullified by the image of the educated woman projected by the popular cinema.

The Sex Object

The changes in society that were swept in with the seventies were so fundamental that even the commercial cinema could no longer ignore them. A strong, vocal movement for women's rights extended to sharp criticism of the media and the images it propagated. The alternate cinema began making inroads into traditional concepts; a few actresses themselves helped to raise (even marginally) a new consciousness about the consistently negative roles they were expected to play. The rigidity of past norms could no longer be unthinkingly upheld. An occasional film did raise issues that were beginning to shake Indian society.

I Demand Justice (*Mujhe Insaaf Chahiye*, 1983) shows a young woman's determination to make her errant boy friend recognize the child she is expecting—without demanding that he marry her—captured the spirit of contemporary attitudes. The woman lawyer who fights her case in court echoed the modern mood. In a fighting speech, she demands that if certain practices are sanctified by the Shastras, then let those Shastras be burned. A few years earlier, such a statement would not have been permitted, or if it had, would have elicited strong protests from traditional-minded audiences. Instead, in audiences at regular shows, man and woman, young and old, applauded statements such as: "If the girl made a mistake, so did the boy. Why should only she be made to pay the price for it." The times have changed, but only a handful of mainstream directors seem aware of it.

In *What Kind of Justice is This* (*Yeh Kaisa Insaaf*, 1979), a young man and woman are each the sole support of their families. Although very much in love, she hesitates to marry him, afraid that she may not be able to continue providing for her widowed mother and young brother. He convinces her that because they are both educated, modern-thinking, and earning, there was no reason why her salary should not go to her mother. They get married. Inevitably, conflicts arise and she leaves her husband saying, "What kind of justice is this where a man is praised for taking care of his parents, but for a married woman to do so is not acceptable." In other words—and it is a thought echoed in many films—a woman who is financially responsible for her family has no right to get married. This is one of the few films that challenged that assertion and the authority of a feudal patriarchal system in which men had a vested interest, which was starting to crumble. In the emerging contradiction, tensions were aggravated by sexual frustration. The cinema, no longer able to close its eyes to the increasingly liberated woman—educated, working, independent—began to distort its presentation of her. She was depicted, on the one hand, as an easy prey to erotic and frequently violent fantasy and, on the other, reduced to an object of decoration, no longer even of desire.

The Scales of Justice (*Insaaf Ka Tarazu*, 1980), a very successful film, is supposedly a cry against rape. It has the voluptuous star Zeenat Aman as a beautiful, successful model. She is not shown as "bad," having none of the attributes associated with "loose" women.

She does not smoke or drink; she is not promiscuous. But she is independent, dresses and works as she pleases, lives alone with a younger sister, and has no family to lend her "responsibility." This is totally unacceptable. It is, as Joan Mellen (1973, 27) says about the pattern in Western cinema, "society's own vengeance upon women. It enslaves those it protects and it rapes and mutilates those who escape its inhibiting norms. . . ."

In a sense, even more significant than the rape in the film is the implicit approval of an inherent hypocrisy. In an early scene where she is shown getting ready to meet her fiancé's parents, she discards her revealing dresses for a sari and modestly covers her head. The parents are delighted. "We never thought a model could be a good girl," they say approvingly. Later, after the rape, when she goes to court and loses the case, they reappear and condemn her immodesty for thus exposing her "shame" to the world. She is made to conform to this notion of "shame" when she rejects the fiancé, who is still willing to marry her. "This body is soiled," she says and goes away. The court scene is equally revealing. The prosecutor (male) is shown as logical and legalistic, while the victim's woman lawyer argues emotionally. Much later, when she kills her violator after he has raped her sister, she is back in the same court, a self-confessed murderer. This time, however, without a lawyer, she makes an emotion-charged speech in her own defense and is allowed to walk out vindicated and go scot-free. The same would-be parents emerge from the wings, and she falls at their feet. "Beti" (daughter), they murmur endearingly, as they embrace her. So much for immodesty, rape, murder, and the law.

Rape scenes are almost *de rigueur* in the popular success formula. In a bizarre confusion of values, kissing is still rarely shown, nudity is taboo, but highly erotic gyrations that pass for dancing are an integral part of most films. These "dances" are performed by a few young women who specialize in such numbers and whose appearance is eagerly awaited by audiences. The obligatory rape scenes are usually the setting from which the action develops. Often it is the rape of a sister, who then dies, that provides the motive for the revenge and vendetta films that dominated the seventies. A possible answer to the significance of these scenes is provided by Wendy Doniger O'Flaherty (1980, 26), who sees rape in Indian films as "the ultimate expression of a highly sublimated eroticism, the dark mirror image of a genre in which the hero and heroine may not be depicted actually kissing."

Through the seventies, the emphasis shifted from love between the hero and heroine to friendship between two men or two brothers. While women are seldom shown as understanding or supporting each other—they are, in fact, each other's worst persecutors—male camaraderie is underlined in most films. An astonishing series of box office super successes featured the charismatic Amitabh Bachchan in the repeated role of the underdog with a chip on his shoulder and a grudge against society. The romantic lover of the sixties gave way to the angry loner of the seventies, romance to sex and violence, song-and-dance sequences to fight numbers choreographed by "fight masters." In the lonely battle against an indifferent society, the hero's main support is friendship—masculine friendship—with mothers and sisters to be protected from a motley collection of shady, underworld characters. In few of the films is there room for marriage. In many of them the romance ends tragically with the hero sacrificing his love at the altar of friendship. Friendship is what endures. In the syndrome of the seventies, which called for "multi-starrers," somebody has to die. Often it is Amitabh Bachchan, perpetuating the image of the outsider, clasped in the arms not of his beloved but of his buddy.

Naturally in such scenarios, women have peripheral roles. Characterization is minimal as they play out the stereotypal mother or sister or girl friend. One major change has occurred. The vamp, who used to represent the dark side of the heroine, has disappeared. Where in earlier films she was the sexy creature wearing revealing Western clothes, leading the man astray, today it is the heroine who is allowed to be sexy-looking and pure-thinking at the same time—both cabaret dancer/singer and good girl.

In the eighties, as the "new" cinema has begun to make its presence felt, if not commercially at least in terms of awards and prestige, the mainstream cinema is acquiring the appurtenances of a social conscience. But the lie behind the appearance is easily detectable. There is no real commitment to the ideas being advanced. Instead, there is exploitation of hurtful reality to wrench the heartstrings of a susceptible audience. Along the way, distortion, fakery, and playacting. But as audience tastes are showing signs of changing, the popular cinema is being forced to take an introspective look at itself.

PARALLEL LINES

If the mainstream cinema in India reflects the dominant ideology of society, the alternate cinema expresses the emerging social concerns of its percipient minority. It is as rooted in realism as the mass cinema is in escapism, as progressive and open-minded as the other is conservative and backward looking. The latter idealizes the past; the former looks ahead to the future.

Nowhere is this illustrated more vividly than in the treatment of women. The most visible change in society in the years since independence in 1947 is in the position and status of women. The proponents of the new cinema portray the transformation that is taking place with all the attendant upheavals in people's lives, perceptions, behavior. Their attitude towards women is the result not of a deliberately thought-out strategy but rather the unconscious extension of their own approach to life, moulded as much by their general cultural education and awareness of contemporary trends as by their intensive exposure to the Western, particularly European, cinema. Their sensibility is almost directly opposed to the commercial film. In a variety of languages, in Bengali, Malayalam, Marathi, Kannada, and Hindi, thought-provoking new directors, cosmopolitan in outlook but committed to the concept of a modern India, are bringing their own contemporary attitudes to bear on the kind of films they are making. In style, and particularly in content, the differences are sharp.

The Precursors

It began in the sixties, in Bengal, with Satyajit Ray and Ritwik Ghatak. Ray's films, particularly those with an urban setting, have always shown the director's fine perception of the tensions of women, the obvious, outward conflicts in *Mahanagar* (1963), the inner emotional world in *Charulata* (1961). *Mahanagar*, in fact, was the first film to take a woman as the central character. Her transformation, when she starts to work out of family necessity, echoes the transformation in society. It is done with the delicacy and lightness of touch that characterize all of Ray's work. The wife, Arati, takes up a job at a hint from her harassed husband when he finds he just cannot meet the extended family's needs from his salary. At first reluctant, she slowly begins to enjoy her discovery of a whole new world. She becomes friendly with an Anglo-Indian colleague, Edith, who presents her with her first lipstick. There is a marvelous scene where Arati tries on the lipstick— shy, timid, infinitely moving, as we watch her growing awareness of herself as a person. Her confidence grows through her competence at work and at contributing to the family income, but she does not lose sight of her basic values and rises to a spirited defense of her friend

Edith when the boss tries to fire her. She resigns from her job to find that her husband has lost his. Both unemployed, but confident they can fight the odds together, the couple are united for the first time as whole persons not as stereotypes of husband and wife. And the relationships within the family have shifted and altered, gently but fundamentally.

Ray is rarely dramatic. Poetry, with him, lies in the little things that make up the canvas of life. Charulata is one of the most graceful, sensitive, emotionally strong, and memorable women to reach the Indian screen. Her strength is the strength of the pure and the innocent. She falls in love with her brother-in-law, but it is in the expression in her eyes, her stillness, and her silence that you feel it most deeply. Set in 1870, a period when upper-class India was almost more Victorian than England, she knows there is no escape for her, nor does she seek it. She accepts her life but awakened now to a full consciousness of it, as her husband has to a full awareness of her as a person. Ray's women are complex, subtle, strong individuals through whom he makes his statements about the mutations that society is experiencing at all levels.

Ritwik Ghatak's women in two of the greatest of his eight films, *Cloud-Capped Star* (*Meghe Dhaka Tara,* 1960) and *Subarnarekha* (1965) are totally different from Ray. Steeped in Indian myth himself, with a sharp intellectual understanding of its strong cultural manifestations and its distortions, he uses it and transforms it in his films. In *Cloud-Capped Star*, says Kumar Shahani, one of Ghatak's most ardent and illustrious disciples, "the breaking up of society is visualized as a three-way division of womanhood. The three principal women characters embody the traditional aspects of feminine power. The heroine, Neeta, has the preserving and nurturing quality; her sister, Geeta, is the sensual woman; their mother represents the cruel aspect. The incapacity of Neeta to combine and contain all these qualities, to retain only the nurturing quality to the exclusion of others, is the source of her tragedy. This split is also reflected in Indian society's inability to combine responsibility with necessary violence to build for itself a real future."

All this in a simple story of a refugee family, victims of the partition of India, where Neeta is the breadwinner. Her elder brother, evading responsibility, is lost in his world of music; Neeta is the only one who believes in his dreams. The younger brother and sister, still studying, and the old parents (illness compels the father to give up his teaching job) are all Neeta's responsibility. The only thing that she can look forward to in life is the return of Sanat, with whom she is in love. But when he does come back, Sanat discovers Geeta, and with the tacit encouragement of the mother, who is terrified of losing Neeta—"What will you eat if Neeta leaves," she screams at her husband—Geeta marries Sanat. The father watches helplessly at the draining away of his beloved elder daughter's life force. As one by one the two brothers and sister become independent, Neeta's nurturing quality is no longer required, and she is at last free to find refuge and release—in death from tuberculosis. But in that very death—as the hills echo her last cry to her now successful musician brother, "I want to live"—is an affirmation of life and hope.

It is the same in *Subarnarekha*, which has outwardly a more melodramatic form. But the figure of the woman transcends the particular to say in Ghatak's own words: "Today we are all refugees, as we have lost the roots of our lives."

Mrinal Sen is the third of Bengal's trinity of greats. Although he started making films in 1956, he really came into his own only in 1979 as a mature filmmaker in full command of his medium with *And Quiet Rolls the Dawn (Ek Din Pratidin)*. This film and three of the four that followed—*In Search of Famine (Aakaler Sandhaney, 1980), The Case is Closed (Kharij, 1982)*, and *The Ruins (Khandhar, 1983)*—have women as their principal protagonists. *And Quiet Rolls the Dawn*, an extraordinarily evocative film, is a single night in the life of an ordinary family where the eldest daughter, once again, is the solitary earning member. On this long night when she does not come back home, the attitudes of the parents and the younger sister, veer from anxiety about her physical safety to anxiety about what the neighbors will say, to anger, to trauma. It exposes the peculiar, unresolved attitudes towards a working daughter as opposed to a working son, leading ultimately to a disintegration of a class and the norms that had sustained it for so long.

The other three films carry forward the theme of confrontation between past and present, the awareness of guilt the underlying thread running through them. Guilt for affluence and prosperity and exploitation in *In Search of Famine,* where a film crew shooting in a village turns the lives of its people upside down and goes its way. But Smita Patil playing Savitri in this film within a film, is shaken to the core in her encounter with reality in the shape of Durga the village girl, whose life is so closely paralleled in the life of Savitri in the fictionalized story.

In *The Case is Closed,* the young wife of the middle-class couple with one small son is shattered by the death of their young servant boy. Not in a direct sense responsible for it, it awakens her nevertheless to the manner in which the class to which she belongs has always taken for granted the exploitation it has always practiced. In *The Ruins,* a young man from the city is haunted by his encounter with a young woman he meets, his friend's cousin, in the course of a weekend spent with friends at a house far away in the countryside. He goes away, back to his work, his frenetic city life; she stays behind, chained to her ailing mother's bedside, profoundly altered by the contact, strengthened rather than weakened by the unfulfilled promise of life it held out momentarily. All the films have ambiguous, open-ended final scenes, leaving you disturbed and questioning of your own assumptions and motivations.

The Early Years

Mrinal Sen's best work came later, but his *Bhuvan Shome,* together with Basu Chatterjee's *Sara Akash* and Mani Kaul's *Uski Roti,* all in Hindi, all in 1969, are taken as the starting point of the New Cinema. Ray and Ghatak had worked in isolation. They had their many admirers, but there were few filmmakers capable of following in their footsteps. By 1969, the groundwork for a movement had been laid. Film societies were proliferating, the Film Institute had been in existence for eight years—with Ghatak as professor for a short, crucial period—and the Film Finance Corporation, set up in 1960, had decided to start financing new, "noncommercial" filmmakers.

In the very first years following 1969, a number of such films were made, and the cinema took off in several different directions and languages at once. The one characteristic they shared was a definite break with the mainstream cinema. It was like coming out of a stuffy, overcrowded, artificially lit, richly brocaded mansion into the fresh, open air. There was a sense of space, of freedom, of movement. And an end to stereotypes.

Bhuvan Shome has been given an irreverent one-line description—Big Bad Bureaucrat Reformed by Rustic Belle. Sen took the camera out on magnificent sweeping landscapes and the irresistible freshness of Suhasini Mulay as the village belle—a genuine free spirit. *Sara Akash* started what was to become known as the Middle Cinema: straight realism with moments of drama and none of the trappings of commercialism. The content was frequently social conflict, the form narrative. It does not always come out clearly on the side of radical change. Indian society, like its filmmakers, is still too confused and contradictory for anything to be totally unambiguous, but the leanings towards it are unmistakable.

In *Sara Akash,* the young wife is educated, but her ability to read is treated with scorn by the other women in the joint family. A continuation of the traditional practice where women are never supportive of each other? It would seem so. Her education, instead of helping her to cope better with the situation into which she is thrust, is shown as serving no useful purpose. A novel merely provides her with an escape from the taunts of her mother-in-law and the sulky silence of the reluctant young husband, forced by family pressure into an unwelcome marriage. It is only his unhappy sister who shows any sympathy for the helpless wife. Abandoned by her own husband for another woman, the sister lives precariously in her father's house. She is obliged to go back to her husband when he comes to claim her, having been himself discarded by the other woman. Her mother pleads for her but without any real hope or conviction, acknowledging that the father is doing the socially accepted thing in sending his daughter back into what everyone knows will be a life of misery. Significantly, none of the younger women take up the cudgels on her behalf. They too are cowed into believing that the woman's place is with her husband, whatever his faults.

This unwitting and uncritical espousal of the governing norms of the time was overthrown definitively a few short years later within the heart of the middle-of-the-road Hindi cinema, as it had been from the very start by the more experimental innovators of the alternate cinema.

The Alternative Statement

In the movement started at this time, cinema moved far away from the stereotypes that people the commercial film. Women emerged as heroines in the drama of daily life, the men as weak, vacillating, and inadequate. The statement is quiet, but authoritative. The premise and the resolution are both in keeping with the role that women are playing in real life. Self-assured, confident, beginning to break out of the economic dependence that had for so long held them in thrall, more and more women are working, some earning more than men. The new films either portray this growing confidence or denounce the society that tramples upon it. India, like its films, functions at many levels.

Mani Kaul, the earliest of these new young filmmakers, in his first film, *Uski Roti,* makes an unsparing critique of a rural woman's dreary, hopeless drudgery in an equally unsparing form. The bleakness and insecurity and silence in which the wife lives out her life, at the whim of her husband's temper or rare moments of kindness, add up to a scathing attack on a system that conspires to oppress and suppress women. But the controversial notice it received centered more on the style, which stood conventional filmmaking on its head.

Kumar Shahani, who was graduated from the Film Institute with Mani Kaul, made *Mirror of Illusion (Maya Darpan)* in 1971, a film of extraordinary sensibility where it is equally absurd to separate content from form. However, the central character is a young woman, living in a decaying, feudal mansion with her father and widowed aunt. She is the subject of the film—not its object. The look, in a total reversal of the conventions of Indian cinema up till this time, is not that of the male, deriving satisfaction from watching the female as an object. It is the inward look of the woman at herself and the world she perceives around her. Kumar Shahani carries this forward in *The Wave (Tarang,* 1983), an infinitely more complex film where the woman protagonist assumes a mythical dimension reminiscent of Ritwik Ghatak's work.

The South

In Karnataka, at the same time, the birth of a new cinema was induced with the assistance of people from literature and the theater. *Funeral Rites (Samskara,* 1970) was based on a novel by U. R. Ananthamurthy and played by members of an amateur theater group called the Madras Players. Prominent among them were the playwright Girish Karnad and Snehalata Reddy, whose husband, Pattabhirama, directed and produced the film. Orthodox Brahmanism is a strong force in Karnataka and the target of many of the new filmmakers. *Funeral Rites* is a metaphor for the decadence and power of the Brahmins. It shows them plunged in a metaphysical dilemma over the cremation of a renegade member of their sect who has defied every caste taboo, going to the extent of living openly with a low-caste woman. Here the woman continues her traditional role as temptress, but in *The Ritual (Ghatasharddha,* 1977), also written by U. R. Anathamurthy and made by another Film Institute alumnus, Girish Kasaravalli, she is the victim, having transgressed the rigid sexual code of the same orthodox Brahmin society. A child widow, now living with her widowed father, she is seduced by the local schoolteacher and becomes pregnant. All crude and cruel abortion attempts fail. The father is forced into performing the funeral rites for his still-living daughter; her head is shaved and she has to leave the village. Another Brahmin offers his sixteen-year-old daughter in marriage to the old widowed father; another tragedy is in the making. The film, in searing images, bitterly questions the fate of women in such a milieu.

Five years after *The Ritual*, a woman director, Prema Karanth, produced *Phaniyamma* (1982) on the same idea. The terrible injustice to child widows in her films spans the whole life of her protagonist, Phani. Married as a child, widowed before she reaches her teens, she has to submit to her head being shaved and wear only plain white for the rest of her life. The lonely young girl's growing up, growing old, and dying is portrayed with compassionate understanding and, underlying it, a seething anger. Through the succeeding generations of women that Phaniyamma loves and tends, the evolution of a society is laid bare. Towards the end a sixteen-year-old girl is widowed but scorns the conventions that still demand, albeit weakly, that she have her head shaved. "Cut off her hair," she cries out defiantly, thrusting her mother-in-law forward. She stalks off, leaving Phaniyamma to say gently to the appalled custodians of the heritage of the past that times have changed and the dehumanization of women, so long sanctified by traditional religious practice, can no longer be continued.

In film after film, sometimes stridently, most often gently, one sees the bastions of male privilege being stormed and falling as the old order changes, yielding place to new.

The poetry of the contemporary Malayalam cinema could be taken for a withdrawal from the fray into a romantic or metaphysical world. But all of Aravindan's films, particularly the latest, *Twilight* (*Pokku veyil*, 1982), reveal a deeply political person, while Adoor Gopalakrishnan in all three of his films—*One's Own Choice* (*Swayamvaram*, 1972), *Ascent* (*Kodiyettam*, 1977), and *Rat Trap* (*Elippathyam*, 1982) —in chronicling the decay of feudalism, shows his concern with what becomes of the women. In *One's Own Choice*, a young couple fleeing parental disapproval are slowly faced with the end of romance and the sordidness of survival. When the husband dies, survival for the pregnant young wife lies only in one appalling direction. What choice does she have? The film leaves you with the terrible question. In *Ascent*, the women are practical and capable, the man an irresponsible vagabond. *Rat Trap*, the most mature and haunting of his films, is as much about the plight of the woman as her brother's inability to cope with life itself. The eldest sister, who has escaped the suffocating confines of the family home, is a no-nonsense matriarch. The youngest sister finds her own way out. It is only the middle sister, the gentle and undemanding nurturing woman, who succumbs. Her escape lies only in illness, and with her departure the brother sinks into paranoia.

The East

Two recent films in Oriya, *The Winter Night* (*Seeta Rati*, 1982) and *The Mirage* (*Maya Miriga*, 1983), indicate the changes in the perceptions of the woman of herself, by the family, and, by extension, society. In *The Winter Night,* Manmohan Mohapatra says it directly; in *The Mirage,* Nirad Mohapatra only suggests it, but with devastating effect. In the former, a love affair in a small village fades out because the young man does not have the courage to stand up to his father, who opposes the match on grounds of disparity in economic and social status. The woman is the one with the strength to face up to life. In *The Mirage,* the portraits of the three women within the extended family reveal in the most delicate manner the roots of the disintegration of a whole way of life. The elder daughter-in-law's rebellion at the end, her disaffection with her traditional role when confronted with the absolute rejection of it by the new, city-bred sister-in-law, consists only in refusing to light the oven to cook the food. In that gesture the seeds of change are planted. The husband, the eldest son in the large family, becomes conscious of the centuries of suppression and exploitation that his wife embodies and determines to reverse it; it signals the end of an era.

In nearby Bengal, three contemporary, politically minded directors also take the latent strength of women to make their points. In Goutam Ghose's *The Occupation* (*Dakhal*, 1981), it is the woman, the young widow, who takes on the combined strength of all the men representing the law, vested interest, male power and, in fighting for her right to her husband's property, defeats it; in Utpalendu Chakraborty's *The Eye* (*Chokh*, 1982), the demonstration against the corrupt establishment with which the film culminates is led by the dead worker's wife. In Buddhadeb Dasgupta's *The Crossroad* (*Grihayuddha*, 1982), right at the end the woman turns down the man she has so long been in love with, saying that if he has lost the will to continue the (political) struggle, she must carry on alone. Yet, she is by no means militant. Caught in the power play of big business, corruption, politics and all the havoc it connotes, she just carries on doing her work, quietly but with such inner strength that she will never succumb to an easy escape.

THE WOMAN 123

In Marathi, Jabbar Patel's *Threshold* (*Umbartha*, 1982) has provoked heated controversy for the image of its principal woman character. It is the story of a married woman's quest for relevance, a revolt against the emptiness of her affluent environment. Married to an understanding husband, the mother of a lovely little daughter, what more could a woman want? The director does not even suggest that it might be a son, so long considered the final fulfillment of a woman's biological role and the pinnacle of her achievement. On the contrary, this film has the courage and the perception to show that the woman today is looking for her own self as an individual, sentient, human being. An interpretation of the woman in *Threshold* as basically restless and dissatisfied, with a neurotic core to her being which some have chosen to see, springs more from a weakness in the script than the director's intention. Beyond her personal evolution and largely responsible for it, is the Center for Deserted Women she manages for two years, leaving her husband and daughter in the large joint family. At the Center many of the problems of women are raised—desertion, rape, prostitution, suicide, and, for the first time, lesbianism. There is a scathing attack on the pomposity, selfishness, and indifference of the managing committee who look on the women as things, without condemning the society that reduces them to such abject misery. Despite its uneven structure, *The Threshold* offers powerful support to the woman's right to choose the way she wants to live.

In the Hindi film, still considered the closest we come to a national cinema, films with controversial images of women are gaining strength and finding increasingly large audiences. Starting out almost tentatively, the image has become more sharply focused, more uncompromising in the last few years.

Shyam Benegal's films have always been noted for his positive women characters—and for discovering talented new actresses to play them. *The Seedling* (*Ankur*, 1974), which introduced the amazing Shabana Azmi, *Night's End* (*Nishant*, 1975), which started Smita Patil on her rise to the top as a dramatic actress, and *The Churning* (*Manthan*, 1976) form a trilogy of oppression against the poor, the dispossessed, and the women. *The Role* (*Bhumika*, 1977) is based on the life of Hansa Wadkar, a great actress who dared to live life on her own terms. In the series of affairs that took her from one man to another with the shadow of her husband hovering over them all, the film shows little development or growth of her as a person. But at least the affairs were of her own choosing. She was never crushed by the defeats that were a part of her experience, and Smita Patil's smoldering presence invested the whole with a rare intensity. With *The Market Place* (*Mandi*, 1983), though enlivened by the brilliant performance of Shabana Azmi as the madame of a brothel, Benegal has inadvertently tarnished his reputation as a champion of women. Prostitution, especially today, is hardly the stuff of comedy, and showing the prostitutes leading gay, happy, companionable lives with the madame like a broody hen has been roundly condemned. Benegal has a strong social conscience, which is manifested even in this film when a terrified girl is sold into the brothel. She ends up killing herself. The intrusion of tragic reality into what appears designed essentially, if misguidedly, as a light comedy unbalances the structure of the film.

Two films, though hardly commercial in the conventionally accepted usage of the term, were surprisingly well-received by the audience: *The Cry of the Wounded* (*Aakrosh*, 1980) and *The Vicious Circle* (*Chakra*, 1980). Smita Patil's incandescence in both lights up the screen. Although still a victim of circumstances, in neither of these films is the woman an insignificant, pale, defeated character.

But the films that have done the most to shatter the Indian traditional mould in which women have been imprisoned are *Once Again* (*Ek Baar Phir*, 1979) and *The Meaning of Life* (*Arth*, 1983). These films were widely shown, proved commercially successful, and are still the subject of heated discussion.

In Vinod Pande's *Once Again*, the wife, torn between a strong sense of duty and her own preferences, finally chooses to walk out on the husband with whose values and way of life she is in complete disagreement. Although the decision to leave is made in order to stay with the man she has fallen in love with, it was nevertheless revolutionary on the Indian scene. The surprise was that it won the wholehearted approval of the women in the audiences. This was reinforced by Mahesh Bhatt's *The Meaning of Life*. Here the man leaves his wife for another woman, but as she descends into hysteria and neurosis, he attempts a reconciliation with her. She, in the meantime, has pulled herself out of her state of shock and mental paralysis to make something of her life. She meets another man, who falls deeply in love with her. Although tempted by his warmth and undeniable charm, she rejects a second marriage, fearing a repetition of the earlier painful experience. When the husband comes to her, she asks him the question no Indian screen wife would have dreamed of asking earlier—"If I had done what you did, would you have taken me back?" When he is honest enough to acknowledge that he would not, she has made her point and turns away to continue with the life she has made for herself and from which she derives a measure of satisfaction. There are certain glaring inconsistencies in this otherwise courageous film in which Shabana Azmi plays the wife and Smita Patil, the other woman. Although the wife is treated with understanding and sympathy, the other woman, in her dress, behavior, and profession (she is a film actress), displays the iconography of the conventional temptress. Her hysteria seems to stem from her longing for marriage, her neurosis both cause and effect of not being able to satisfy it. The wife finds the courage to live life on her own because she has taken on the responsibility for her maidservant's little daughter. By implication, then, total fulfillment comes from either a husband or a child. It is an ambiguous statement if one examines it closely. In general, however, most women identify with the wife and applaud her conduct—her dignity, self-sufficiency, and courage.

All these years the cinema, new and commercial, has been the near-exclusive preserve of male directors and writers. But now more and more women are entering the field. Entirely different from each other in approach and theme, Aparna Sen and Sai Paranjpye are both their own scriptwriters. Aparna Sen is very conscious of herself as a woman; Sai Paranjpye prefers to be a director first and a woman second. Aparna Sen's first film, *36 Chowringhee Lane* (1981), in English, though a study in loneliness, shows the inherent strength of the central woman character. Sai Paranjpye's forte is comedy, but the viewpoint is the result of a strong male conditioning.

Other women directors are waiting to complete their films. But whether they show a particularly feminine sensibility or not, the new Indian cinema is rich with promise.

References

Lal, P.
  1981   *The Ramayana of Valmiki*. New Delhi: Vikas Publishing House.
Mellen, Joan
  1973   *Women and their Sexuality in the New Film*. London: Davis-Poynter Ltd.
O'Flaherty, Wendy Doniger
  1980   "The Mythological in Disguise: An Analysis of *Karz*," *India International Centre Quarterly*, 8, 1:23–29.

9
The Painted Face of Politics: The Actor-Politicians of South India

Chidananda Das Gupta

A SPECTER is haunting Indian politics—the specter of cinema. Film stars, it seems, have nothing to lose, except their makeup, to become ministers. Some don't even have that much to lose. Two states of South India already have their top film stars as chief ministers; in the two others composing this region, the local matinee idols are waiting in the wings and making off-stage noises. In the rest of the country, too, there is an uneasy feeling about the superstar of the all-India (Hindi-language) film whose family has been very close to the family of Indira Gandhi for decades. In case of need, it is said, he may be persuaded to take the field, especially if the star politicians of the South develop all-India ambitions. The strange case of N. T. Rama Rao, top star of the Telegu-language film, suggests that the cinema is becoming the voice of the proletariat in a country led so far by an English-educated elite.

What manner of men are these—M. G. Ramachandran (MGR), chief minister of Tamil Nadu, and N. T. Rama Rao (NTR), chief minister of Andhra Pradesh? What sort of films have they made? Does the nature of the films have anything to do with their climb to the top and with the nature of the leadership they provide? How did they get to the top anyway? Finally, is this having an effect on all-India politics?

It would be best to begin by looking at the rise of N. T. Rama Rao in Andhra Pradesh, a bizarre instance of cinema taking over government, before a flashback to the earlier success story of MGR of Tamil Nadu, whom NTR regards as his *anna*, or elder brother.

A sixteenth-century astrologer in a hamlet in Andhra Pradesh is said to have made some startling predictions about the future of the country. The book in which these were made, *Kalagyanam (Knowledge of*

Time), is much in demand today and is being translated, among other languages, into English. Some examples for the twentieth century: "A Bania [merchant] will bring freedom to the country"; "A widow will rule India." Mahatma Gandhi did belong to a merchant community; and Indira Gandhi, India's prime minister from 1966 until 1984 (except for an interlude of three years), was indeed a widow.

Early in 1982, the superstar of Telegu films was asked to play the role of this astrologer, Veera Brahmendra Swami, in a film about him. He was given the book of predictions to read in preparation for playing the role of its author. Poring through it, superstar N. T. Rama Rao came across a line predicting that, around 1982–83, "a man with a painted face will rule Andhra." He sat up: "But that's me!" Within a few weeks he had formed a party, Telegu Desam (Telegu Country, named after the language of the state), and after nine months of inspired campaigning, he defeated Indira Gandhi's long-ensconced party in the state elections, becoming the second film-star chief minister of a state in India. (Another version of the story has it that this episode brought to a head an already incipient resolve.)

In deciding that the prediction was about him, N. T. Rama Rao was not being vain, but factual. At age fifty-nine, the foremost actor of Andhra Pradesh carried a big load of paint on his face, transforming his dark skin into a glowing pink that contrasted vividly with jet black eyebrows and bright lipstick. Since he mostly played gods or god-like men, the paint was a must, for all gods, with the exception of Krishna and (in the South) Rama, are supposed to have been Caucasian in the fairness of their skin.

The time was ripe for a film actor with a god-like image to take over the affairs of state. Frequent changes of chief minister, dictated by New Delhi, had caused deep resentment, compounded the problems of corruption and maladministration, and highly incensed a proud people who had played an imperial role in ancient and medieval India. According to many political commentators, the chief ministers were chosen not for their regional following but for their loyalty to Delhi. As one local wag quipped, "Mrs. Gandhi changes Andhra's chief minister as frequently as her saree."

The main NTR film playing in Andhra's theaters through 1982 was *The Tiger of Bobbili (Bobbili Puli)*. A much-decorated Indian army officer is turned into a deserter and an outlaw by the machinations of his villainous father. He escapes from prison, forms his own band of followers, rounds up the judge and the police officers in a cave, and treats them to a homily on the evils of modern society and on the nature of true justice. "Whenever virtue is on the decline," he tells them in stentorian tones, "I appear on earth to rescue the good and punish the bad." The words had been spoken by Krishna in the ancient scripture *Gita* when he was persuading the reluctant Arjuna to fight against his evil enemies. The film heralded NTR wherever he went and played an important role in bringing him victory in the elections.

The audience in the cinema not only cheered loudly but threw confetti on the screen. The ragged urchins in the front rows seemed to carry an inexhaustible supply in their pockets. The theater is so small, decrepit, and tucked away in the rear of a slum, miles out of the nearest town, that it took hours to find it. Found, it proved to be empty inside and besieged by a crowd outside, waiting patiently all day for the power failure to end. Evening came, but power did not. One had to come back the next day to contend with ticket holders of both days. Finally the manager arranged for us to see the film standing in the projection booth. All around, the buildings bore the signs of the recent elections. The initials NTR still remained stenciled on urinal walls; torn "Vote for NTR" posters flapped in the wind.

Cinema in South India

The power of the cinema in South India has to be seen to be believed. Like a tropical jungle speeded up by stop-motion photography, it grows before one's eyes, sprouting out of the streets of the cities and the ears of their citizens, overflowing everything, covering the sidewalks and the walls with its lush undergrowth, threatening to engulf not only politics, but life itself. Fifty-foot cutouts of film stars glower down upon Madras pedestrians, patches of tinsel shimmering over their many-colored costumes; rows of posters, large and small, cover all available wall space, surround the open areas and drape the trees with a restless, grasping energy. Thousands of fan clubs rally to the support of their favorite stars, fulfilling their every wish and defending them if not to the death, at least to a few broken limbs.

The entire length of Kingsway, Secunderabad's main road (now named after the president of India), is dominated by rows of film distribution offices displaying paper posters and painted hoardings. A few shops for industrial durables are uncomfortably wedged in between them. An enormous painted cutout of superstar Kamalahasan, flanked by his heroines in various states of undress, stands in a dynamic diagonal against Hyderabad's huge Hussain Sagar Lake, large tufts of his underarm hair swept back in deft strokes of the sign painter's art.

The huge cinema theaters (two of the best in Hyderabad are owned by the chief minister's family) gleam in shining metal and etched glass, dusted and wiped on the hour, their lobbies decked out with kitschy Christs and Krishnas leading their devotees up shining ramps and escalators with colored lights. These are the temples of modern India. Monumental in size, cleaner than most city hospitals, they are to the common people what the five-star hotels are to the newfangled industrial executives.

South India makes the bulk of India's 700-odd feature films a year; the ratio of cinema sets to the population is more than twice the national average. Unlike other parts of the country, the South has a large number of "touring cinemas," thatched huts with projectors that set up shop in small towns and large rural villages like the nickelodeons of the United States, or, in a way, the world-trudging salesmen of the Lumière Brothers. The center of production used to be Madras, the capital city of Tamil Nadu (ruled by a film star chief minister). No matter which of the four Southern languages was spoken in a film, it would be shot in a Madras studio. Today, regional production centers have come up, and much of the filmmaking in South India has become decentralized. Yet Madras remains a focal point of the film industry. The Hindi film, which is shown all over India, also has a large following in the South. Many Hindi films are made in Madras and are often mere remakes of South Indian films. All-India film stars play in Tamil and Telegu films constantly. Bombay, which used to dominate the production scene, has yielded the pride of place to Madras.

What kinds of film are these that seem to turn superstars into arbiters of the nation's destiny? By and large, they are variety shows loaded with song-and-dance numbers, fight scenes, cabarets, car chases, and high drama of coincidences and deus ex machina connected by a thin story line and a sturdy actor. The characters are types, not individuals; they are derived from folk forms to the extent that good and evil are clearly defined with no grey shades around. They celebrate notions such as: whatever is modern and Western is bad, especially the modern working woman; the village is good, the city is wicked; traditional values, religion, filial piety, patriotism, family honor must be upheld—but not before a Cook's tour of delectable sin with rape and seminude, hip-and-breast-shaking dances. The acting derives its hamming from the forms bred in the all-night, open-air rural traditional theaters and puts them into the intimacy of the cinema screen. The older rural forms required loud voices that could be heard and exaggerated gestures that could be seen from a distance. There is no question in the cinema that follows them of the inner logic of a character's motivations and development. The songs are interregnums—they hold up the action, which is promptly resumed after the song is over. Sometimes the song is also a commentary on the action. There is a lot of sexual innuendo and sensual buildup toward a climax that is never shown. Kissing is adroitly bypassed, although the censors do allow it if it is considered a necessary part of the story telling. The place of the kiss and the sexual union is taken by the song, which bursts forth orgasmically like a flood breaking out of a dam. There is much brandishing of "modernity," but because it is not integrated into the lives of either the screen characters or the audience, it becomes a form of clowning. NTR will thus dress in a chocolate jacket with white lapels and dance on a green hillside with a heroine who wears unrealistically skimpy clothes, both flailing their arms and jumping around to the rhythm without any choreography or system of steps. The expression on the actor's face could only be described as a permanent leer fixed upon the hip-wiggling heroine. Double to multiple roles for a star are common and considered a feather in his or her cap. Two people who are patiently played by the same performer are presented as different—father and son, mother and daughter, twins or sometimes even friends, one with a moustache, one without. As a Telegu reviewer points out, in the film *Prema-Simhasana,* "K. R. Vijaya is both NTR's mother and wife," for NTR plays both father and son. The threshold of suspension of disbelief is extremely low. Little heed is paid to realism. South Indian actors will often make up their faces, neglecting the rest of the body. The skin tone of the hand may be startlingly different from that of the face. The main characters will be made up, the others left as they are. Standards of lighting and photography are, on the whole, higher in Bombay than in the South; the dances there are cut with more skill, and many films have individual sequences of international standard. Some Bombay films attempt more complex themes of marital relations and conflicts of old and new, touch sensitive spots before returning to conventional denouements. Such departures from the traditional are fewer in the soap operas of the South. Stars as in Bombay often act in three different films a day, in different shifts, starting at 7 A.M. and going on till after midnight. In Tamil Nadu, an actor may appear for the first shift in Madras and for the second in Coimbatore, 500 miles away. His time is so precious that the cameraman has no chance to light him properly. One cameraman is in the habit of asking the main actor where he is going—Salem or Coimbatore. He will then bark his order: "Salem Lights!" or just "Coimbatore!" Salem is nearer, so some refinement in the lighting is possible; Coimbatore is too far for anything beyond plain visibility.

There is a tendency in India to regard all films other than those in Hindi as regional, because their circulation is confined to their own linguistic areas. However, there is little that is regional about South Indian-language cinemas, especially the Tamil and the Telegu, other than the language. The recipe is the same: dances and songs, high-pitched melodrama, rape and mother-worship, fights and "love scenes" (always played in the copious lap of nature—hills and dales, flowers and tress), coincidences, multiple roles by the main performers. Over the years, the differences between the all-India film and the regional film have narrowed, especially in the South, because more and more, the Hindi formulae have come to be accepted as the model. In fact, the Tamil and Telegu films have outdone the Hindi film at its own game; Bombay now regularly remakes South Indian successes, especially in Telegu. Thus the Telegu *Justice Chowdhury*, with N. T. Rama Rao in the lead in the inevitable double role, was remade in Hindi within the same year. If anything, the Bombay film is a shade less inane and accommodates more of high art and the intermediate product than the mass cinema in the South.

It is the "new cinema" promoted by federal government loans (and subsidies in some states) that seeks to act as social catalyst of change. These films are closer to Western films of tight narrative illusion and sophisticated cinematic techniques. Yet in some ways they are more Indian, less imitative of the West. These films support constitutional goals and severely criticize the establishment for not implementing them. In the process, they are blamed by the chauvinists for parading India's problems abroad—much to the embarrassment of the country's ambassadors. some films are Marxist and Brechtian, self-consciously seeking identity with Indian tradition or to help the forces of democracy and modernization. Many of the films (beside Satyajit Ray's) are sensitive and well-crafted and have won acclaim nationally and internationally. Most of them are beyond the understanding of the semiliterate and illiterate lumpen that forms the bulk of the mass audience, or anathema to them because of their serious treatment of important themes. They have met the needs of the urban elite but have not, perhaps cannot, reach the large audience. The distribution system is built around the blockbuster. It is difficult for the low-budget films of the "new cinema" to break through. Yet some films are slipping through the net these days, and a few sophisticated filmmakers are trying to reach the wider audience with partial success. A small sector of the in-between film acceptable to both the educated and the uneducated has also been in existence for some time. But the vast majority of the 700-odd feature-length films made every year remain mindless soap operas that reinforce religious orthodoxy and societal values of a bygone era, breeding contempt for the present and dividing rather than integrating mass attitudes torn between the old ideas and new practices. It is in this context that one must see the rise of N. T. Rama Rao and the continuing rule of M. G. Ramachandran.

THE ELECTION OF N. T. RAMA RAO

Asked about his policies as a chief minister in an interview, NTR said: "You have seen the film [*Bobbili Puli*]. There is a man who punishes the bad; there is a man who does justice; there is a man who always sides with the wronged sections of the people. So naturally there is sympathy for the hero. That is the style of role I perform. So the people expect good things to come of my service to them."

It is evident that the chief minister has a simple and strong sense of mission. His sincerity is never in doubt, even to his worst enemies. It was never in doubt when he was campaigning for nine months across his large state, often following or preceding Mrs. Gandhi. People saw in him the savior they had seen in 292 films. In most of these he had played the gods and their incarnations and supermen. For decades they had flocked to see him and bow to him, and now they were doing so again. Riding a 1940 Chevrolet turned into a caravan with a platform and a public address system on top, the god of cinema had crisscrossed the state's 275,000 square kilometers to be greeted with rousing receptions everywhere. The members of his six hundred fan clubs served as his emissaries, and people came to his meetings in hordes. "He would begin his day at 7 A.M. and end at 2 A.M. the next morning," says his biographer, Venkatanarayan. "During the last 19 days of the campaign, the travelling became a round-the-clock affair. He carried just two paris of khaki trousers and full-sleeved bush shirts, bread, butter, honey, lemon juice and soda. Inside the van, he would sit in an aircraft-type seat, surrounded by garlands collected at the meetings and boxes containing cassettes of his speeches to be distributed to party workers."

As soon as the driver alerted him to an approaching crowd, he would climb through a hatch onto the roof and speak to the thousands who ran towards the NTR "chariot" as soon as they heard it coming. In the early hours of the morning, the caravan would stop wherever it was. After three hours of sleep, NTR would wake up, sit by the roadside or near a well, shave, bathe, wash his clothes, eat out of a leaf held in his hand, and then carry on again. On the red-letter day, a record number of 21,496,754 voters exercised their franchise, of whom 9,623,361 voted for NTR's Telegu Desam party, giving it 199 seats in the legislature of 286. And thus the cinema swept to power in one of India's largest and most backward states, weighed down with poverty and illiteracy. As the large, handsome chief minister sat straight on a big chair in his office at six in the morning, dressed in the saffron robes of a religious mendicant, an earring dangling from his left ear (as prescribed by his astrologer), it was impossible not to remember the lines from the *Gita* in his recent film, about God appearing on earth "to rescue the good and punish the evil."

Sincerity is all very well, cynics ask, but what about policies? What does a film actor know about politics? A handsome face and burning eyes may solve problems in films, but in real life? Does he understand economic issues, industrial development, or integrated perspective planning? Poverty is not something you remove with bare hands, however hairy and strong. Talking to a group of intellectuals in New Delhi soon after his triumph, NTR confessed: "I am new to politics, but I want to learn. I want to do something for the people. Please help by telling me how to go about it." Predictably, the hard-boiled eggheads were disarmed. However, some of the naivete may have been assumed for effect. The Telegu Desam party had produced a clear-cut twenty-nine-point preelection manifesto. Since taking over, NTR has been trying to implement the program and, wisely, to avoid confrontation with the federal government. "If the body wants to be strong, the limbs must be strong," he repeats every time the question of regional parties undermining the integrity of the country comes up. Soon after coming to power, NTR announced a grandiose plan for getting together all opposition leaders, including chiefs of states ruled by parties other than Indira Gandhi's. It seemed impossible, but he brought it off. The *mahanadu,* or great assembly, at Vijaywada became the biggest all-India gathering of nonestablishment parties ever seen. Keeping true to his dramatic instincts, NTR kept everybody in style, except himself. He stayed in a hut while other leaders were housed in stately buildings. Agreement among the leaders was achieved on issues so broad as to mean little, but the great assembly nonetheless pointed to the possibility of a national alternative to Indira Gandhi. Atal Bihari Vajpayee, India's foreign minister for the three years (1977–1979) during which Mrs. Gandhi was in limbo, declared astutely that it was time India had a prime minister from the South (so far they have all come from the North, all but one from the Northern state of Uttar Pradesh). In other words, there was a hint that NTR would be acceptable to the opposition parties as the national leader. If this ever comes to pass, the cinema will have taken over power in a country of 730 million.

Cinema and Mass Culture

It is not only in his Southern origin or his mythological image that Rama Rao is different from the national and state leaders India has so far had. For some two hundred years the evolution of modern India has been guided by a Western-educated intellectual elite. Gandhi achieved an extraordinary identity with the common man; yet he had been educated in England and had practiced ballroom dancing and law. He was against the caste system and the feudal hierarchy, cornerstones of India's social tradition, and valued the concepts of individuality, freedom, and equality derived from the West. Today's India owes a tremendous lot to Jawaharlal Nehru, Gandhi's nominated successor. He was the son of a very rich lawyer and a product of Harrow and Cambridge, an embodiment of the "brown Englishman" that Macaulay's education plan for India had envisaged. However, this particular "brown Englishman" had a complete commitment to democracy without shortcuts. Nehru extended the Gandhian concept of individual self-sufficiency to national self-sufficiency as the key to true independence, and this has been responsible for much of India's progress. In the social integration and modernization of India, too, his leadership resulted in a sometimes violent churning-up of a tradition-bound society whose stability has depended on its hierarchical system. Despite his patrician upbringing and Western education, his love for his people and his identity with India's history and tradition were never in doubt.

Yet the fact remains that his was the voice of the elite; the reforms he brought about were initiated in the councils of the great, meant to filter down to the masses. But this filtration invariably clogged up on the way down because a good part of the governmental and party administration had other ideas, shaped to its own vested interest. As a result, large masses of people were left below the poverty line, and the participation of people at the grass-roots level in the planning of the country's progress was never achieved. India's industrial revolution thus followed the outdated model of a Dickensian England muddling through urban destitution, rural displacement, and all-round exploitation of the poor. This is precisely what Nehru had hoped to bypass with his Fabian socialism and did not succeed in doing. The process became more complicated after him. As the infrastructure he had laid down began to create an industrial upsurge, the scramble for the fruits of development intensified, leading to greater corruption and exploitation and rearguard action against all liberalism by powerful feudal forces. The regional power centers became less and less Nehruvian and more and more intent on systems that secured their regional pride and their traditional right to exploit.

Another aspect of this was the fostering of high art and the neglect of mass culture. Nowhere is this more evident than in the cinema. Mainly through governmental impetus, India has quickly developed remarkable range of high- and middle-brow cinema for the urban educated (Satyajit Ray, Mrinal Sen, Shyam Benegal, and others), leaving the mass cinema virtually untouched. Since this has been true of the entire field of culture, with folk forms perishing in the hothouses of urban museology, the masses have not had the benefit of a cultural interpretation of the new scientific-industrial phenomena developing around them. Tradition and scientific advance have remained for them disparate, unreconciled opposites. They have learned to use the products of science without accepting the values of science—the right to doubt, for instance. In fact, while seeking the products of industry, they also despise them as manifestations of an evil, godless era—in the style of Ayatollah Khomeini. In the absence of this interpretation, either by the elite or by traditional folk performers, the cinema has stepped into the breach to supply the cultural leadership. It is the cinema that tells people the difference between good and evil, East and West, the traditional and the modern, the scientific and the religious. The cinema sets up models of behavior and of attitudes. Today the value system of the urban majority and its rural periphery is almost

THE PAINTED FACE OF POLITICS 137

entirely the product of the cinema. The cinema is to India what television is to the United States. Its hold is even more absolute because for vast masses of people, it is literally the sole medium of entertainment or communication for which they care.

Despite all the breast-beating of the intellectuals over this debasement of popular culture, the fact is that cinema has become the arbiter of popular taste, the Pierre Cardin and the Yves St. Laurent of the common man. What is more, it has now become the instrument of a grass-roots revolt against the domination of elite culture. Andhra Pradesh has the highest number of cinema theaters—and touring rural cinemas—of any state in India, followed by neighboring Tamil Nadu. Both the states are today ruled by superstars of the cinema. The cultural domination of the cinema has, inevitably but imperceptibly, turned into a political domination. It is also significant that in the two states ruled by superstars of the mass film, the "new cinema" has made little headway. Asked if he thought film appreciation should be taught in schools and colleges, the chief minister of Andhra Pradesh nearly had a fit. There was nothing wrong with the Telegu cinema, and in any case, good films needed no teaching. It was neighboring Karnataka and Kerala that had taken the lead in bringing about a more cinematic and socially aware film in the South. Veerappan, MGR's information minister, bitterly attacked film clubs for showing uncensored foreign films (a facility granted by the federal government through the Federation of Film Societies, presided over by Satyajit Ray) and lifestyles that corrupt the culture and tradition of Tamils.

THE EDUCATION OF RAMA RAO

If any leader could ever be the total opposite of Jawaharlal Nehru, it is Nandamuru Taraka Rama Rao. He was the son of a farmer, born on May 28, 1923, in the small village of Nimakuru, then inhabited by fewer than five hundred people. The village had no school of its own; a teacher used to come walking 5 kilometers to take classes in a shed. Few people in those days had money with which to pay the teacher. Says Rama Rao: "If I close my eyes, I can see my master coming to our village, helping the villagers and teaching us the whole day and walking back to his place, with vegetables in one hand, a tumbler of buttermilk in the other, and a sack of two of rice on his head." His farmer father was determined that Rama Rao should be properly educated, unlike himself and other farmers of the day. If it rained, father would carry son to school on his shoulders along the muddy paths through the rice fields and, once there, wash his feet and wipe them and leave him in the care of the venerable teacher. Eventually, he sent the boy to college. Here Rama Rao caught the eye of his Telegu professor, who was a playwright. The handsome young man was cajoled into playing the role of the heroine (there was no question of girls acting with boys in those days). Rama Rao was ready to go on stage when the professor arrived in the green room and ordered him to shave his moustache. The future superstar of Telegu cinema politely but firmly declined to remove what he called "the symbol of manhood." In a frantic last-minute compromise, Rama Rao went on with his moustache hidden under a pile of make-up. He was an instant success and earned the nickname Meesala Nangamma—moustachioed Nangamma (the name of the woman he played).

At twenty, Rama Rao married Basavarama Taraka, his wife and the mother of his seven sons and four daughters. He recalls that marriage so absorbed him that he twice failed in his examination. Finally he passed his BAA and found a government job after a long wait, but gave it up to get into films.

In his first day's shooting, Rama Rao played a police officer asked to punish a group of antigovernment demonstrators. "Like a bull in a china shop, Rama Rao ran after the volunteers for about 500 yards without a break and beyond the gates of the studio, Prasad (his director's) protestations that he was moving out of the camera, and that he shouldn't beat the poor extras so hard, fell on deaf ears." Later he learned to stay within camera range, but never to pretend to fight. The musclemen in fight scenes in his recent films allege that he would pummel them with all his might. Asked why they did not hit back instead of taking it from him, one of them said: "Sir, it's an honor to be beaten up by NTR."

Bull in a china shop—that's what some people think he is in politics. He tries hard to fulfill his campaign promises—fast. He has no time for commissions and expert committees and even, according to some commentators, consultation with cabinet colleagues. He appears to be impatient with the democratic process in the running, if not the election, of government. On a number of issues, he has had to backtrack and whittle down impetuous promises, sometimes creating new problems in the process. Thus his free lunch program for all school children has had to be pruned continually until it came down to children from the low caste and backward communities. The result is a peculiar caste- and community-based discrimination in school at lunch time, dividing the children. Suddenly he reduced the retirement age for government employees from fifty-eight to fifty-five, without notice, two months before the end of the fiscal year, causing untold problems to those who had to retire without preparation and to those who remained to prepare the government budget for presentation to the legislature. As the realities of finance began to dawn on him, he blamed his inability to save the poor, like other opposition chief ministers, on the federal government's alleged refusal to cooperate and on an unjust division of revenues between center and state. But one can't say he is daunted by the odds against him. He has a simple faith in God's intervention on behalf of those who want to do good. Since he left college, he is reputed to have read no book except film scripts and religious scriptures. Humble in origin, superstar of a plebeian art, NTR's voice is of the grass roots of the village and the street, unencumbered by the niceties of the elite, and addressed to the heart rather than the head. Recently, NTR took *sanyas*, or the renouncement of worldly happiness, shaving his head and wearing saffron robes. "I am no longer the lustful and gorgeous-looking Rama Rao, but a yogic chief minister."

FILM AND POLITICAL POWER IN TAMIL NADU

The cinema's rise to power in the neighboring state of Tamil Nadu is of a longer standing. It is the outcome of a vastly more conscious orchestration of the film medium in order to seize political leadership.

Tamil is an ancient language and the Tamilians a brilliant people with a glorious tradition in literature and the arts and a leading role in virtually every aspect of the country's progress today. In many ways, Tamil Nadu is the repository of ancient Hindu tradition unmutated by Muslim influence, which was much stronger in the North. It is at the same time one of the think tanks of contemporary India. For about a hundred years, Indologists, mostly British and German, had held that the Aryans came from the Caspian-Caucasian region through Iran into India; that they were a tall, fair-skinned and handsome, nomadic and warlike, Sanskrit-speaking people who rode into India on horses, conquering the North around 1500 B.C.; and that they were absorbed into the subcontinent well before the beginning of the Christian era. The discovery of the vast remains of a Bronze Age civilization in the Indus valley in the 1920s sparked more theories, based on evidence from

Indian and Iranian scriptures, of Aryan destruction of the cities of the original inhabitants, phallus-worshiping Dravidians, who were equated with dark-skinned, short-statured Southerners, important among them the people of what is today Tamil Nadu. This theory has of late been under severe attack from a new crop of Indian, Pakistani, European, and American archeologists. But the previous hypotheses (not yet wholly discredited) have held sway for so long that the stereotypes generated by them still provide the format for a great North-South divide. The epic of the *Ramayana*, in an extension of this view, is the story of the Aryan conquest of the South, ultimately resulting in the hegemony of the Brahmins, mostly fair-skinned. When independent India came to be dominated by leaders from the North who persuaded the majority to accept Hindi, a widespread language in the North, as the national language, there was resistance from the South, which hardened as the power of vested interest—economic and political—in the promotion of Hindi became increasingly apparent to Southerners. The position of the Brahmin, who was supposed to have come from the North and dominated religion as well as the services and the professions, came under attack from people unable to wrest cultural leadership from him. An anti-Brahmin, anti-religion, anti-North, anti-Hindi, and anti-Sanskrit movement gradually took shape in Tamil Nadu in the 1950s under E. V. Ramaswamy Naicker. The *Ramayana* was burned in the streets and the Brahmins showered with insult. The movement curiously took up the cinema as its propaganda weapon and wielded it with great skill. Beginning with the "Self-Respect" movement of the Justice party before independence, the agitation turned into Dravida Kashagam (Dravidian movement, or DK), later the Dravida Munnetra Kashagam (movement for the uplifting of the Dravidians, or DMK), and brought a number of film scenarists into its ranks. These writers held such power over the film industry that they were billed above the directors. Among them was C. N. Annadorai, the leader of the DMK. Especially under him, films steadily promoted the colors of the DMK flag and insinuated anti-Brahmin, anti-North, and anti-Hindu sentiments into their narratives. Annadorai's script for the film *Maidservant (Velaikari)* made him an idol from 1949 onward. The film ran for months, and its dialogue was on the lips of the people all the time. M. G. Ramachandran, himself not a Tamil but a refugee from Sri Lanka of Keralan origin (Kerala is the extreme southwestern coastal state of India, a long strip looking a little like Chile), was by that time a popular actor in Tamil films whom Annadorai took under his wing. "We need your image," Anna said, and MGR gave it ungrudgingly. "If he appears at a meeting, we get 40,000 votes; if he speaks, we get 400,000." By the early 1960s, MGR was running neck to neck with Shivaji Ganesan, a supporter of the Congress (Nehru-Indira Gandhi) party and by all accounts a finer actor than MGR.

Film historian S. Krishnaswamy explains the dominance of the MGR image: "In acting talent, Shivaji is head and shoulders above MGR; but Shivaji has played a great variety of roles. He is often the tragic hero; people sympathize with him, but do not idealize him. MGR is always portrayed as the savior. As a result Shivaji has never been a vote-getter." The engineering of the MGR image was conducted with finesse. Grid by grid, the proletariat was systematically covered; a film about fishermen, another about rickshaw-pullers, then about nurses, about clerks, and so on, were made, covering every section of the working population. In each, MGR plays the good man, the Robin Hood, the dispenser of justice, the savior of the distressed. A maidservant came back home sobbing: she had just seen "MGR killing a tiger to save his mother's life—in this day and age." He never entered the grey areas, not to speak of playing villains or unfavorable characters. "Between the mid-50s and the early 70s," says Krishnaswamy, "if MGR played in 100 films, not in one did he die." But unlike NTR, he never played gods or mythological characters, because the DMK began on an anti-Brahmin and therefore anti-God platform, since entry to God's temples was guarded by the Brahmin.

However, to bring Christians into the fold (the South has a long Christian tradition, going back, it is said, to the fourth century and conversions by St. Thomas himself), in 1969, MGR launched, on December 26, *The Life of Jesus Christ*. It was a great occasion that looked, according to American researcher Robert Hardgrave, like "a wedding of the DMK and the Church, presided over by Christ Himself. At the long table before assembled guests, MGR, properly attired for the occasion, was joined on one side by the Archbishop of Madras and on the other by Chief Minister N. Karunanidhi, leader of the ruling Dravida Munnetra Kazhagam." The cunning with which this was done is plain in the eyes of MGR playing Christ—except, of course, to himself and his followers, typical of their unawareness of the intimate vibrations given off by the cinematic image. All that the situation lacked was a Luis Buñuel to film this first supper.

MGR's information minister, Veerappan, used to be his production manager; his party's sprightly propaganda secretary, Jayalalitha, had played heroine to him in a number of films. Asked about her personal relationship with MGR (who is better known for his amorous exploits than NTR), Jayalalitha delicately referred to a Hindu god: "Lord Muruga has two wives, one is Valli, the other is Devayani. Janaki (MGR's wife) is Valli and I am Devayani." The weekly that published this carried a cartoon alongside showing Lord Muruga sitting on a peacock with Janaki on his right and Jayalalitha on his left. Like the party boss, its propaganda chief has always played the good girl, in some 113 pictures. She speaks a number of languages fluently, including English (unlike MGR, who hardly speaks any), which she learned in a convent school. A good public speaker and a bright conversationalist, she makes a propaganda secretary no political party would be ashamed of.

MGR's production company symbol shows the DMK flag; stories and dialogue constantly refer to Dravida glory, some of them going back to great periods of Tamil history. Very often MGR wears a red shirt and black pants—the colors of the DMK flag. Films often begin with Annadorai's portrait and end with the rising sun, symbol of the DMK party. Within the film, there would often be a portrait of Anna on the wall alongside one of Mahatma Gandhi. An adaptation of *Prisoner of Zenda* has MGR as the king issuing a decree that reads like the DMK party manifesto. Screen populism was steadily supported by real-life paternalism; when there was incessant rain for days in Madras, MGR bought raincoats for six hundred rickshaw-pullers emblazoned with the DMK's rising sun. A film on rickshaw-pullers reinforced both the charity and the film's sales.

Ironically, MGR's popularity was actively promoted by his political enemies. More than a hundred Congress party legislators owned cinema theaters, and for well over a decade, they constantly played MGR's films full of DMK slogans and symbols in their theaters. Finally, when battle was joined in the 1967 state elections, the DMK won a landslide victory. C. N. Annadorai's first cabinet consisted of ten members, nine of whom came from the film industry. After Annadorai's death in 1969, there was the inevitable battle of succession, which was won by film writer Karunanidhi. But when he tried to build up his son as a superstar, presumably to produce a surrogate for MGR, the two fell out. The party was split between the DMK and MGR's AIADMK (All India Annadorai DMK). In 1979, M. G. Ramachandran became chief minister and but for a brief interregnum has remained so.

The Mingling of Myth and Fact

Mircea Eliade has commented on the traditional separation of myth and fact in India. He gives the example of millions of religious-minded women pouring libations upon the *lingam,* which they know to be a representation of the male member resting in the female but have learned to see it as a symbol of a divine creative principle. As they pour their offerings upon it, nothing can be further from their minds than sex. The cinema has stood this traditional relationship of myth and fact on its head. Myth has become fact. The film star who plays God has become God. The cinema is too palpable, too naturalistic for its gods to be turned into mere symbols. Decades ago, Prem Adib, a Muslim, used to play the role of Rama (god-hero of the ancient epic, the *Ramayana*); devout Hindus would pick him up from the studio before he could take off his costume and makeup and make him stand in their homes while men and women would prostrate themselves before him and worship him. "Devadu! Devadu!" (God! God!), the crowd assembled every morning before his house would shout when N. T. Rama Rao, god hero of hundreds of mythological films, would appear on his balcony early every morning to great his devotees genuflecting below. The practice has continued since he became chief minister. The assembly forms by about six in the morning, because NTR the film star worked three shifts a day in the studio starting at seven, and NTR the chief minister now begins his day even earlier.

MGR avoids seeing people individually, as far as possible; but he too makes his periodic public appearances, emerging from his splendid isolation. The mingling of myth and fact is reflected in the curious popular indifference to the actual achievements of the star-ministers. They are not the objects of judgment but of blind loyalty. Image is more important than fact. MGR knows this well, and his populism is always directed toward the image. It is said that he does not see anyone—not even his cabinet colleagues—until he has his cap on to cover his baldness and his dark glasses to hide the pouches under his eyes (some say he has a pigmentation problem). Keeping up appearances became a particular problem with him after a fellow actor, M. R. Radha, who used to play the villain opposite him in film upon film, shot him in the neck in the course of an argument, impairing his voice and generally aging him. At a railway station in Coimbatore, one is told, a little boy was garlanding the chief minister and accidentally knocked off his cap, revealing his bald pate. MGR slapped him hard and ruled that henceforth no one was allowed to garland him; garlands must be handed to him, from a safe distance, and he would hand them over to his secretary. Very recently, a press photographer managed to take a shot of him without notice. An aide promptly snatched the camera from the man. It was later returned to him, with the developed film intact—except for the shot of MGR.

According to most observers, economic indicators show a decline in Tamil Nadu. The spurt in industrial growth in the fifties and early sixties has run out of steam; power is in chronically short supply, and so lately is water. After years in the saddle, MGR's populist image building has yielded little concrete result. Madras city's per capita water consumption is one of the lowest in India—70 liters a day against Calcutta's 128 liters, Bombay's 178, and New Delhi's 218. That 70 liters has, at the time of writing, been cut to about 30 a day. Journalist S. V. Mani paints a lurid picture: "Witness the rapidly expanding poverty scene: The thousands living like worms in the slums and pavements of Madras, the hundreds walking miles for a pot of drinking water in the villages or long water queues in the cities; human beings suddenly emerging from sewerage wells and shaking off the muck and slime. . . . this is the reality, the outcome of the politics of illusion."

Yet MGR's stardom doesn't seem to have lost any of its shine. Nor, of course, has the more recent NTR's. As the two chief ministers sit in their offices deliberating matters of state, their painted faces and ornate bodies flicker on the screen, reinforcing their image. NTR's latest film, released simultaneously in ninety-three theaters on his birthday on May 28, 1983, is significantly called *The Dictator (Chandasa-sanadu)*. Reruns of MGR's films fill many theaters of Tamil Nadu. With more than 250 films under each chief minister's belt, these reruns have a certain inexhaustibility.

The fact that the chief ministers of these states are constantly seen frolicking with the girls, throwing punches at musclemen, or dancing like lunatics at night clubs and on mountain slopes does not impair the admiration of their subjects. The gods have their own morals that mortal men regard as awesome. Besides, monogamy, although prescribed on the statute book, does not flaw the macho of polygamy and concubinage in a traditional society. And so the supermen ride their chariots across the wastelands of lowly lives, bringing thrills to those who subsist on dreams.

Whenever anything goes askew, people blame the party men or the bureaucrats; the fault, dear Brutus, is not in our stars but their underlings. Fans still throng the theaters on opening night of reruns of MGR's films and get into fights with supporters of rival stars, much like soccer fans in Europe and Latin America. Many will go without meals for days to buy a ticket on the black market for the opening show. And now they are graduating to a private army, if one is to judge by reports of a Youth Front (described as storm troopers by one journalist) launched by MGR some years ago. Trained in combat skills, this youth corps would be made up of "lumpen students and unemployed and the marginally employed." According to one report, the president of the All-World MGR Fans Association claims a following of 1.5 million registered in 27,000 units in Tamil Nadu, and half a million musclemen were expected to form a youth front that would carry out the leader's orders without ever asking why. "When three civil liberties organisations in Tamil Nadu jointly sponsored a national enquiry into the killing of 20 harijans ('untouchables') and agricultural workers in North Arcot and Dharampurin districts in 1980," said the *Sunday Observer*, "a 300-strong mob attacked the lodge where they were staying. The mob banged open the doors, destroyed their baggage, beat them up and made sure they had no material to document." MGR is himself reported to have said at the launching of the front: "If the officials tried to put obstacles in the way of the youth, the party would not be silent," sending a chill down the spines of even the police force. In his efforts to tame the press with a draconian bill, MGR had to beat a retreat—but not before a protracted battle.

In Andhra Pradesh, NTR's fans and party men repeatedly threatened half a million government employees on strike for nineteen days six months after he took over—half a million for whom the charisma had worn off. It was a senior official who adroitly ended a confrontation with the iron-willed chief minister. His party henchmen are said to be restive—because a very rich chief minister wants them to spend their time in their constituencies instead of feathering their nests in the capital, where they can manipulate the officials and distribute patronage to the moneybags. How long their lack of riches can be reconciled to their loyalty to divine charisma remains an open question.

On the other hand, the two star politicians signed an agreement over the sharing of river waters, bringing a long dispute between the two states to a close and possible relief for Tamil Nadu's chronic water shortage. A Council of Southern States has been formed to coordinate policies and might bring some benefits to the region. NTR has introduced legislation to give women equal rights to parental property.

The Political Future of the Cinema

Of the four Southern states, two have actor chief ministers; in the two others, there are stars waiting in the wings. Karnataka's matinee idol Raj Kumar came out stridently in support of a language policy that would compel everyone living in that state to use Kannada, the language of the state, in offices and schools and all governmental institutions. This could have the effect of gradually sealing off the state from communication with all others. (English remains the unavoidable medium of interstate communication, especially at the leadership level —a language MGR can barely speak and NTR has in rather rudimentary fashion.) The present non-Congress coalition government of Karnataka is handling the issue with kid gloves without giving in to such isolationism. The situation is not ripe yet for Raj Kumar to ride to power amidst language riots. But the gunpowder may be piling up. In the fourth state, Kerala, the cinema is as popular as in the other three, and superstar Prem Nazir has served notice, after some hesitant hiccups. But Kerala has a literacy rate of 70 percent, the highest in India, a large middle class, and a highly politicized electorate able to keep myth and fact strictly apart. Newspaper circulation is very high; libraries abound in rural areas. Like West Bengal, Kerala has a large Communist party, which has been in power for long stretches. Communism here has a devout face; the Marxist must bow to religion. Unlike the rest of India, Hindus cannot dominate here, because of very large Muslim and Christian minorities. Political commentators think Kerala will be the last state to fall to the cinema, and perhaps it never will—even though Prem Nazir is the holder of the *Guiness Book of World Records* title for having acted in six hundred films, that is, more than NTR and MGR put together.

A still larger question looms on the horizon: What if the rest of India develops the same ratio of cinema seats to population as the South, which has twice the national average? There are at present only eleven thousand cinema theaters in the country, which works out to seven per one thousand population, where UNESCO recommends twenty-seven. The present government projection is of thirty thousand theaters by the year 2000—almost three times the present figure. Will this catapult the cinema into an all-India vortex of political power? What will be the effect of the entry into politics of Amitabh Bachchan? He is the biggest all-India star, playing in Hindi films that also play in the South side by side with the local product. What is more, he is an old family friend, close to Rajiv Gandhi. Amitabh is a great performer, more a cabaret artist than an actor, but one who can hold an audience in thrall with his singing and dancing, both technically amateurish but full of a verve that never fails to wow the crowds. When he was in hospital for a serious injury, Prime Minister Indira Gandhi visited him, and at least half the nation was praying for his recovery morning and evening. Bachchan has denied having political ambitions—many times. Some think he is protesting too much.

A comparison of NTR and MGR can be interesting. One is earthy, accessible, spontaneous, sincere, religious, and naive, sometimes to the extent of trying to reinvent the wheel. The other is conscious and deliberate, keeps himself away behind makeup and dark glasses and cap except to appear before the millions. Both are determined, charismatic, paternalistic and dictatorial, intellectually unprepossessing, virtually bereft of broader scientific perspectives or integrated national-global points of view. It can be said in their defense, however, that they are no worse than nonactor chief ministers holding the fort today. The antics of Antulay in Maharashtra and Jagannath Mishra in Bihar (both of whom were brought down basically by the press) were, if anything, more bizarre and more brazenly evil.

But the question really is not whether certain chief ministers are actors or nonactors. Many of the other chief ministers are practically nonentities, dependent on the will of the federal government; the actors are not. They have their own dangerously blind following, sworn to unquestioning loyalty. Their populist measures are criticized for having little to do with real economic growth. Their populace, many people feel, when frustrated by realities, could easily turn to totalism, finding scapegoats in groups that are different from themselves—in language or religion or region or whatever. Will the cinema, as the voice of the common man, help create a more democratic India by bringing its rulers closer to the grass roots? Or will it act as a force towards populist, parochial, "benevolent" dictatorships? With the projected threefold increase in cinema seats in the coming two decades without a perceptible change in the nature of the soap opera, the chances of the popular cinema's values overwhelming the elite culture (that at present guides the country) and seizing political control are considerable. C. N. Annadorai, himself a highly literate person, provided a clue to the new culture sometime before capturing power (quoted by the *Sunday Observer,* July 11, 1982): "In the next ten years, there is going to be a big increase in the semi-literate population. I shall be their leader. My determination will be to keep them semi-literate."

10
Songs in Hindi Films: Nature and Function

Teri Skillman

Bombay Hindi film song has developed as a musical genre since the introduction of synchronized sound film in India in 1930. The film songs discussed here are from films classified as commercial rather than art films. The examples come from commercial films that did not receive financial assistance or a film award from the government of India—in other words, films regarded as popular among the Indian audience and not those promoted by a government agency.

From ancient India to the present, music, dance, and drama have been regarded as interrelated and inseparable, in both classical and folk traditions. In the late nineteenth century, under the influence of British dramatic traditions, there was a renaissance of classical theater among the English-educated Indian minority. As the renaissance spread, the folk dramatic tradition with its reservoir of songs and dances became the primary resource for a new theatrical tradition.

When French films were introduced to India in 1896, theatrical drama was presented as silent film with musicians hired to accompany the film. Beginning in 1912, when Indian-produced silent films were screened, Indian musical instruments—the harmonium and tabla— were used for musical accompaniment (Rangoonwalla 1983, 69).

The introduction of synchronized sound film in 1930 began the music-drama tradition of the Indian screen. *Alam Ara*, the first Indian sound film, which included seven songs with instrumental accompaniment, became the model for the music-drama films that followed. Thus, music became an important element in the production of sound films and gave Indian films their unique character. The immediate popularity of the sound films is attributed to the popularity of stage drama and silent films and especially to the audience's fascination with seeing a song dramatized. The film songs were not full-length songs as we know them today; rather, they were short intonations of prose sung by the actor-singers. The tunes tended to be based on popular theater songs derived from Indian classical and folk melodies. In this first decade, the theme of the film had priority over the melodic material (Sharma 1980, 57).

Song lyrics reflected film themes: untouchability, interreligion marriage, poverty, caste, and social system inequality. Melodies were predominantly borrowed from folk and classical repertory but altered for use in film by changing instrumentation and sometimes rhythms (Barnouw and Krishnaswamy 1980, 72). In the late 1930s, the instruments used to accompany the voice were those associated with North Indian classical music—sitar, tabla, harmonium, sarod—and also the violin.

Film songs of the 1930s were frequently referred to as light classical songs because of the use of Indian classical instruments, melodic materials, and song forms and the development of a characteristic singing style, now known as "crooning." K. L. Saigal is credited with introducing this singing style, which was popularized through other movies and phonograph recordings of the film songs.

In 1935, R. C. Boral, a film music composer, discovered that the solution to recording film songs for actors who could not sing was lip-synchronization or "playback song" (Rangoonwalla 1983, 84). Songs would be recorded, and the actors would lip-synch the lyrics. This permitted actors who were incapable of singing to perform in song scenes by lip-synching a singer's voice. The effects of using the playback technique were manifold: songs could be recorded in advance, thereby cutting costs, and the songs could be released in advance, for publicity purposes, on discs to radio broadcasters and the commercial market just prior to a film's premiere.

The radio was responsible for popularizing singers and film songs by making the sound track available to those who could not afford the luxury of a phonograph or frequent visits to the cinema hall. The radio network, introduced in India in 1927, made the songs accessible to the vast Indian public. By the end of the 1930s, phonograph discs and radio broadcasts had popularized film songs across the vast Indian subcontinent.

In the 1940s, the Indian independence movement, World War II, and the unwillingness of many Indians to support the British war effort all had adverse effects on Bombay Hindi films. The war years led to drastic changes in the internal structure of the film industry.

These changes were caused by the Indian black market, the Film Censor Board, and the radio network. As a result, "formula films" and playback songs became the trademark of Indian commercial films.

During World War II, the shortage of raw film stock, which had to be imported from the West, and the British ban on political films led to a shift in themes from social criticism to humorous musical entertainment. Films acquired a formulaic structure in which the emphasis was placed on entertainment in song-and-dance scenes; these films were quite similar to Hollywood musicals of the 1940s. With these light musical films, songs became musical entities with memorable texts and tunes (Rangoonwalla 1983, 77), which the Indian audience remembered and sang outside the context of the film setting and the cinema halls where they viewed the film.

The "formula film" has been described as a film that has at least one major star as the hero or the heroine, if not two, a villain, fight scenes, and approximately six songs and dances. The films were primarily romantic in theme, and the stories were written to glorify the stars. The plots contained numerous coincidences, requiring a "willing suspension of disbelief" on the audience's part (Sarkar 1975, 105). The scenes were often filmed in unconventional settings in sometimes equally unconventional circumstances (Barnouw and Krishnaswamy 1980, 155), such as a coincidental meeting of long-lost brothers at the scene of an accident. Stereotyped opposites were juxtaposed to create dramatic tension, as, for example, a fight between the hero and the villain. The songs and dances were inserted into this pattern of formulaic coincidences with their stereotyped situations and characters to provide an emotional outlet for one of the stars, comic relief in an awkward situation, or romantic interplay, or to convey a message reflecting traditional Indian values. A characteristic of a formula film was that it never ended in tragedy. Formula films became the popular form of entertainment: social, political, and religious issues slowly disappeared as themes over the next decade. Emphasis was placed on glamorous and superficial conflicts between good and evil and not on the serious issues that India was facing due to rapid social change and the influence of Western culture and technology.

Song became the highlight of the 1940s film. Folk songs from the northern provinces were used as a melodic base for the film songs, and harmony was introduced by Christian musicians from Goa (Chandavarkar 1980, 72). During this decade, the lyrics and the melodies became increasingly more important, and in many cases, either one or both came to be borrowed from foreign musical traditions. The plot was of secondary importance. The playback technique was commonly used, and as a result, actors were no longer required to sing.

By the 1940s, film production costs had escalated enormously for stage-set films. The success of a film depended on the popularity of the star, so by employing one or two big-name stars, who were not necessarily singers as they had been in the 1930s, a film could be made for a quick profit. An independent producer could make a low-budget film by filming, for example, on location in a hill station and by using the playback technique for all song scenes to eliminate the necessity of coordinating the singing and acting. With this technique of low-budget filming, playback singers were rarely informed of the context or story in which a song would be set, often because it was not known at the time of the recording. Critics of the Bombay film song genre attribute the somewhat emotionless and mechanical sound of some songs to the fact that they are recorded in isolation (Sarkar 1975, 104). Some singers who attained prominence or a monopoly on the recording market, such as Lata Mangeshkar, were able to demand that their songs fit the context of the film. The process of filming on location and using the playback technique minimized the cost for sets, stage personnel, and orchestra musicians; thus, song lyrics, the music director-composers, musicians, and singers gained importance and incredible wealth.

Singers—Lata Mangeshkar is a typical example—who gained a monopoly on recording film songs would sing for a variety of characters; singers' voices were not chosen to match a stereotyped character from movie to movie. For example, in Raj Kapoor's film *Shree 420* (1955), the heroine lip-synched to Lata's voice. In the 1957 movie *Ab Delhi Dur Nahin,* Lata's voice was used for the young hero's songs. Each character is different, and the sentiments expressed in the songs do not always reflect an emotion logically associated with the character. The Indian audience is primarily concerned with how well a singer renders a song, rather than with the logic of what a character sings or the fact that the same voice is used for different characters; the Indian audience's second concern is the visual enactment of the lyrics. Therefore, the audience is not concerned with the standardization of a character type with a specific voice. The emphasis is on the context, action, and emotion being expressed and not whether it is appropriate to the character. The sentiment a character expresses often reflects the audiences' emotion.

SONGS IN HINDI FILMS 153

After Indian independence in 1947, the Indian Censor Board, an institution previously established by the British, issued strict regulations in an effort to reform the film industry. These regulations pertained to physical contact between the sexes on the screen (Barnouw and Krishnaswamy 1980, 140) and the "Westernization" of film songs. The censors were mostly concerned with blatant physical contact, so producers developed an overly suggestive body language to compensate for the prohibition of physical contact and used songs as vehicles for such expressions. To quote Indian film critic Kobita Sarkar (1975, 106):

> Since our censors and perhaps the general public might disapprove of any direct statement—the song is the traditional way out of the impasse. If a girl says 'I love you', this makes her brash and unfeminine. If she borrows some famous singer's sound track and warbles on through endless miles of footage on the subject of dil [heart] and mohabat [love] and the like . . . the proprieties will be maintained and audiences will approve vociferously.

Songs were used to express sentiments that could not be spoken, and when dramatized in film, the body language, covered by the veil of a song, suggested a display of affection, which was forbidden in public.

At approximately the same time the Censor Board established this new policy, the introduction of Western technology began to revolutionize the film song recording industry. In 1948, magnetic recording machines and sound tapes were introduced to India. These allowed performers to immediately hear the product instead of having to wait for the sound tape to be processed. In addition, Arriflex cameras were being used to shoot film scenes. The picture quality was improved, but due to excessive machine noise, the entire film required overdubbing (Singh 1981). By the early 1950s, film phonographs or "playback machines" were beginning to be manufactured in India (Film Enquiry Committee 1951, 161). These advances in technology enabled producers to accelerate production of film songs for long-playing discs.

In 1952, Dr. B. V. Keshkar was appointed minister of information and broadcasting, which gave him authority over All India Radio, the Film Division, and the Central Board of Film Censors. Keshkar was directly responsible for the change in the broadcasting policy of All India Radio. The Central Programme Advisory Committee (1953, 361) defined the purpose of the new policy in the following statement:

> From its [radio's] power for good or evil has arisen the necessity of directing its use in such a manner as to make it serve the purpose of the

cultural and moral progress of society as well as its healthy entertainment. It must aim at the same time to express, satisfy and guide public taste and impart information as well as instruction in its widest sense. Its aim should be to satisfy the cultural and recreational need of the people in the most attractive manner. It should reflect the inner urges of our national life, make our people realise their responsibilities and inspire them with enthusiasm for the development and progress of the country.

The purpose of such a puritanical policy was to limit the broadcast time of film songs. The Censor Board determined that film music had become overly influenced by elements of Western music, namely, by the tuning system and the use of Western musical instruments. The use in film songs of such instruments as the piano, harmonium, vibraphone, xylophone, and saxophone involved adoption of the Western tempered scale. This, it was felt, was rapidly blunting Indian ears to the nuances of traditional Indian music (Barnouw and Krishnaswamy 1980, 209). The Censor Board considered traditional Indian music to be North Indian classical music, which in fact was not widely popular in India, nor was it the music of the masses. According to Naushad Ali, a prominent film music composer (Barnouw and Krishnaswamy 1980, 212),

> classical sangeet [music] has never been the art of the masses. It flourished in the glamourous courts of the Rajas, Maharajas and Nawabs. . . . The common people, who had no access to the great durbars [courts], were never offered the opportunity of listening to classical music. They could not, therefore, acquire an appreciative ear for it.

Keshkar had a strong preference for Indian classical music and saw All India Radio as the medium for its revival. Keshkar began a drive against "hybrid music" by cutting down the broadcast time for film songs to a bare minimum. In its place he aired classical Indian music. In addition, the titles of the films from which these film songs came were not to be announced on the air as Keshkar considered this to be an advertisement (Barnouw and Krishnaswamy 1980, 208–209). In a survey article on radio broadcasting in India, Keshkar was sharply criticized for the new broadcasting policy (Central Programme Advisory Committee 1953, 361).

> The "exorcising" of film music could have been brought about in a better though indirect manner, by taking measures to improve standards in cooperation with the film producers. The effect of a sudden and drastic withdrawal of the "savoury" menu, which it is claimed as many as 90

percent of listeners demanded, is to insist on an instantaneous reversal in listener taste which is bound to affect demand or the extent of listening in. What has been less subject to criticism, and indeed has been welcomed in many quarters, is the attention that is being paid by the Ministry of Information and Broadcasting to the revival and stimulation of traditional or classical music.

The Indian masses identified with film songs instead of with classical music and were fascinated by the instrumentation. In order to continue listening to film songs, the All India Radio audience switched to Radio Ceylon and Radio Goa.

Film producers had been using the radio for the promotion of film songs. Prior to a film's release, producers released disc recordings of the film songs to All India Radio (A.I.R.) and to the commercial market. These songs functioned as advertisements for the film and encouraged people to see the songs actually being performed in the cinemas (Barnouw and Krishnaswamy 1980, 157). With Keshkar's restrictions on the broadcast of film songs, producers looked to Radio Ceylon for assistance. During the 1950s, Radio Ceylon began developing its short-wave broadcasting system and eagerly accepted the opportunity to broadcast Bombay Hindi film songs on an unrestricted basis. Radio Ceylon broadcast the latest hits from Bombay once a week on the "Binaca Toothpaste Hour" (Binaca Geet Mala). This program became the Indian radio version of the televised "American Bandstand." Each hour featured the hit parade of film songs and, as a result, aided in further popularizing a song prior to a film's release.

Radio Ceylon dominated the subcontinent's broadcasting market through the 1950s and 1960s. Only in 1957 did the broadcasting policies of All India Radio change to include regional folk songs, light classical music, and popular film songs. This more liberal policy is attributed to the addition of two major short-wave broadcasting stations in Bombay and Madras, built to challenge the Radio Ceylon monopoly (Barnouw and Krishnaswamy 1980, 203). In the late 1950s, the Censor Board heeded popular demand, and film songs were broadcast on All India Radio and later (in the 1970s) on television.

By 1955, Indian films were being purchased in the international film market, which encouraged the use of foreign musical elements so that the films would appeal to a wider audience. Film producers used stereotyped scales and rhythms and combinations of Indian and foreign instruments to achieve a semblance of the sounds and styles they desired—American popular, Western classical, Iberian, Oriental, and

Latin American. "Murdmurd ke na dekh," a song from Raj Kapoor's 1955 film, *Shree 420,* has the flamenco guitar and the Strauss waltz styles interwoven as the instrumental introduction. The size of the orchestra in the 1950s grew to more than fifty musicians. The musical result sounded Western to Indian purists and Indian to Westerners. "Hybrid music," a popular term of derogation among Indian purists, increasingly came to be used to describe the film song genre.

The most significant influences on film song during the 1960s and 1970s were from Hollywood, Anglo-American popular culture, and Western classical music. Plots and songs were often plagiarized—some song texts were translated word for word into Hindi or melodies duplicated note by note (Sarkar 1975, 108). For example, in the 1961 film, *Chhaya,* the first theme from the first movement of Mozart's Symphony No. 40 in G Minor was beautifully adapted for a film song, "Itna na mujhse tu pyaar jita, ki amin ek badal awara" [Do not express so much love for me, I am just a wandering cloud] (Chandavarkar 1980, 74). Settings in which songs and dances most commonly occurred were dream sequences, parties, cabarets, and rustic scenes (Sarkar 1975, 105). One of the most popular themes for songs was love, but other themes were also used, such as patriotism, travelogues, moral and philosophical obligations, character autobiographies, and hippies and drugs. The invasion of marijuana-smoking hippies into Indian society in the late 1960s and early 1970s was satirized in Dev Anand's 1972 movie, *Hare Ram, Hare Krishna.* In the song, "Dum Maro Dum," the use of electric guitars, the heavy rock beat, and a slurred vocal quality parodies the psychedelic experience.

Non-Indian musical elements that were incorporated into Bombay Hindi film songs were frequently introduced via Anglo-American popular culture (including Latin-American rhythms and various other ethnic musics that inspired popular songs). Indian composers did not adopt popular Western styles in their entirety but selected elements such as rhythmic patterns, melodic figures, and instruments that fit the Indian conception of the style. The most easily discernible of the borrowed styles are jazz styles, Latin-American dances, rock-and-roll (specifically, Elvis Presley and the Beatles), Hawaiian "hapa-haole" songs, Western classical, cabaret, and disco.

Along with the introduction of non-Indian musical styles came the use of advanced technology, especially electric instruments and sound-recording equipment. Advanced technology has affected Bombay Hindi film songs both directly and indirectly; the use of electric guitars, synthesizers, and advanced sound-recording equipment have altered the sound of film music, especially in the 1970s. Improved mass communication commercial technology has made audio equipment, such as radios, cassette recorders, stereos, television sets, and now, video machines, available and somewhat more affordable to the Indian consumer. In 1978, Delhi television broadcast two weekly programs devoted to films: "Chitrahar" and the "Hindi Sunday Night Movie." "Chitrahar" is a half-hour program that presents three to four screenings of songs from various films (not always Bombay Hindi films). This program is similar to rock videos on television in America and Europe. Like the "Binaca Toothpaste Hour," its radio predecessor, "Chitrahar" encourages the audience to see the film in order to understand the context of the song.

In the 1960s, the New Wave film movement, a movement concerned with socioeconomic issues in India, emerged as a reaction to the formula films produced in Bombay. In the 1970s, a Middle Cinema movement began among some producers. This movement was affected by the realism of the New Wave movement and attempted to bring the reality of Indian life into popular films. The effect of this on music was immediately noticeable. The songs from these films were set in situations which were complementary to the character and story of the film. For example, "Come Alive," from the 1978 Shyam Benegal film, *Junoon,* is an English song in a ballad style, sung by the actress who plays the part of an Anglo-Indian lady at the time of the Sepoy Mutiny in 1857. Songs from the Middle Cinema were appropriate to the period, location, and social setting of the film and were used to enhance the drama. Overall, an element of realism was used in tying the song scenes to the action of the film.

To summarize, Bombay Hindi film song has become widely accepted throughout India. It is most popular in the urban centers and is rapidly becoming more widespread in the rural areas due to radio broadcasts and travelling cinema shows. Film song is the popular Indian music and has achieved this status through transcending cultural, religious, linguistic, caste, and class barriers by appealing to the ethos common to all Indian traditions and societies. Film song can be heard on every kind of occasion and in all locations—at weddings, religious celebrations, political rallies, in tea shops, temples, and private homes.

The development of Bombay Hindi film songs has, to date, responded to Hollywood, New Wave and Middle Cinemas, and to rapid advancements in technology. Film song is India's bridge between the traditional and the rapidly developing modern society.

References

Barnouw, Erik, and S. Krishnaswamy
    1980   *Indian Film*. New York: Oxford University Press.

Central Programme Advisory Committee (India)
    1953   *Report of the Central Programme Advisory Committee.*

Chandavarkar, Bhaskar
    1980   "The Great Film Song Controversy," *Cinema Vision India*, 1, 4 (October).

Film Enquiry Committee (India)
    1951   *Report of the Film Enquiry Committee.*

Rangoonwalla, Firoze
    1983   *Indian Cinema, Past and Present*. New Delhi: Clarion Books.

Sarkar, Kobita
    1975   *Indian Cinema Today—An Analysis*. New Delhi: Sterling Publishers Pvt. Ltd.

Sharma, Pt. Narendra
    1980   "Half a Century of Song," *Cinema Vision India*, 1, 4 (October).

Singh, Kuldip
    1981   "The Road to Sophistication," *50 Years of Indian Talkies (1931–1981)*. Bombay: Indian Academy of Motion Picture Arts and Sciences.

PART 3
China

Chinese Cinema

ALTHOUGH CHINA was exposed to the art of cinema from 1896 onward, film was until very recent times perceived as an imported and alien form of communication. Indeed, it is not without significance that, at the beginning, cinema was referred to by the Chinese as "Western peep shows." This sense of foreignness was discernible at a number of different levels. Until 1949, much of the cinematic diet offered to the Chinese was of foreign origin; many of the films actually shot in China were made by foreign companies. A substantial number of films produced in China were based on Western works ranging from Shakespeare to Hardy, as well as on Russian and Japanese works. All of these factors, no doubt, contributed to the growing feeling that cinema and foreignness were closely linked. Or to phrase it differently, the feeling that the art of cinematography was not an indigenous art form pervaded the consciousness of the Chinese. However, as a consequence of the social and political climate generated in the 1980s and the emergence of remarkably gifted filmmakers of the caliber of Chen Kaige, Zhang Junzhao, and Tian Zhungzhuang, the situation has changed considerably. One can observe a distinct Chinese sensibility, often drawing on the richness of inherited traditions, animating the better films made in recent times.

From the very early period, there was established in the minds of both filmmakers and audiences a close relationship between cinema and didacticism, which later gave way to political messages. Seeing the vast potential that film had for inculcating a political consciousness in the mass of people, the Communist party established the first film organization in 1932. The Communist party and left-wing intellectuals exercised a profound influence on filmmaking in China. This is, of course, not to suggest that foreign influences—mostly those emerging from capitalistic societies—and questions of profit making and commercial impulses were absent.

By the 1940s, one could observe an interesting linkage between the art of cinematography and the literary and dramatic arts. Most film directors were deeply familiar with and sometimes involved in theater and literature. This close association between literature and cinema had two important consequences. First, as literature was held in high regard by the educated in China, it served to legitimate the newly introduced art of cinema and make it more respectable as a form of entertainment. Second, until a few decades ago, cinema in China evolved as a literary art in which the writer of the screenplay seemed to assume a greater importance than the director.

After the Communist revolution in 1949, the importance of cinema as a form of mass communication was increasingly realized by the policymakers. Although a link had been forged between cinema and political consciousness-raising, it was evident to the top officials of the party that cinema had yet to establish itself as a nationally popular mode of entertainment. Up until that time, cinema had catered to specialized audiences drawn mainly from elite groups. One of the primary objectives now was to win a national audience for the art of cinema.

As a consequence of this urge to make cinema a medium of political education, as well as the desire to gain a national audience, films that subscribed to the credo of "socialist realism" began to be produced in increasing numbers, the Soviet Union providing the model and impetus. Themes dealing with revolutionary zeal and fervor, the actions of positive heroes who had the interests of the masses in mind, class struggle, and the triumph of progressive forces over reactionary forces were given greater emphasis. As films exported from other countries except Soviet Russia were banned, locally made Chinese films had a far bigger market than they had had before 1949.

With the launching of the Cultural Revolution in 1964, with its unmitigated fervor and the exercise of largely unchallenged authority by the followers of Jiang Qing, these tendencies were strengthened. One can, on the basis of the available evidence, say that the Cultural Revolution sought to focus attention on two themes, which were, of course, interrelated: the importance of indigenous art forms and the political function of art. Consequently, there was to be seen a concerted effort to make use of traditional art forms to convey modern experiences and a vision of society that was in keeping with the

CHINESE CINEMA 163

accepted political agenda. Revolutionary operas like *Taking Tiger Mountain by Strategy* were offered as models to be emulated. However, in terms of the exploration of complex human experiences, and the imaginative use of the medium, these films clearly left much to be desired. In retrospect, a prominent trend that merits closer analysis if one is interested in the question of cultural identity and cinema is the abandonment of the cosmopolitan approach to the art of cinematography that gradually had been taking shape and the attempt to create a more Chinese style of filmmaking based on the traditional art forms, most notably, the opera. The Cultural Revolution proved to be a disaster. In October 1976, the so-called Gang of Four, who spearheaded the Cultural Revolution, were arrested and disgraced; questions were raised regarding the wisdom of some of the actions of Mao Zedong himself. Since Deng Xiaoping's assumption of power and the inauguration of a more liberal atmosphere, the film industry has begun to display signs of health and vitality. The bitter experiences of the Cultural Revolution, the exposure to good Western cinema, and the constructive role played by the Beijing Film Academy have, no doubt, contributed significantly to this state of affairs. A film like *The Yellow Earth* is emblematic of this new vitality.

In order to understand the present ferment in Chinese cinema, we have to give close consideration to the fifth generation of filmmakers. During the past three years or so, a number of extremely gifted film directors have attracted the attention of internationally oriented film critics and scholars. Many of these directors were trained in the Beijing Film Academy and display a sensitivity to and comprehension of the art of cinema that their predecessors did not. Among them, Chen Kaige, Huang Jianxin, and Zhang Junzhao deserve special mention.

Chen Kaige's *The Yellow Earth* deals with a fairly simple story. A soldier comes to a mountainous village to collect folk songs. He lives in a house where a young girl is married to an older man to whom she had been betrothed in infancy. He explains to the young girl how women are now treated in the capital of Yan'an under Communist rule. The young girl sets out in search of the city and is drowned. Chen Kaige presents this simple story very movingly on the screen, using exquisitely chosen visual images. The cinematographer, Zhang Yimou, assists greatly in this effort. The presentation of the landscape and of the relationship between man and nature is deeply reminiscent of classical Chinese paintings. Mountains and earth occupy much of the frame, and human beings are portrayed as being overwhelmed in the topography. The pace of the film, as well as the lucidity, reflects a distinctly Chinese sensibility. Huang Jianxin's *The Black Cannon Incident* and *The Stand-in,* two other films that bear testimony to the vigor and purposefulness of the films made by the fifth generation of Chinese filmmakers, take a critical look at the bureaucracy. Both of these films contain a rich vein of satire.

These filmmakers are, of course, not without their critics and adversaries in China. Some have contended that *The Yellow Earth* does not adequately portray the power and capability of the Communist party to solve the problems of the peasants. Similarly, *The Black Cannon Incident* generated a great deal of controversy. The ideologues have not given up on their strictures, and currently the cinema in China has become a field of contention for power between ideologues and innovative young filmmakers. It is difficult to predict who will win out in the end, but at least for the time being there is reason for optimism concerning the innovativeness and artistic commitment of some of the young filmmakers in China.

11
Chinese Film in the 1980s: Art and Industry

Ma Qiang

AFTER THREE long decades of devastating political movements after the founding of New China, the Communist party began devoting itself to the economic reconstruction of the most populous country in the world before entering the decade of the 1980s. The highly acclaimed and hotly debated economic reform movement that started in 1979 first achieved tremendous success in the rural areas and soon swept the urban areas, where the emphasis has been put on the decentralization of the national production system and the priority development of coastal cities. The most important aim has been to open up the country to the outside world.

Along with its economic achievements, the movement toward reform has also begun to affect other elements of the society: ways of life, values, and traditions. While importing urgently needed Western technologies and machines, China is inevitably exposing herself to Western culture, which some people are afraid will bring in "decadent elements of bourgeois thoughts." As reform proceeds, it is being considered as a kind of experiment instead of as the only solution to the country's problems.

The Chinese film, a proven barometer of the political climate in China, reflects, and in turn is changed by, the economic reform movement. The following thoughts will try to give an analytical account of the development of the Chinese film in the 1980s, with the hope of providing a better understanding of the current economic movement.

Before proceeding to view the development of the Chinese film industry in the 1980s, it should be of some help to take a retrospective look at the industry from its very beginning. The Chinese first saw films in 1896, when agents of the Lumière brothers screened a film at a tea house in Shanghai, the future center of the Chinese film industry. The following decade saw the rapid development of the film industry in China, partly as a consequence of the gaining of a "sphere of influence" over China by European powers, the United States, and Japan.

By the end of World War I, the film industry in China was recognized as a source of profit by local industrialists. In 1917, the Commercial Press set up a Department of Motion Pictures, which in 1921 produced the first feature-length film (*Yan Ruisheng*, 10 reels) and in 1923 built the first film studio. In 1920, the first Chinese film, a piece of Beijing opera, had been produced in Beijing; this was followed by two short films (*The Difficult Couple* and *Zhuangzi Tries His Wife*). However, they had little significance in the development of the local film industry because the market at that time was dominated by foreign films. A few local films, much outnumbered by films from abroad, were produced by Chinese filmmakers with imported film equipment and film stock. In the period after the establishment of the first film studio, about twenty large and small film studios were set up in Shanghai. These studios produced a large number of commercial films, which, although criticized later by some progressive film critics as being stereotyped and of low taste, paved the way for technical sophistication in the national film industry.

The Chinese film industry in the 1930s and 1940s was characterized by the activities of left-wing filmmakers whose works were popular among audiences in cinemas where foreign films were shown. However, development of the film industry was hampered by the invasion of the Japanese army. Film studios were either closed or destroyed, cameras and film stock were hard to find, and filmmakers were among the refugees who fled to the hinterland, where they managed to produce some short subjects about the war.

Films after the war, especially during the period 1946–1949, experienced a kind of renaissance, which was created mainly by the activities of progressive filmmakers in areas, such as Shanghai, that were ruled by the Nationalists, but also by their counterparts in Yan'an, who began their careers by making documentaries in the "liberated areas." Films produced during this period laid the foundation on which the film industry in China developed through the years of vicissitudes after the founding of the People's Republic.

After 1949, almost all films from abroad, except those from the Soviet Union, were banned. This left a large market to be satisfied exclusively by the national film industry, which had been nationalized by 1953. All film studios and other film institutions were managed and regulated by the government, which made national plans for financing, production, distribution, and promotion. Quotas were allocated to each film studio. The same pattern was repeated after the Cultural Revolution (1966–1976), during which filmmaking was virtually stopped. In recent years, film studios have begun to enjoy a certain flexibility in choosing the subject matter of films to be made and in distributing films they feel could be profitable.

The Chinese film industry entered the 1980s with a mixed feeling of optimism and pessimism. Even after the Cultural Revolution was officially over, the aftermath still was felt in the following years. The damage that the revolution did to the film industry was devastating. Thousands of film workers were sent down to the countryside; some were persecuted, some even killed, and film studios were closed for several years. No one knew when the film industry might recover.

On the other hand, the film industry had reason to be optimistic. The medium once again had the opportunity to draw a large audience, as it had after the founding of the People's Republic, when all foreign films were banned and a huge market was left for local films. During the period 1976 to 1979, other means of entertainment—classical concerts, Beijing or local opera, weekend dance parties—were virtually nonexistent. The national network's TV programs were so boring that people used to watch only 30 minutes of daily news coverage. The people had just survived a revolution during which no films other than eight "model Beijing operas" could be seen, and they still had no other means of entertainment. Thus, they rushed to the theaters to see a newly released film or film that was being reshown. Even though fewer than one hundred feature films were produced in the years between 1976 and 1979, the Chinese film industry was fortunate to be able to rerelease more than two thousand films, among which were 997 imported films. These films had first been shown before the Cultural Revolution and now could be enjoyed again by the whole nation, which had been forced to see nothing but the aforementioned eight "model" modern Beijing operas for more than ten years.

Thus, the Chinese film industry enjoyed rapid development in the first half of the decade. In 1980, 84 feature films were produced, with the number of moviegoers totalling 234 billion, which meant an average of 29 films per person that year. In 1984, 144 films were produced, a number exceeding even the expectations of the government.

There are thirteen film studios in China that are entitled, according to the regulations of the State Council, to produce feature films. Their output ranges from two (Tianshan and Inner Mongolia Film Studios) to sixteen (Shanghai Film Studio) films a year. In addition, at least one film studio in every province is entitled to make newsreels and documentaries. Since feature films have become so profitable, this second group of studios has proceeded to produce feature films. Film-related institutions that were entitled to perform other activities also have invested in film productions. Furthermore, new film institutions have been mushrooming. In 1985, they increased to 190,000, with fifteen million employees.

However, the optimism experienced by the film industry at the beginning of the 1980s was short-lived. With the further opening up of the country to the outside world and the consequent awakening of the people from a rigid system, audiences that had had no choice of entertainment began to be drawn to a great variety of cultural events, from drama to rock-'n'-roll dances. The proliferation of television sets has provided the people in the remotest corners of the country with programs imported from Hong Kong, Japan, the United States, and other countries. Furthermore, video shops, which are mushrooming throughout the country, also draw a large number of viewers. As a result, the number of moviegoers has fallen to the lowest since 1980. In 1984, only twenty-six billion tickets were sold, down 10 percent from 1980. In the first quarter of 1985, the moviegoing audience was 30 percent smaller than during the same period the previous year. The result has been a loss of revenue of RMB 9.36 million ($3.12 million).

What is even more critical to the film industry is the fact that the aforementioned filmgoers went to the cinema not to see locally made films but to enjoy films imported from foreign countries and Hong Kong. Take, for instance, a billboard announcing the film schedule for the month of May, 1985, put up by a railway workers' club in Beijing: Among the seven feature films to be shown that month, two were from Hong Kong, one from the United States, one from West Germany, and the rest from France. Not a single Chinese film was scheduled. This is by no means the only case. On September 12, 1985, *People's Daily* (overseas edition) carried a letter from a reader who complained that fewer than fifty people were present when he saw the Chinese film, *Border Town;* by the time it was over, thirty-odd remained. It should be noted here that the film in question was far from a critical failure. Based on a novel of the same name by Shen Congwen, the veteran writer of the May Fourth movement, and directed by the equally eminent director, Ling Zifeng, this film was highly acclaimed when it was shown at the Montreal Film Festival.

It seems that commercialism, scorned by the Chinese since 1949, has played a vital role in the development—or rather, the decline—of the once politics-oriented medium of film. In the same letter mentioned above, the reader continues to detail the publicity given to films that are potentially profitable. Most of them are *kung fu* films from Hong Kong and commercial films from other countries. While *Border Town* was scheduled for one day with three shows only, the U.S.-made *Rambo: First Blood* was given such overwhelming publicity that when it was shown throughout the country, one could hardly get a ticket.

Authorities' responses to the decline of the film industry are different, as are their explanations of the decline. In a letter to the director of the Film Bureau, published in *People's Daily* of June 15, 1985, Xia Yan, chairman of the China Film Association, expressed his dissatisfaction after seeing forty-four films produced in the first half of 1985. According to the letter, of the films he saw, 60 percent to 70 percent were *kung fu* and detective stories. There were virtually no films that reflected the "vigorous" economic reform movement. Xia, at the age of eighty-two, was unable to sleep the night after he read the annual film production plan for 1985. He demanded that every film studio make more than one film about contemporary issues, that is, the economic reform. Otherwise, he told the director, "the Party and people will criticize us, and our life for next year will not be smooth." He forgot that only five years before, when the Fourth Annual Conference for Film Workers was held in Beijing, he had told representatives from all over the country that a distance should be kept between artistic creativity and current political movements. He had then quite correctly pointed out that it was very difficult for a film to "truly" reflect current politics and sometimes "it is very dangerous." He also forgot that at about the same time he wrote to the director, Deng Xiaoping, in a talk with a foreign leader, expressed his worries about the fate of the reform by telling his guest that "the reform is only an experiment; it might succeed, and it might fail as well."

Yuan Wenshu, the vice chairman of the China Film Association, has the same view as Xia Yan. In addition, he urges filmmakers to make films appealing to ordinary people, and he assures them that creative freedom and administrative flexibility have been offered by the government. But he denies that the Chinese film industry is facing a crisis. Ding Qiao, the deputy minister of culture in charge of film production, concluded during a symposium on documentary films that film production, in the face of competition from television and other cultural activities, would not be able to enjoy a steady increase but would develop in a spiral way. Although he denied, as Yuan did, that film was in crisis, he did point out the fact that the film industry, once a source of lucrative profits, was now in danger of losing money.

It cannot be denied that the Chinese film industry is facing a crisis. However, it is a crisis that is also being faced by other art forms in China, especially such traditional ones as Beijing opera, folk dance, and music. Seemingly in contrast to this, popular culture, which has a heavy touch of Western culture, is thriving. Li Delun, the conductor of the Central Symphony Orchestra, is reported to have said: "Since World War II, 'mass culture' from the U.S.—from jazz to disco—has conquered the world; China is the last battleground—and we are hardly putting up any resistance." It is significant that while *The One and the Eight*, the groundbreaking first film of a young director, was being heavily censored before it could be released, *Huo Yuanjia*, a Hong Kong television series, was sweeping through the country. Many reasons can be given for the decline of the film industry in China, from limited artistic freedom to mismanagement of the system, but one point needs to be explored thoroughly before we can find the solution: contradictions between the deep-rooted bureaucracy and the new flexibility, and between long and heavy traditions and foreign influences.

While the film industry in China has been suffering a financial crisis, film as an art in China has been making obvious progress. Some film critics call this another "golden day" of the Chinese film, like that of the 1930s.

Despite the fact that mainstream films are still being produced as poor propaganda or crude entertainment, some relatively new directors who have been exposed to a large number of foreign films and contemporary film theories, and who have enjoyed the freedom of artistic expression that previous generations never had, have made a number of films that have been internationally acclaimed, even though they have often been failures at the box office. These directors, who make up the so-called fourth generation, were graduated from the Beijing Film Academy before the Cultural Revolution broke out and did not have a chance to make any films until it was over. Together with the "fifth generation" of filmmakers—the first graduates after the Cultural Revolution—these directors have set trends in the recent development of the Chinese film.

Since the founding of the new China, film has been considered a reliable tool for political propaganda; therefore, filmmakers have been apt to make films that extol the revolutionary and historical glories. In other words, these films have been made to educate people or to support the current political movements. When the 1980s began, with more relaxed cultural policies and the awakening of the people from a rigid system, a number of films began to focus on more personal and philosophical aspects of people's lives instead of portraying their heroic deeds in the bitter years of war or their miserable lives during the Cultural Revolution. The film that started this trend is *Seagull,* which tells the story of a woman volleyball player who sacrifices all her life to gain the world championship for her team, only to find that her goal cannot be achieved in her generation. She then becomes a coach and finally, in a wheelchair, watches on a television screen as the Chinese team defeats the Japanese. Zhang Nuanxin, the director, explains, "I dedicate my film to those strong and decided who, like Sha-ou ["sea gull" in Chinese], fail to realize their ideal, to those heroes who cannot succeed. . . . Life is ruthless and success doesn't come to everybody's hand." What she does not mention here but expresses clearly in her film is that individual and common interest are dependent on each other and the individual must be determined to be the master of his own fate before he can contribute to the common interest. The message was evidently accepted by the younger generation, for when the film was released in 1982, it immediately became popular among college students.

During the Cultural Revolution, hundreds of thousands of young students were sent down to the country to be "reeducated." In those years that they spent with peasants, many young students, after becoming disillusioned with the revolution, began to think, thereby gaining a better understanding of the revolution, of the country, and of themselves. *Our Fields,* a film directed by Xie Fei of the Beijing Youth Film Studio, tells the story of one "reeducated" student who returns to the country after being graduated from the university in 1982. The film truly reflects young people's lives, their frustrations, and their hopes. The same theme appears in several other films made before and after this one—*Sacrifice of Youth, Back-lit Picture,* and *Wakening Up,* to name a few. With different stories and characters, the directors of these films express their philosophy of life, their understanding of history, and their hope for the future. Although the number of this kind of film is small, and although they were quite controversial when released, these films were artistically welcomed and did quite well at the box office.

It needs to be pointed out that these films are basically about young people from big cities. Though some films might be set in the country, their heroes are often educated young people who come from cities. If we look at the history of the Chinese cinema, we find that most films produced in the course of eighty years—like films throughout the world—have focused on city life. In the new China, even though the government has constantly urged filmmakers to make films about rural life, films thus made have been anything but true reflections of the feelings of the peasants. Looking from this background, we can see another trend developing in Chinese film. A large number of films are being made to reflect the fate, feeling, frustrations, and hopes of the millions of peasants. These films are no longer trying to propagate the government's policies; what they show to the audience are the poverty and backwardness of rural China and, at the same time, the hope and future there. Films in this group include *When Winds Blow, The Reed Pipe Sounds, Sounds from Home, Xumao and His Daughters, River Without Buoys,* and *The Yellow Earth*. Most of these films were directed by the young generation of filmmakers in China. They have a remarkable perspective on the reality and history of China, and they have gained, through their personal sufferings in the countryside during the Cultural Revolution, a profound understanding of the relationship between the people and the land. Therefore, the films they have made are true pictures of rural China. It is not difficult to predict that among these filmmakers will emerge some great artists in the future. In fact, films such as *River Without Buoys* and *The Yellow Earth* have been internationally recognized.

The Chinese film has not only moved from the city to the countryside, it has further moved to the remotest areas of the countryside. As filmmakers focus on rural life, they often find remarkable scenery in those remote areas, scenery that is visually astonishing to these mostly city-bred filmmakers. A film critic recently used the phrase "western movies," borrowed from the American cinema, to describe films made on location in Northwest China, such as *The Yellow Earth, Life, The Sun,* and *Waves of the Desert*. Northwest China, through which the Yellow River flows, is considered to be the cradle of Chinese civilization. It is a rather undeveloped area with vast stretches of arid, yellow land. However, it also the site of the richest and most colorful folk arts. It is not surprising to see that films made there are made with deep feelings for the land and profound understanding of the people and history.

It is difficult to predict how long these trends can survive in the wave of commercialism that is currently sweeping the country, nor how far they can advance against the still rigid system. Despite their artistic merits, the aforementioned films are not always favored by the authorities. However, film in China is no longer merely a tool for political propaganda. While it has developed as an industry, it has also made great progress as a form of art. In the past five years, the concept of film as an art form has gradually replaced the concept of film as a means of education among filmmakers, while films have been considered as entertainment instead of political propaganda among filmgoers in China. With a further relaxation of cultural policies and a continuing opening up of the country to the outside world, along with a higher level of education among filmmakers and a relatively high level of film literacy among the people, film in China will make tremendous progress in the future.

During an interview, Chen Kaige, the director of *The Yellow Earth,* said: "In China the east is mountainous, the west is flat; the west is poor, and the east is rich. Chinese history is full of examples of revolutionary movements that spread from west to east. In this spirit, we, recent graduates of the Beijing Film Academy, have chosen this yellow earth—poor, barren, and yet full of possibilities—to begin our artistic careers." In the same sense, the new Chinese cinema will break through the strict censorship and through the new commercialism and will advance towards a great cinema.

12
The Sinification of Cinema: The Foreignness of Film in China

PAUL CLARK

FILM IS the most foreign art introduced into China in the Westernizing cultural upsurge known as the May Fourth movement at the beginning of the twentieth century. Film (along with modern-style spoken drama) was totally new, with no precursors in traditional Chinese literary and artistic activities. The modern novel or short story, in contrast, had antecedents centuries old. Indeed, a nationalist Chinese might argue that these artistic forms had been invented in China. The technical complexity of the film medium compounded its foreignness: until the 1920s, few Chinese had managed to assemble the specialized talent and capital needed to create films. Until at least 1955 most films that Chinese audiences saw were foreign-made. During the three recent decades, the men and women charged with shaping and implementing cultural policy have continued to regard films as an imported and therefore perhaps more suspect medium. Until recently, film artists have not been strongly inclined to disagree.

This paper will outline some of the reasons for the persistence of this attitude towards cinema in China and will suggest some of the factors that have inhibited the development of a distinguishably Chinese film art. A 1984 film from China will be cited as an indication of the paradox that the sinification of cinema may be achieved by an internationalization of film in China.

Using the term "sinification" implies the assumption of a spectrum of "Chineseness," from complete and autochthonous cultural forms to fully imported ones. Constructing such a spectrum would be a misleading and meaningless exercise, except for nativistic culturalists. Even if such a spectrum existed, cinema would probably not find a place on it. For Chinese of a range of political persuasions have at least unconsciously tended to regard film as something from outside the culture. By implication, it must remain somewhat separate and exotic. This sort of attitude is less easy to find in the case of other cultural activities. Sinification in this context merely refers to a process whereby the connections between film art and the rest of Chinese culture, and between film and Chinese society, are strengthened. Defining what is Chinese will be left to the philosophers and to critics of "spiritual pollution."

We should usefully keep in mind that throughout the nine decades of film history in China the most successful, popular films have been foreign. Before 1949, more than three-quarters of the films that filled China's screens were imported, mostly from Hollywood. In the 1950s Soviet films took the place of the American product, although they occupied perhaps only a quarter of screen time. Foreign films continued to attract audiences throughout the subsequent two decades. Since 1976, and the end of the Cultural Revolution, during which Chinese filmgoers could view the best that P'yŏngyang and Tirana could offer, imported features have continued to be the most closely watched films.

From this bold statement two things should be apparent. First, some of the worst films on China's screens have been imported ones. Second, the association of film art with foreignness is overwhelming. Filmgoers in China have watched films perhaps more for their origins from abroad than for their quality. Tirana is not yet a world cinema capital. To be sure, the choice of the Tirana studios as supplier of the imports that filled the void when Chinese film production stopped for almost five years after 1966 was a political one, when China and Albania were largely isolated from the wider intercourse of nations. But to most Chinese film viewers perhaps this did not matter as much as the fact that what was on the screen was a window to a wider world, even if that world was Hoxha's Albania or Kim Il-sŏng's Korea.

Needless to say, the first films shown in China, as in most parts of the world, were from abroad. In 1896 the Chinese and foreign clients of a Shanghai tearoom enjoyed a moving picture show (probably from Lumière brothers) in addition to the usual, indigenous entertainment. The empress dowager, Cixi, was another early film viewer, until a narrow escape from involuntary immolation by a flaming projector made her lose interest in the cinema.

During the First World War, when films, like other imports in the Chinese market, were harder to find, indigenous entrepreneurs saw the commercial potential of the medium. Hundreds of film companies were capitalized, registered, and collapsed during the 1920s. A few survived into the next decade, struggling with foreign competition and audiences' tastes nourished by the imported product.

After 1930, however, a national Chinese cinema began to find an important, though small, place in the film market. The men and women who helped create this domestic cinema remained active in Chinese filmmaking well after 1949. A few still served as the elder statesmen and women of China's film world in the 1980s.

Social and political changes that made possible the emergence of Chinese filmmaking are easy to outline, though harder to relate concretely to the work of this new generation of film artists. The intellectuals who in the 1920s had regarded film as a curiosity for the amusement of the lower classes took more interest in cinema in the 1930s. One of the reasons for this change of attitude was undoubtedly the rise of nationalist sentiment in the 1930s, as imperial Japan invaded Chinese territory. Similar Japanese designs on Chinese sovereignty had encouraged the patriotic May Fourth demonstrations of 1919, which gave the label May Fourth to the whole movement for social reform and the modern, cultural regeneration of China which dominated intellectual, as well as political, life in the first half of the twentieth century. In the early 1930s many May Fourth intellectuals began to recognize the potential of film art as a medium for the political and social mobilization of a Chinese public that largely ignored them. One such band of intellectuals formed a film group within the thinly disguised Communist-front organization, the League of Left-Wing Writers.

What followed in the 1930s was an uneasy and frequently disrupted combination of mercantilist greed and progressive zeal. While social reformers and alienated intellectuals saw in cinema a means to transform mass society, the owners of film studios in Shanghai saw a chance to transform their bank accounts. The nature of the medium—its need for considerable capital investment and for skilled technicians and artists—made the alliance between capitalist and artist unsurprising. After 1949, the alliance was replaced in large measure by a combination of Party cultural bureaucrats and filmmakers. As in the 1930s, the imperatives of film production meant that each side needed the other.

The films made in Chinese studios in the 1930s needed audiences. For all its potential as a mass medium, foreign and domestic films reached a decidedly narrow segment of Chinese society, until well into the 1950s and even 1960s. In 1927 one count found 106 "picture theaters" in China, although most of these places probably provided other entertainment as well. By 1949 places where films were shown had increased to about seven hundred, in a country of more than four hundred million people. In the 1930s the majority of filmgoers lived in the most non-Chinese parts of the nation: in the treaty ports like Shanghai, Guangzhou (Canton), and Tianjin and in the riverine hinterland. All these places were most accessible to foreign influence and commerce.

Within these places, film patrons were a self-selected narrow slice of the population, at least until the late 1940s. Most films in the cinemas were from abroad. Filmgoers needed the time and money to attend a film show, and also the familiarity with or curiosity about foreign customs, people, and places, which filled most screens. Foreign films in the 1930s were not dubbed; that was too expensive. A Chinese narrator (like the Japanese *benshi*) and, more often in the 1930s, side-titles aided audiences' understanding of Hollywood and other movies. Even most of the comparatively few Chinese-produced films in the cinemas reflected the cosmopolitanism of 1930s audiences. The average film from Chinese studios had an urban setting, with middle-class characters: perhaps mixed-up "modern girls" or conscience-stricken scholars in love with factory workers.

This is not to underestimate the extraordinary achievements of some Shanghai artists in the 1930s. Films like *The Goddess (Shennü)*, which presented a sympathetic but unvarnished story of a prostitute, essayed subject matter not seen in other countries' cinemas for years to come. *Spring Silkworms (Chuncan)*, an adaptation of Mao Dun's May Fourth short story, gave central place to work in an innovative depiction of production. The emphasis on adolescent physicality in *The Highway (Dalu)* is still astonishing fifty years after its production. A single long tracking shot from an arriving taxi across the pavement, into and across the hotel lobby in *Plunder of Peach and Plum (Tao li jie)* was an extraordinary effect for a 1934 film.

Two catastrophic, national events have shaped Chinese history in the twentieth century more profoundly than any other: the War of Resistance to Japan (1937–1945) and the Cultural Revolution (1966–1976). Both had considerable impact on the development of film in China.

THE SINIFICATION OF CINEMA 179

When cinemas reopened at the end of the war and as the Shanghai studios resumed production, more filmgoers began to watch Chinese films than had been the case in the prewar decade. Movies began to resemble a mass medium. One reason for this change was the vividness in which films from the late 1940s like *The Spring River Flows East (Yijiang chunshui xiang dong liu)*, *Crows and Sparrows (Wuya yu maque)*, and *Lights of Ten Thousand Homes (Wanjia denghuo)* presented the nationwide experience of the war against Japan and its aftermath. Filmmakers during these years had been forced out of the cosmopolitan enclaves of Shanghai. They had been exposed to conditions and parts of society far from the treaty ports. This unprecedented, and hard to explain, coincidence of audience and artists' concerns helps account for the success of these postwar films. Artistically they built on the achievements of the 1930s: this was only natural, because the filmmakers of these two decades were largely the same people. The war had changed the nation: it seemed that only a widely accessible medium like film could adequately represent this transformation.

But the accomplishments of the late 1940s were not sustained. The War of Resistance to Japan had laid the foundation for the success of the Red Army in the civil war against the Guomindang. Also during the war Mao Zedong had encapsulated the Communist party's views on the social role of art in his *Talks* on the subject in the wartime headquarters in Yan'an.

It would be hard to find a place more distant culturally and politically from Shanghai than the mountain town of Yan'an in northern Shaanxi province. In this unlikely setting, where the peasants may not have even seen a film before the arrival of the Red Army in 1936, a pattern of Party control of cultural production and emphasis on the popularization and elevation of taste in art and literature were established. In the subsequent four decades, for the Chinese film enterprise as for the rest of cultural activity, the Yan'an legacy represented a relative emphasis on popular, native forms, simplicity and directness, and Party strictures. In contrast, what we might call the Shanghai legacy is less easy to characterize. As we have seen, many progressive filmmakers since 1930 had subscribed to Party guidance. But the Shanghai experience had been an international, Westernized, and underground one. Filmmakers, cultural bureaucrats, and others encountered problems in the transition to open control of the new cultural enterprise, and to the need to appeal to broader audiences. Having taken over the asylum in 1949, the inmates (both Party cadres and artists) felt at something of a loss.

By 1953 Hollywood films had disappeared from China's screens. Production of new-style Chinese features, modeled loosely on Stalinist "socialist realism," was slow to develop. To fill empty screens, dubbed Soviet and other socialist films were shown. Audiences expanded rapidly. Like the businessmen of the 1920s and the progressive intellectuals of the 1930s, the Party leadership was attracted by the potentials of this mass medium to reach the widest, in this case political, audiences. Despite its foreign associations, film was burdened with the task of promulgating a mass, national culture, comprehensible to all citizens in all parts of the country, not just in Shanghai. Filmmakers had to earn responsibility and trust from the cultural leadership. The result was a half-decade delay in the growth of the film industry. The insistence on the change from one foreign model (Hollywood) to another (Moscow, via Yan'an) compounded the problem of the development of a distinctly Chinese cinema. Filmmakers were encouraged to ignore their own achievements of the late 1940s in using film to reflect the national psyche.

This pre-1949 "progressive" film tradition enjoyed a brief revival in 1956–1957 during the Hundred Flowers campaign, in which Mao Zedong invited intellectuals and artists to assess progress since 1949. Some of the assessments proved too blunt, and many critics were suppressed during the subsequent "Anti-Rightist" campaign. Soon Party and popular energies were caught up in the Great Leap Forward, a Maoist lunge towards instant modernization of China's economy on Chinese terms.

The move towards Chinese solutions to economic problems was paralleled by the replacement of "socialist realism" (which had never been fully implemented) by a new slogan. "Combining revolutionary realism and revolutionary romanticism" was a looser cultural ethos. The latter term in particular allowed for greater recognition of China's folk arts and performing traditions. Filmmakers produced more musical and opera films, drawing on the riches of China's cultural legacy, in its "reformed," Party-approved guise.

The establishment of film studios in interior cities, such as Xi'an, Chengdu, and Huhehaote (in Inner Mongolia), suggested that film was losing its close association with the Westernized outlook of Shanghai. Ambitious plans for a feature-film studio in every provincial capital were soon abandoned. But younger filmmakers in the interior studios, because of the absence of senior artistic staff who had first call on limited film stock and other resources, were able to direct their first features. Strict hierarchies in the older studios in Changchun, Beijing, and Shanghai frustrated younger talents there. This pattern of innovation from the provinces was repeated in the early 1980s, with promising results.

The Party effort to use the imported medium of film as a purveyor of a mass, national culture reached its height during the Cultural Revolution. When feature-film production resumed in 1970, after a five-year hiatus, the first new features were the "model performances" promoted by the Party insurgents under Jiang Qing. These stage shows were mostly modernized operas, carefully crafted attempts to update traditional Chinese forms with modern, revolutionary content. The people who made the films were some of the artists who had been active since the 1930s in Shanghai filmmaking. The specialized nature of the medium gave the Party leadership no choice but to rely on these old hands. Despite the care taken in the celluloid adaptation of the model operas and ballets (another foreign form given nativistic treatment in these years), they failed to map a new path for the sinification of film art. The absence of any other films, except for Albanian, North Korean, and a few other imports, ensured rapid audience saturation. *Taking Tiger Mountain by Strategy (Zhiqu Weihushan)*, for example, was seen by 7.3 billion viewers between its late-1970 release and the end of 1974. This suggests that every man, woman, and child in China had seen the film at least seven times in four years. In these circumstances, interest in the modernization of an ancient art rapidly gave way to resentment and indifference.

After 1974 new-style feature films began to appear to relieve audiences of a steady diet of "model performances." But the (often collective) creators of these films draw upon the limited aesthetic of the model operas. In an art like film, with its potential for naturalism and range of expression, the new features were bound to disappoint both their makers and long-suffering Chinese audiences. Given the time it took to produce new scripts, the effects of this failed aesthetic lasted well after the fall of the Party insurgents in late 1976.

In the 1980s Chinese cinema has been in turmoil and under threat. These conditions have caused alarm but also have fostered some interesting and potentially revolutionary developments in the sinification of film. Foreign films emerged yet again as the most popular films in

China. Audiences packed early-morning screenings of Indian films. American Film Weeks played to overflow houses whenever they were held in major cities. Local filmmakers felt resentment at the success of these Hollywood and other imports. They also saw the rapid increase in television ownership and demands on studios to make films available for television broadcast as a threat to the hitherto preeminence of film as the most effective mass medium in China.

The most common response from filmmakers was to try to beat the imports and changing audience tastes at their own game. Films made in China became faster paced, with more emphasis on action and love stories. Techniques like the split screen, slow motion, and freeze frame were put to ill-use in these new stories. Such imitation merely compounded the problem of foreign competition in this still apparently foreign medium.

A more recent and reasoned response to the dilemmas of a film future was the work of a new generation of filmmakers. These young men and women had received part of their education during the Cultural Revolution, when many educated youths underwent internal exile. Like the earlier generation of Shanghai artists who had been exposed to life outside the metropolis during the War of Resistance to Japan, this new generation had gained during their years of exile or enforced idleness an understanding of the totality of Chinese society and of popular attitudes to politics. These young artists got the rest of their training at the Beijing Film Academy, where the first new degree class in more than a decade enrolled in 1978.

Most of the older generations of filmmakers in China had an ambiguous attitude to film, especially because of its nontraditional, foreign associations. The Shanghai artists of the 1930s and 1940s often were skilled proponents of other literary or artistic pursuits. Experiment with the Hollywood-derived medium at least started as something of a hobby or adjunct to writing and painting, the only "true" arts to a Chinese intellectual. The early emphasis on the film script has continued to be strong and is a reflection of the primacy of literature in Chinese culture. Even the generation trained after 1949 not infrequently regarded film as a means to bring other arts (particularly fiction and stage performances) to the screen. Many regarded the reverential adaptation of the great works of May Fourth writers as their classic achievements.

Members of the new, 1980s generation see themselves as film artists first and last. Film is their chosen and perhaps only medium of artistic expression. They have had more exposure to a wider range of international cinemas than any previous generation of Chinese filmmakers. Much of their new work suggests that this awareness of international film styles has given these young artists the confidence to turn to Chinese culture and experiment more thoroughly than their predecessors with the combination of film art and indigenous styles.

A film by Chen Kaige, a 1982 graduate of the Beijing Film Academy, illustrates the potential of the new generation. *The Yellow Earth (Huang tudi)* was produced in 1984 at the Guangxi Film Studio, where the newness and remoteness of the studio allowed younger artists like Chen and cinematographer Zhang Yimou opportunities hard to find in more established studios.

The contrasts between this film and most ordinary features made in the same year is striking. Pacing is slow and deliberate, to reinforce the film's presentation of the stasis and desperation of peasant society in 1939 Shaanxi province. The framing of the shots and their montage are reminiscent of turning the pages of a Chinese picture or comic book. The earth fills the frame, with only a narrow strip at the top of the screen for human figures. Style and theme mesh more closely than in most films made since 1949. The peasants are presented, as in traditional painting, as part of nature. They drink the fine silt suspended in the water of the Yellow River, in this region which was the cradle of Chinese civilization. The millet they wrest from the earth and grind on their millstones even looks like the dirt from which it came. The subtle presentation of the story and characters is unusual: most films made in China after 1949 did not allow their viewers such imagination and intelligence. Chen and his collaborators have taken the elements of a more run-of-the-mill post-1949 feature: a revolutionary setting, direct reference to the promise and achievement of the Communist party, and soldier and peasant heroes. From familiarity with the artistic possibilities seen in international cinema, they have presented these familiar elements in new, profoundly effective ways.

There is a paradox in the achievement of *The Yellow Earth*. The first generation of Chinese film artists watched and competed with films from Hollywood in the Shanghai of the 1930s and 1940s. Their experiments in "neorealism" and mise-en-scène are only now being recognized in China and abroad for their uniqueness. After 1949, a new generation (and these older artists) turned to a new foreign model, Moscow, and made films according to the artistic strictures established in rural, wartime Yan'an. *The Yellow Earth* has a message and setting derived from Yan'an: but its style is as international as the older Shanghai film and artistic tradition. Whether by this it can represent a new step in the sinification of film art remained to be seen in the late 1980s.

References

Material for this paper is drawn from my book, *Chinese Cinema: Culture and Politics since 1949*, to be published by Cambridge University Press in the Cambridge Studies in Film series in late 1987.

13
The Position of Women in New Chinese Cinema

TONY RAYNS

WOMEN have been treated as badly in Chinese cinema as in any other national cinema; they have been stereotyped as helpless victims or self-sacrificing saints and have suffered the usual varieties of sexist exploitation. At the same time, though, Chinese culture is significantly less patriarchal than neighboring cultures like those of Korea and Japan, and it has produced at least its share of strong and independent-minded female role models. Admittedly, most of these involve women either standing in for men or impersonating men, but progressive Chinese culture of the twentieth century (notably work developed under the aegis of the May Fourth Movement since the 1920s) has managed to build on the latter tradition, often characterizing women as bearers of knowledge or as fighters for social change. This strand of thought inevitably found its way into the progressive Shanghai cinema of the 1930s and set some important precedents for the representation of women in Chinese cinema of later years.

The following notes have no pretensions to offer a comprehensive account of the representation of women in Chinese cinema. They content themselves with examining some of the tensions and contradictions found in the depiction of women in some recent Chinese films, all of which belong to a notional "New Wave." The underlying contention is that Chinese cinema of the present is fully embroiled in the struggle for a new representation of women, albeit a struggle that lacks the theoretical perspectives of Western feminism. For the purposes of argument, I have chosen to focus on three films, one from each of the major Chinese film industries: Ann Hui's *The Spooky*

Bunch (*Zhuang dao zheng*, 1980) from Hong Kong, Edward Yang's *Taipei Story* (*Qingmei zhuma*, 1985) from Taiwan, and Chen Kaige's *The Yellow Earth* (*Huang tudi*, 1984) from the People's Republic.

It is first necessary to establish exactly what is meant by "New Chinese Cinema," since there are obvious historical and political differences among the three centers of production.

The first New Wave in Chinese cinema appeared in Hong Kong in 1979, when a large group of young directors (many of them trained in Western film schools) made the transition from television production to the film industry. They entered an industry that had been dominated by the martial arts genre (and its subsequent variant, the "kung-fu comedy") since the start of the decade, at a point when the generation gap between veteran directors and their young audience was becoming embarrassingly noticeable. Diminishing audiences and the ever-increasing formulariness of Hong Kong cinema had left a palpable space for innovation, and a number of small independent production companies simultaneously took the initiative of hiring new directors who were markedly closer in age to the majority audience than their industry peers. The chief underlying significance of this development was that it brought images of contemporary Hong Kong back to the cinema: whereas most of the veteran directors were born in the mainland and tended to make studio-bound movies that were entirely disengaged from the immediate realities of Hong Kong, the young directors were all born or reared in Hong Kong and they felt a natural impulse to deal with their experience of their home environment. The result was not a New Wave in the Althusserian sense of a radical break with cinema of the past, but it did (at least in the short term) liberate Hong Kong cinema from a set of dismally stale conventions.

The Hong Kong initiative, and the excitement that greeted the first films of Allen Fong, Ann Hui, Tsui Hark, and others, had an inevitable "knock-on" effect in the film industry of Taiwan, which was even more strangled by outworn conventions than the Hong Kong film industry had been. In Taiwan, the first initiatives were taken by the Guomindang government, the largest investor in the film industry through its Central Motion Picture Corporation (CMPC). The CMPC began producing portmanteau films in 1981, each comprising three or four distinct episodes and each designed to give new directors their first breaks or to allow young directors already working in the industry a chance to undertake more ambitious work. One of the features so produced was the three-part *The Sandwich Man* (*Erzi de da wan'ou*, 1982), which cemented a connection between the new spirit in cinema and the nativist school that had recently revived Taiwanese literature, since all three parts of the film were based on stories by the leading nativist writer Huang Chunming. All the directors who contributed episodes to these portmanteau films went on to direct features in their own right, sometimes for the CMPC and sometimes for independent producers. Many of them, too, were Western-trained, and their relative familiarity with other national cinemas helped to open their eyes to the possibility of using their films to deal with their feelings about and experiences of Taiwan. As in Hong Kong, this New Wave has not, in the main, produced radically innovative work, but it has effectively served to displace the work of older, established directors in the film industry.

The New Wave in Mainland China's cinema is more recent and less well established, but it shows signs of representing a far more radical break with the past than has been the case in Hong Kong or Taiwan. In China, the initiative came not from the top but from the grass roots: the first generation of filmmakers born after the 1949 Communist victory came of age and felt an almost militant dissatisfaction with both the prevailing standards of Chinese cinema and the existing structure of the film industry. These new directors are all recent graduates from Beijing Film Academy, China's film school, and most of them (although automatically assigned to work in one of the state film studios) got their first opportunities to direct from television. They owe their film careers to the Chinese government's decentralization policies: assignment to a major studio like those in Beijing, Shanghai, or Guangzhou is tantamount to a sentence of twenty years as an assistant director, since those studios have large staffs of established directors with priority claims to the year's ration of film stock and production finance, whereas assignment to one of the new regional studios like Guangxi, Xi'an, or Kunming means that a young director is likely to have the opportunity to direct without delay, since the new studios are small, have no veteran staff, and are not bound by an institutional pecking order. Accordingly, new directors like Zhang Junzhao, Chen Kaige, and Tian Zhuangzhuang have requested postings to these studios and have found their way clear to make films and tackle subjects of interest and relevance to their generation. Their work is proving to be innovative in both theme and form, and its innovations embody implicit criticisms of the manifold failings of Chinese cinema in recent years. Whereas the mainstream of Chinese movie production since the death of Mao has been resolutely escapist and romantic, the work of the young directors seems to be committedly political: they are not afraid (or, more accurately, are determined) to broach issues that the older generation would prefer to leave untouched.

All three of these New Waves have appeared against backgrounds of rapid social change: in Hong Kong, the debates and uncertainty surrounding the territory's future after 1997; in Taiwan, the belated modernization of Taipei as a financial and manufacturing center; in China, the pragmatic reforms associated with Deng Xiaoping. The young directors of all three New Waves belong to the post-1949 generation and are thus comparatively unmarked by the political and other struggles of the 1930s and 1940s. Few of them see themselves as belonging to a specifically Chinese film tradition, although all of them are actively committed to an engagement with the social and cultural changes around them. It is this, rather than any formal trait, which gives their work its cultural specificity. The other factor that links young filmmakers in Hong Kong, Taipei, and China is the fact that they have had a great deal more exposure to non-Chinese cinema than any previous generation of Chinese filmmakers; many have also enjoyed opportunities for travel (and hence for first-hand acquaintance with other cultures) that were not available to earlier generations. In short, they are both Chinese and cosmopolitan, and their work reflects that equivocation precisely. It is as if their films reach for a place in the mainstream of international cinema that Chinese cinema does not, in fact, yet have.

This brings us back to the question of women. Some of the new directors (principally in Hong Kong) *are* women; many are men who have gone out of their way to privilege female characters and issues in their work. There is no feminist movement (in the Western sense) in Hong Kong, Taiwan, or China, but filmmakers in all three production centers are generally informed about the contemporary Western interest in feminist issues, including the debates surrounding the representation of women in films. Needless to add, they are also working in societies that offer women a substantially wider range of roles than was the case as little as twenty years ago, and it is hardly surprising that their work reflects that development, at least indirectly. Rather than attempt an overview of their achievements and failures in this area, I prefer to turn now to analyses of the three particular films mentioned above, with a view to drawing some tentative theoretical conclusions from the concrete evidence of these examples.

THE SPOOKY BUNCH (ZHUANG DAO ZHENG)

The Spooky Bunch is unique in Hong Kong cinema in being produced, written, and directed by women. It was initiated as a project by its producer and star, Siu Fong-Fong (in Mandarin: Xiao Fangfang), a leading actress in Cantonese films since the late 1950s, and it was produced by Ms. Siu's own company, Hi-Pitch Productions. Ms. Siu was one of many independent producers in 1979–80 who saw that the emergence of a new group of young directors offered an opportunity to get away from the venerable formulas of Hong Kong cinema. Ann Hui (in Mandarin: Xu Anhua) was one of the most prominent new directors, thanks to a distinguished career in television, and she had just completed her first cinema feature. Ms. Siu approached her and invited her to formulate a film that she could both produce and star in. Ann Hui worked with her (then regular) script collaborator Joyce Chan and came up with *The Spooky Bunch*. The film was released with above-average success in 1980.

The film is a supernatural comedy with elements of suspense, cruelty, romance, and sentimentality. It deals with a fourth-rate Cantonese opera troupe, which arrives to perform on the relatively undeveloped island of Cheung Chau, one of the few areas in the territory of Hong Kong that still evokes the rhythms and flavor of rural China. From the day of its promotional parade through the streets of the small town, the opera troupe is plagued by ghostly apparitions. It gradually becomes clear that the chief supernatural agent is a mischievous female spirit named Catshit, who is possessing one member of the troupe after another and forcing them into self-destructive acts. Catshit's prime target is the troupe's leading actor, who is forced into embarrassing displays of effeminacy. Against this background, an incipient romance develops between Ah Chee, the troupe's scatterbrained leading actress, and the sophisticated, Westernized son of a Hong Kong businessman who is visiting the island for family reasons. It emerges that Catshit is the harbinger of an entire platoon of vengeful ghosts: a nineteenth-century military squadron that was poisoned to death by an ancestor of Ah Chee's. A Buddhist monk is brought in to give advice, and he undertakes to trap the ghosts. Ah Chee's prospective boyfriend valiantly presents himself as a scapegoat to Catshit and succeeds in deflecting her assaults. Ah Chee and her boyfriend can finally be alone together, but the last shot (of a mysterious bouncing ball) signals that Catshit is not "dead" yet.

The first thing to establish about *The Spooky Bunch* is that it has no manifest feminist content at all. The film registers first as an offbeat genre piece, second as a formal experiment (much of it is shot in extended, hand-held takes, using only available light, a device that gives it an unexpected, documentary-like immediacy), and sexual politics seem firmly pushed to one side. And yet even a cursory study of the synopsis reveals a number of challenges to traditional Chinese gender stereotypes: the fact that the chief ghost is female, the undermining of the troupe leader's masculinity (wickedly emphasized when Catshit possesses him while he is naked in the bath), the general inadequacy and unreliability of the men, the eventual survival of the women. The film "rhymes" Ah Chee with Catshit (played respectively by Siu Fong-Fong and Tina Liu, the film's executive producer and producer), presenting the ghost's ruthless malice as the inverted mirror image of the heroine's daffy innocence. In one sense, the film follows convention by thus presenting its women protagonists as trouble, but it squarely departs from convention by actively *celebrating* them as such. In marked contrast with the traditions of melodrama, this female trouble is neither tamed nor harnessed but triumphant. Catshit survives; Ah Chee gets her (recalcitrant) man.

The film's main theme is one with particular relevance to Hong Kong: the way that the present is haunted by the past. Using a location that is a throwback to an earlier phase of Hong Kong's development, the film explores the notion of lingering guilt for past crimes and underlines phenomena like the widespread persistence of superstition—which it implicitly compares with the survival of less-than-lustrous touring Cantonese opera troupes. The idea that the world is a veil of illusion is, of course, a Buddhist one, and it underpins the film's vision of a corner of Hong Kong where the old ways hold strong and where the past cannot be repressed. But the film's wit lies in its insistence on reading these themes across its play with gender stereotypes. In a way, *The Spooky Bunch* is the Chinese cinema's answer to a Hollywood film like *Bringing Up Baby*.

THE YELLOW EARTH (HUANG TUDI)

The chief thrusts of Chen Kaige's remarkable debut feature are political and formal, and it will be useful to examine them before moving on to consider the role of the film's young female protagonist. *The Yellow Earth* is set in Northern Shaanxi province in 1939 and shows a middle-aged Communist soldier named Gu Qing coming to an isolated mountain village some distance from the Yellow River. He has been detailed to collect folk songs for possible adaptation to use as political campaign songs. He is billeted with one of the village's poorest families, comprising a prematurely aged widower and his two children, the fourteen-year-old girl Cuiqiao and her younger brother. Gu gradually establishes a working relationship with these taciturn and grindingly poor people and begins to collect songs. He has already witnessed an arranged marriage for a teenage girl in the village, and he offers Cuiqiao utopian promises that such things will be outlawed when the Communists come to power. But Cuiqiao soon finds herself facing a similar arranged marriage to a much older man, and Gu realizes helplessly that he is powerless to intervene. He leaves on a trip to his base in Yan'an. While he is gone, Cuiqiao decides to abscond from her marriage and is last seen taking a boat across the Yellow River at night, going in the direction of Yan'an; we hear her voice singing a Party song that Gu taught her, but it breaks off in mid-phrase—with the implication that she has been swept away or, more likely, that she has drowned herself. Gu returns to the village to find full-scale traditional prayers for rain in progress, and he has to swim against a tide of humanity in a vain attempt to reestablish contact with Cuiqiao's younger brother.

Leaving aside the larger resonances of the setting (the Yellow River valley was, of course, the cradle of Chinese civilization, but it offers notoriously fickle terrain that erodes fertile land as fast as the river deposits it), Gu Qing's sojourn in the village is clearly a summary and cipher of the Chinese Communist party (CCP) quest for a rural power base in the China of the 1930s. Previous films on this period in modern Chinese history have invariably shown the Party member as a privileged intellectual bringing enlightenment to the more or less receptive rural masses. *The Yellow Earth* is notably more objective in representing the period as an encounter of two worlds, two ways of seeing, and in showing each saddened and disappointed in the other. By emphasizing the enormous inherited weight of China's peasant culture and by pointing to a weakness at the root of the CCP's struggle to transform China, the film makes a momentous contribution to present-day political and cultural debates in China. At the same time, the film proposes viable new ways of drawing on the old Chinese cultural traditions: its own images are patterned after Shaanxi peasant paintings, especially in their use of great expanses of foreground space. The film is aesthetically innovative in all its formal devices: its use of silence and song rather than dialogue to advance its argument, its almost trigonometric camera movements, its insistence on natural light, and its eloquent play with reaction shots. And these strategies are complemented by the subtlety of its colors and textures, the confidence of its visual and dramatic rhythms.

Given all these characteristics and qualities, what does it mean to the film to choose the fourteen-year-old girl Cuiqiao as the person in the village most receptive to Gu Qing's vision of a changed society? And what does it mean that Cuiqiao disappears while on her own quest for the basis of that vision? Aside from the other child bride glimpsed in the opening scenes, Cuiqiao is the only woman featured in the film, and so the filmmakers are ostentatiously privileging her as a bearer of hope and knowledge. In doing so, they are both acknowledging the particular oppression of women in feudal society *and* implicitly criticizing the idealized depictions of women as feudal victims in earlier Chinese films. Cuiqiao has the spark of resistance within her, but the filmmakers are neither naive nor overoptimistic enough to believe that this alone will "save" her. She is quick to grasp the implications of Gu Qing's vision but inevitably lacks the maturity and perspective that would allow her to relate them to her own position. If she is a victim, it is only partly because she has no option but to submit to an early arranged marriage; it is also because nothing has adequately prepared her to deal with the concept of change. In one sense, Gu Qing is adding to her oppression by promising her a communist utopia; the film adds one more item to the long catalogue of ways in which men can oppress women.

TAIPEI STORY (QINGMEI ZHUMA)

Edward Yang's second feature is as ground-breaking in its way as *The Yellow Earth*. It offers an extraordinarily comprehensive panorama of recent social changes in the city of Taipei, focusing on a central couple (engaged since adolescence but never married) and some ten other characters of various ages around them. According to Yang himself, the film was conceived schematically, with the individual characters chosen and developed to represent different types, attitudes, and classes. The film's most striking achievement is that this genesis is virtually invisible: the characters are not mere ciphers, but living, plausible, understandable people.

The film's fiction is unusually dense, to the extent that it almost resists synopsis. Chin,[1] the central woman, works as personal assistant to an apparently unmarried career-woman executive; when their company is taken over by a larger conglomerate, Chin decides to follow her boss in leaving. She thus spends the main body of the film out of work, with unaccustomed time on her hands. She has also recently broken with convention by moving away from her parents and into an apartment of her own, despite not yet being married; her gesture reflects both her own sense of upward mobility and her growing dislike of her father (and particularly of the way he has treated her mother). Lon, her long-standing fiancé, is a perennial failure in business, torn between a lingering childhood passion for baseball and dreams of starting a new business venture with his brother-in-law in California. He, by contrast, feels great sympathy for Chin's father and bails him out of financial difficulties; but he finds a channel for the release of his own sense of failure by projecting it onto a friend from childhood in a much worse state than himself, a taxi driver stuck in a poverty trap with a sluttish wife and two ill-cared-for children. The film traces the on-again, off-again relationship between Chin and Lon through a period of a few weeks that prove crucial to both of them. Innumerable plot strands are interwoven, and the film moves freely between high-rise offices and tumbledown trading streets, affluent villas and virtual slums.

The film's approach to this material has been called Westernized, and it is certainly true that Yang's cool, controlled images have a precision and a visual resonance not unworthy of Antonioni or Wenders. *Taipei Story* is none the less completely culturally specific in its address to immediate issues in Taiwan, from the infatuation of Chin's younger sister with all things Japanese to the rowdy bike gang that roars past the presidential palace during the Double Tenth celebrations (10 October, the old Republican National Day, still observed in Taiwan). The patchwork structure serves Yang's purpose precisely: the city itself becomes the subject, crisscrossed with human passions and tensions that it ultimately dwarfs.

Chin is in many ways the film's most interesting figure, and there is clearly especial point in Yang's choosing (not for the first time in his career) to focus on a woman. She suspects Lon of maintaining contact with another former girlfriend (now unhappily married in Japan) and hovers on the brink of two affairs herself. The first is with a married architect who is apparently feeling the seven-year itch; the second is with a young man who shares a squat with her sister. She passes up the architect but perhaps spends the night with the young man (on the rebound from a row with Lon), only to realize her foolishness next day. Her sexual choices mirror her social options exactly: if the architect represents middle-class affluence and conformity, the young man represents dropout dissidence, and the faltering, independent Lon represents a far-from-reliable path between the two. But Yang has the very good sense to impose another, more fundamental perspective on the relationship between Chin and Lon. In this perspective, Lon represents the past (clinging to adolescent obsessions, respecting traditional family structures, lamenting change) while Chin represents the future. She breaks with traditions, takes a successful female executive as her role model, and refuses to sentimentalize the things that are lost in the process of social change. She is, in short, a modern individual, prey to moments to alienation, doubt, and loneliness but ultimately self-assured, self-sufficient, and secure in her survival. She embodies the tensions and contradictions necessary for survival in a modern city. Yang's decision to make this character a woman rather than a man has an almost polemic force.

None of the three films discussed above is typical of the film industry in which it was made, and so it is necessary to ask to what degree they are exceptions.

In the cinemas of both Hong Kong and Taiwan, it remains common to find female characters reduced to the level of the most reactionary stereotypes: brassy hookers and strippers, bossy mothers and mothers-in-law, meekly subservient wives and fiancées. (Needless to add, the sexual stereotypes are depicted less explicitly in the puritanical context of Taiwan cinema than they are in Hong Kong.) At the time of writing, Pat Ha, one of the most accomplished of young Chinese actresses, can be seen in two films that happen to be in simultaneous release in Hong Kong: in one (an inept variation on the American *Police Academy* films) she plays a virginal daughter who falls "purely" in love with a police cadet, while in the other (directed by a woman) she plays a ruthless prostitute who tries to suppress every humane impulse. Less than a year ago, Ms. Ha played the lead in Eddie Fong's *An Amorous Woman of the Tang Dynasty (Tangchao haofang nü)*, a modernist period movie about a woman's social and sexual emancipation; her current roles are sadly much more typical of the way she has to earn her living.

WOMEN IN NEW CHINESE CINEMA   195

In this context, representations of women like those found in *The Spooky Bunch* and *Taipei Story* are exceptional—but they are not unique. In Hong Kong, Ann Hui has repeatedly focused on women characters who either insist on defining themselves (by acting rather than reacting) or are provocatively shown as victims of male social engineering. Her latest film, for instance, adapts a short story by Eileen Chang (Zhang Ailing) about a young widow who experiences difficulties in entering a new relationship; the governing metaphor is the Peking Opera, in which a woman's every move is preordained and judged only by its competence in the execution of an unchanging mise-en-scène. Ann Hui's initiatives in this area have been echoed by some other directors of her generation: Yim Ho's *Homecoming (Si shui liu nian)* centers on an intense friendship between two women whose lives have diverged, Stanley Kwan's *Women (Nüren xin)* tackles the lives and loves of a group of career women, and Allen Fong's *Ah Ying (Banbianren)* deals with the family obligations and professional aspirations of a young working-class woman. The more backward-looking Taiwan film industry has not yet produced a second Edward Yang, although its roots in the Shanghai film industry of the 1930s and 1940s have provided other young directors like Zhang Yi with a heritage of melodrama that allows them to deal with the inner resilience of suffering women. Yang's only cinematic equal in Taiwan is Hou Xiaoxian, who has so far failed to produce female characters of any real substance in his work, doubtless because it is at present strongly autobiographical.

Circumstances are, of course, different in mainland China, where a feminist movement of sorts was institutionalized by the Communist government in the 1950s. This has produced a large body of cinema about women, almost all of it dedicated to the need to break the shackles of feudalism. For every *Li Shuangshuang* (a lively satire on the fight for female equality in the rural communes of the early 1960s) there have been a dozen or more films like *Song of Youth (Qingchun zhi ge)* in which the dawning radical consciousness of a young woman student is dramatized entirely in terms of her relationships with her male teachers. There have also been numerous Chinese equivalents of *Mother Courage*, celebrating the indomitable spirit of women as they traverse history, serving as oracles of orthodox Maoist wisdom as they go. These regrettable clichés have certainly impeded the production of alternative images of women and may also explain why China's few women directors have generally chosen to make films about men or families. In this context, *The Yellow Earth* is—if hardly a radical breakthrough in the representation of women—at least a refreshingly clear account of the traps that await Chinese women. As such, it seems to stand alone for the moment, but changes are occurring so rapidly in China that it would be premature to write off the possibility of a more radical feminism in the work of Chen Kaige's contemporaries.

By and large, then, the films outlined above *are* exceptions. What conclusions can be drawn from their representations of women?

The first, obvious conclusion is that the Chinese cinema, both capitalist and communist, is as formulary and entrenched as any other national cinema. Opportunities for change and for the introduction of new ideas will arise only in very particular circumstances: in Hong Kong and Taiwan, when market forces give producers no option but to innovate in order to protect their vested interests; in China, when the bureaucracy governing the film industry creates new spaces for production, especially when these spaces are in unglamorous, far-flung areas of the country. In these circumstances, it would be naive to expect to see a Chinese New Wave of the sort that appeared in France in the late 1950s or in West Germany in the late 1960s.

Second, it is clear that there can be no such thing as a radical-feminist Chinese cinema until social and political changes in the three Chinese territories pave the way for it. The three films discussed above *could* be co-opted into a Western concept of art cinema, but the bottom line is that *all* Chinese cinema is inherently popular cinema at present; cinema remains a genuine mass medium in China, Hong Kong, and Taiwan, and its strength is predicated on its success in addressing a large and responsive audience. No film can exist in a social vacuum, a Chinese film least of all.

Third, the strategies open to directors who are interested in formulating new images of women are limited. They are more a matter of delicate shifts in balance than of wrenching, sudden changes. Unless a director is willing to risk complete commercial failure (as Edward Yang perhaps was when he made *Taipei Story*), the best that she or he can hope to achieve is to adjust an established formula to her or his own ends, whether the formula be a genre, a plotline, or a set of more-or-less stereotyped characters.

Fourth, the fact that *The Spooky Bunch, The Yellow Earth,* and *Taipei Story* have been made in the last five years proves that change is in the air. Neither they nor any of the other films that could have served as examples can be construed as feminist or subversive, but all three succeed in constructing images of women that are significantly different from the norm. Indeed, it could be argued that their construction of "unliberated" women characters is actually more progressive and useful in many respects than most of the examples one could pick from contemporary Western popular cinema, which seems to have come to terms with the concept of "virilized" women but not with any more female-oriented concept of women *as women.*

Fifth, without resorting to rhetoric or crude dramatic manipulation, all three films manage to place women on the cutting edge of the struggle between tradition and emancipation. All three of them privilege women at the expense of men. The appearance of these films at this time suggests that a full feminist consciousness in Chinese cinema is not too far off.

Note

1. I follow the form of names used in the film's own subtitles, which observe no known rules of transliteration from Chinese.

14

Chinese Film Amidst the Tide of Reform

Shao Mujun

A TIDE of reform has been sweeping China since important reforms began in 1981 in the rural areas. With emphasis on overcoming the long-standing "left" mistakes in the guidance of agriculture, the reform of the mode of production has taken shape step by step: from restoring and expanding the decision-making power of the rural communes' production brigades and teams, and restoring private plots, to gradually introducing a system of responsibility for production in which payment is linked to output. As a result, marked changes have taken place in Chinese villages, where families with annual incomes of more than ten thousand *yuan* have emerged.

This tremendous success now acts as a powerful impetus to the reform of the urban sector, which is expected to enter its full-fledged stage very soon. The rural reform also serves to further strengthen the confidence of the staunch defenders of reform and helps to dispel the misgivings of those who may still feel some hesitation in accepting the movement. The handful of hardboiled diehards who stubbornly insist that any reform invariably means the restoration of capitalism is becoming more and more isolated in the nationwide support for reform.

The reform in China is a reform of the economic management system based on the premise of persisting in socialism. It does not touch on the public ownership of the means of production. In the initial period after Liberation, the high speed of economic construction and rapid amelioration of people's living conditions had taught the masses the superiority of socialism in its very concrete forms. But too soon the "left" ideology began to take the lead and expanded to absolute predominance. Mistake after mistake, which culminated in the "cultural revolution," brought the justice of adopting the new system in question. More and more people began to doubt whether socialism could really do them any good and whether it is true that the slogan, "poverty is superior to wealth," as advocated by the Gang of Four, really represented the true essence of socialism. It was only after the smashing of the Jiang Qing counterrevolutionary clique in 1976 and, in particular, after the Third Plenary Session of the Eleventh Central Committee, held in December 1978, that the important question of what is the true face of socialism began to be addressed. In this sense, the present reform movement is in fact a revolution in an effort to rehabilitate the reputation of socialism.

I am not a politician, nor an economist. What I care about is the destiny of Chinese cinema. But film is both an art and an industry (as André Malraux, among others, has noted). It poses questions more complicated than other forms of art amidst the tide of reform.

Chinese film is a colossal industry. There are more than five hundred thousand people working in it, and it used to bring an annual profit of several hundred millions. Its three main centers, Beijing, Shanghai, and Changchun, have huge film studios, each with a staff of from two thousand to three thousand. China has a big film market, though the number of annual releases is comparatively small. In 1983, for instance, 109 domestic films and 35 imported films were released. But the annual attendance is counted in billions. China's film industry has acquired some characteristics of the pre-fifties Hollywood studio system in that the country's nineteen film studios not only have their own sound stages and laboratories but also their own scriptwriters, directors, performers, and technicians. The biggest studios even have their own orchestras and troupes.

Examined from the viewpoint of the mode of production, the most serious malady of the Chinese film industry is what we call "eating from a big rice bowl." In the years before 1982 the state took in all completed films at a unified price regardless of their quality. The studios were thus guaranteed a fixed amount of profit. The film distribution companies run no risk of loss, since the Chinese people still succumb to movie mania, because of the lack of other recreational activities. Even the most didactical stuff can make money when it is treated as political teaching material for cadres and workers and the unions of factories or work units make a block booking.

The disadvantages of practices of this sort outweigh any advantages. Irresponsibility and laziness tend to find encouragement: what-

CHINESE FILMS AMIDST REFORM 201

Table 1. Number of Feature Films Produced in 1983

Film Studio	Planned number	Completed number
Beijing	11	12
Shanghai	16	19
Changchun	16	19
First August	8	8
Zhujiang	7	10
Xi'an	7	10
Emei	7	8
Xiaoxiang	4	1
Guangxi	4	4
Tianshan	2	3
Neimeng	2	2
Childfilm	2	2
Youth	2	2
Documentary	2	2
Outside the Plan		23
TOTAL	90	125

ever film you produce will make money, and nobody will care about the problem of quality. As film studios are such profit-making paradises, they become dutybound to arrange for the placement of more jobless youngsters. The result is that almost all the nation's film studios are overstaffed. The Beijing Film Studio, for instance, has a staff of 1,317 in name, but actually more than two thousand people are "working" in it. The studio made only fifteen films in 1984, and even fewer in past years. Many smaller studios, making between two and eight films a year, also have staffs of more than one thousand (see Table 1).

In the most recent years the Film Distribution Company has changed its practice of indiscriminate purchase to a new system, which requires the film studios to send sample copies of their new films first to provincial distributors to let them decide how many copies they would order. This change in practice, which aims at augmenting the sense of responsibility on the part of the film producers, however, has produced very little effect, as the general pattern of "eating from a big rice bowl" remains unchanged.

The egalitarian system of remuneration is another evil. With earnings of 60 to 80 *yuan* a month, and a bonus of several hundred *yuan* for one film, Chinese actors and actresses, however popular they may be, hardly reap the fortunes of their highly paid Western counterparts. Film directors can draw an extra bonus of 700 *yuan* for one film, but they have to share it among their crews, unless it is the director's last film. Directors and performers of films that win the government's "best film" prize will be awarded a small sum of money, but those who get the Golden Rooster or Hundred Flowers Awards can only enjoy the trappings of fame, without material rewards. (Most recently, the award winners have been given moderate remuneration by their studios.)

After the Film Distribution Company adopted its new system of purchase, the number of copies of different films began to vary. Films of high quality (but in most cases, of more entertainment value) can reap a rich reward for the studios with 250 to 300 copies at the price of 9,000 *yuan* each for the studios. The record lowest price paid for a film is 25 *yuan*.

This egalitarian practice hampers the improvement of the quality of products, although the harm it has done is largely in the technical sphere. Those who lose their enthusiasm are mainly studio crews. Our artists care for their reputation much more than for their income. They are never willing, because of inequitable rewards, to do things in a rough and slipshod way. Studio crews take a different attitude. The film studios are so overstaffed that there are always quite a number of people loitering around the lot. Since working or sauntering, working conscientiously or perfunctorily will make no difference in payment, few will care to do their utmost. Thus in the studios the director always finds his artistic intentions and designs distorted and thwarted by irresponsible or disobedient stagehands. The aggrieved director has no way but to try to fawn on them, even to beg for their support, since he is not in a position to fire anyone.

Despite these unhealthy tendencies, the Chinese film industry so far is a profit-making sector of the national economy. Though attendance has suffered a heavy fall since 1980 (from 1980 to 1983 city audiences dropped by two billion, and urban film release revenues fell at a rate of 25 million *yuan* a year), the situation is still tolerable. In 1983, among the 109 domestic films released, only 11 were sold at a rate of fewer than 50 copies. The average number of copies was 116. Since most Chinese films are made on very low budgets, the return to the studios from 40 or 50 copies of a film will cover costs well.

What, then, has made the leading personalities in the Chinese film industry feel a sense of urgency about the coming reforms? They share a sense of approaching crisis.

All those working in the Chinese film industry know that domestic films win their profits not from their quality but because of two factors. First, the Chinese have very few places of entertainment. Even in big cities like Beijing and Shanghai people find filmgoing the best way to kill time. The extraordinarily low admission prices for city cinemas, ranging from twenty to thirty-five Chinese cents, well suit the financial condition of most urban families. The mobile projection teams that serve rural audiences charge even lower prices. They act on the principle of "many a pickle makes a nickle." Second, film is considered a means of ideological education and political mobilization in China. Party and government organizations, factories and enterprises, military units, and even agricultural communes accordingly all have a special fund for booking films. Any film, however turgid its ideological fare may be, can earn recompense from this fund.

The Chinese film industry had its best time in the years immediately after the smashing of the Gang of Four in 1976. Because the industry had come to a standstill during the 1966–1976 "cultural revolution," Chinese filmgoers were spiritually hungry. They flocked to the cinema to watch any film that was showing. They were described as hungry men eager to eat anything edible. Box office receipts soared to unprecedented heights. Any artistic or technical flaws in the new films were virtually ignored.

But the heyday has gradually come to an end since 1982. The "villain" in this decline is the "open door" policy which got underway at that time. Although the open policy has not touched the cultural field so far, along with the growth of tourism and foreign trade, more and more foreigners and foreign (mostly Western) things have been flooding into the country. They have exercised a considerable influence on the masses of the people, especially youths and intellectuals. Though very few imported films (mainly Western films, as Soviet films were stamped out long ago) are shown, the increasingly colorful real world outside the cinemas made the monotonous and dull life portrayed on screen even more distasteful.

In 1984, attendance, in both the cities and the villages, showed another alarming drop. Nearly half of the year's releases were in the red. The financial condition of the film industry approached a critical stage of minimum returns. According to polls conducted by several public institutions, films, once consistently the favorite form of recrea-

Table 2. Student Poll on Recreation and Film Preferences

A student poll was conducted in February 1984 by the Movielovers' Society of Beijing University. Four hundred twenty-nine students from eight universities and colleges gave their answers.

Question A: Among the following items of cultural life, which is your most favorite?

Question B: On which activity do you spend most of your leisure time?

Activity	Question A Answers returned	Question B Answers returned
Reading books	166 (38.7%)	255 (59.4%)
Listening to music	108 (25.2%)	134 (31.2%)
Watching movies	85 (19.8%)	112 (26.1%)
Watching sports (including telecasts)	69 (16.1%)	96 (22.4%)
Watching TV	38 (8.9%)	81 (18.9%)
Attending lecture courses	19 (4.4%)	28 (6.5%)
Playing chess or cards	17 (4.0%)	24 (5.6%)
Watching stage plays	10 (2.3%)	8 (1.9%)
Watching other performances	7 (1.6%)	5 (1.2%)

Question C: What film subjects move you most?

Subject	Answers returned	Percentage
Life's hardships and difficulties	219	51.0
Beauty of humanity	152	35.4
Greatness of love	56	13.1
Revolutionary heroism	39	9.1
Others	16	3.7

Note: Total number of answers exceeds 429 because some students chose two items.

tion, have fallen to third or fourth place (see Table 2). The annual readership poll for best movies and performers conducted by China's biggest magazine, *Popular Cinema (Dazhong dianying),* in the past has attracted ballots from several million fans. In 1983 and 1984, however, the number of ballots fell drastically. There is also talk that, along with the general reinforcement of the responsibility system in factories and enterprises, the fund for ideological films is likely to be cancelled. All these ominous signs indicate that a crisis is looming on the horizon for the Chinese film industry.

The crisis is one of quality. To be sure, the broad domestic film market still exists, for the Chinese have by no means lost their interest in filmgoing. Public places of entertainment are scarce in China. Cinema houses remain a favorite haunt of young lovers, since coffee houses and tearooms are a rarity, even in big cities. Television in recent years has given some competition to films, but it is still far from a serious menace. Although new films are shown occasionally on television (to date there are no legal stipulations on the relationship between television and films), people still flock to cinemas to catch a feature film that really interests them. At least one reason is that almost all Chinese films nowadays are in color. Few families have color television sets. Evidently people have begun to shun cinemas because they find the films shown there plain boring. The *China Daily* recently quoted one filmgoer as saying: "Some new films are so boring that I cannot sit through them, even when I want to kill time."

Since the problems are of an ideological and artistic nature, the approaching crisis obviously cannot be relieved through a reform of the mode of production and economic management system.

With the vigorous development of the reform movement, many believe that the reinforcement of the responsibility system for film studio production will soon be realized. It is hard to imagine the film industry being able to remain independent of the new economic system by resisting the trend of the times and the desire of the people. However, if filmmakers cannot enjoy full freedom of creative expression in the future, then improvement of the quality of films is inconceivable.

Some people here are quite loath to admit that there is a problem of freedom of expression in filmmaking. To talk about it is even considered a reactionary tendency of bourgeois liberalization. It is supposed that under the socialist system, only people who are considered antisocialist elements are to be deprived of such freedom. Demanding freedom of expression is therefore politically intolerable.

This is fallacious because the fetters on the hands and feet of filmmakers really exist. The cry for untying fetters, so popular in the domain of economic management, is also applicable to filmmaking. To give filmmakers full freedom of creative expression is an important measure to save Chinese filmmaking from its looming crisis.

Film in China has been treated as a most powerful means of political propaganda, the most effective tool to illustrate the politics of the moment. Its power has been not only highly estimated but also more often exaggerated. Although the contents of Chinese films are known to be healthy, they have tended to serve as scapegoats for unhealthy social trends. Criminals often take films as their abettors, and even public security organs have been accusing filmmakers on hearsay evidence. During the "cultural revolution" years, film people were among the most cruelly persecuted. The overestimation of film's influence had put filmmakers in an awkward predicament, so that almost anyone could interfere with their work. Persons in charge of the examination and approval of new films became so cautious that they feared that any small detail in a film might instigate certain social maladies or unhealthy trends. Representatives of the professional sectors whose work was featured in a film were invited to participate in the examination of unreleased films, and their amateurish, even unreasonable, opinions were not easily discarded. In some extreme cases, even protests from individual audiences could lead to the banning of a film. Some time ago I heard a famous middle-aged director complain about the plight in which he had found himself. He wanted to make a film about criminals. His intention was to expose the crime and warn young people about criminals' tricks. But when he went to ask the local public security organs for their opinions, he was advised that he should not show how criminals commit crimes. Otherwise, he was told, potential criminals would have an opportunity to learn the craft. Nor should the film show the process of police investigation, for fear of teaching wanted criminals how to cover their tracks.

In those days, if a film showed a branch party secretary as a negative character, sanctions would follow: the higher the rank of the negative character, the more severe the accusations. What was left for filmmakers to do was to evade the dark side and play up the bright side of life. Fulsome praises plus dry moralization helped to kill art but foster an inglorious success.

Malpractice of this sort culminated during the "cultural revolution," but the repercussions remain prevalent to this day. In recent years, the Party has rightly pointed out that there should be no "crude interference" with the creation of art and literature and replaced the long-established dogma about art and literature serving politics with new claims: art and literature should serve the people and socialism. Accordingly, we began to see hopes for amelioration of the interference. But we also know that the pernicious influence of the "Left" line is quite difficult to eliminate. Lingering fear on the part of film workers allows the evil trends to linger on or recur in masked form. To serve the people and socialism can too easily be interpreted as also being to adhere to the politics of the moment. Therefore, a main target of the Chinese film industry on its road to reform is to fight for full freedom of creative expression, stand against "crude interference," and break away from the agitprop task of illustrating current policies.

Most of us firmly believe that the responsibility system for film production and the acquisition of full freedom of creative expression will open up vast and beautiful vistas for the development of Chinese socialist cinema. This is possible because the real life of today's China is ready to provide the prerequisite for prosperity in film creation.

As we all know, real life is the source of artistic creation. A colorful screen world cannot but be a reflection of a colorful reality. Film artists can portray a character with distinct individuality and an active and lucid mind on the screen only when an archetype of this sort exists in real life. Chinese films are often criticized for their oversimplified plots, false displays of emotion, stereotyped characterization, and high-sounding words. Film artists were invariably treated as responsible for these faults. Strictly speaking, this was not entirely fair. The fettered film artists may be partly responsible because of their lack of originality and resourcefulness. But the main reason is that real life itself has been exactly or almost the same as it was shown on the screen. This is particularly true of the "cultural revolution" years. It was in those years that the suppression of normal human feelings and individual traits reached its extreme. One was deprived of the right to think independently, any display of individuality was condemned as "nursing a grievance against the Party," and concern about personal gains or losses was a crime. The result was a universal loss of initiative. No one would dare to let out his or her innermost thoughts and feelings. He would rather keep his mouth shut until he knew for sure what he should say. Even young people became inert and numb with fear, not to mention the aged. The decade of turmoil confounded the criteria for judging right and wrong, good and evil, and beauty and ugliness. Hypocrisy replaced sincerity, and cowardliness was taken as prudence.

To undo the grave spiritual consequences of the "cultural revolution" would mean to bring the masses of the people from this terrible state of apathy and fearfulness back to a normal state of mind. This is a very difficult task. Today, eight years after the smashing of the Jiang Qing clique, we can say the process of rectification has begun to produce its desired results. The tremendous success of rural reform has greatly accelerated the process. The concrete facts eventually convinced the masses to give up their lingering fears about the possibility of another political movement being mounted. When I write these words, I am writing from personal experience.

Chinese cinema is fortunate in the sense that new possibilities are open to it on the brink of the potential crisis turning into a reality. Vigorous social reform has been providing rich materials for film creation. The gradual strengthening of the legal system will guarantee full freedom of expression against undue interference. Reform of the economic management system will cure the egalitarian malady in film production and distribution. These three reforms are prerequisites for the renaissance of Chinese cinema. They will make Chinese films the expression of the true face of modern Chinese culture.

Index

Aakaler Sandhaney, 117
Aakrosh, 87, 124
Achut Kanya, 74
Aizen Katsura, 63
Akanishi Kakita, 37
Alam Ara, 74, 149
All India Radio, 153 4
Anand, Dev, 73, 156
Ananthamurthy, U. R., 120
Anderson, Joseph, 30
Anderson, Lindsay, 105
Andhi Galli, 87
Andhra Pradesh, 73, 127, 137
Ankur, 87, 123
Annadorai, C. N., 140, 142, 147
Aparajito, 75, 93–106
Apu Sansar, 75, 93–106
Aranyer din Ratri, 105
Aravindan, G., 74–5, 88, 105, 121
Ardh Satya, 87
Arth, 124
Azmi, Shabana, 85, 108, 123–5

Bachchan, Amitabh, 81, 86, 146–7
Beijing Film Academy, 163, 170, 182–3, 187
Beijing opera, 166–7, 170, 195
Benegal, Shyam, 75, 83, 87, 123–4, 136, 157
Bergman, Ingmar, 54
Bhatt, Mahesh, 124
Bhumika, 123
Bhuvan Shome, 82, 118
Black Cannon Incident, 164
Bobbili Puli, 128, 133
Border Town, 168

Borzage, Frank, 16
Bresson, Robert, 88
Burch, Noel, 29, 31
Buruma, Ian, 10–11

Capra, Frank, 16
Ceremony, 62
Chakra, 124
Chakroborty, Utpalendu, 122
Chandasa-sanadu, 144
Charulata, 6, 75, 115
Chatterji, Basu, 76, 118
Chen, Kaige, 161, 163, 173, 183, 186–7, 192, 196
Chetna, 110
Chopra, B. R., 73
Chopra, Yash, 86
Chokh, 122
Clark, T. W., 98
Communist Party, 161, 165, 179, 181, 183, 207
Coolie, 86
Cultural identity, 1–11, 74
Cultural Revolution, 162 3, 167, 170–1, 178, 181, 200, 206–7

Dakhal, 122
Dasgupta, Buddhadeb, 75, 87, 122
Das Gupta, Chidananda, 5, 11, 100
Dean, James, 51
Deewar, 86
Dening, Greg, 3, 12
Deng, Xiaoping, 163, 188
Derzu Uzala, 17
Desai, Manmohan, 73, 86
De Sica, Vittorio, 104

Devadas, 74, 110
Devi, 75
Do Anjane, 109
Dodeskaden, 56
Dooratwa, 87
Dr. Madhurika, 110
Drunken Angel, 47
Duniya Na Mane, 74, 109
Dutt, Guru, 73

Eastwood, Clint, 56
Eisenstein, Sergei M., 24
Ek Baar Phir, 124
Ek Din Pratidin, 117

Fall Guy, 18
Family Game, 18, 61
Fellini, Federico, 35, 48, 54
Floating Clouds, 54–5
Folk drama, 149
Fong, Allen, 186, 195
Ford, John, 10
Fukasaki, Kenji, 18
Funeral, 18, 62

Gandhi, Indira, 127, 133–5
Gandhi, Mahatma, 103, 128, 135
Gandhi, Rajiv, 146
Gang of Four, 163, 200, 203
Gate of Hell, 55
Geertz, Clifford, 3, 12, 94–5, 106
Ghatak, Ritwik, 78, 82–3, 88, 115, 117, 120
Ghatasharddha, 120–1
Ghose, Goutam, 75, 87, 122
Goddess, 178
Godfather, 56
Gopalakrishnan, Adoor, 73, 75, 88, 105, 121
Gosha, Hideo, 56
Goyokin, 56
Graduate, 56
Griffith, D. W., 16

Haha, 65
Haha Kōbai, 65
Haha Sannin, 65
Harada, Kai, 37–8
Harakiri, 56
High, Peter B., 28–9
Hinde, John, 80
Hollywood, 8–10, 78–9, 82, 91, 176, 182, 200

Homecoming, 195
Houston, Penelope, 101
Huang Jianxin, 163–4
Hui, Ann, 11–12, 185–6, 189

I am You, You Are Me, 61
Ichikawa, Kon, 15–16, 22, 27, 29, 67
Ikebana, 20
Ikuru, 6
Imai, Tadashi, 28
Imamura, Shohei, 15
Inquilaab, 81
Insaaf Ka Tarazu, 112
Internationalization, 7
In the Realm of the Senses, 57
Itami, Juzō, 35
Itami, Mansaku, 18, 36–8

Jalsaghar, 75
Jiang, Qing, 162, 181, 200, 207
Justice Chowdhury, 132

Kaadu, 87
Kabuki, 15, 21, 29, 33, 40, 45–9, 51–2, 56, 59
Kael, Pauline, 103
Kagemusha, 17, 61
Kapoor, Raj, 73, 152, 156
Karanth, Prema, 85–6, 121
Karnad, Girish, 87, 105, 120
Karunanidhi, M., 141
Kaul, Mani, 75, 88, 118, 119–20
Khandhar, 117–8
Kharij, 117
Kimi no Nawa, 64
Kinoshita, Keisuke, 15–6, 64
Kobayashi, Masaki, 15, 36, 40, 42–3, 56
Kodiyettam, 121
Kondo, Isamu, 35
Krishnaswamy, S., 141
Kumar, Dilip, 73
Kurosawa, Akira, 6, 15–16, 18, 22, 24–5, 27, 33, 34, 36, 39, 40, 43, 46–8, 52, 54, 56, 58, 60–1
Kwan, Stanley, 195

Late Spring, 46, 56
Leone, Sergio, 56
Life of Jesus Christ, 141
Life of Oharu, 55
Ling, Zifeng, 169
Lubitsch, Ernst, 16

INDEX

Maa Bhoomi, 87
Mahabharata, 74, 77, 81
Mahanagar, 115
Mandi, 124
Mangeshkar, Lata, 152
Manthan, 84, 123
Mao, Zedong, 163, 180, 188
Mass communication, 74
Mast, Gerald, 102
Max Mon Amour, 17
Maya Miriga, 88, 122
May Fourth Movement, 175–6, 182, 185
McQueen, Steve, 51
Meghe Dhaka Tara, 83, 116
Mehta, Ketan, 75, 89
Mehta, Vijaya, 85
Meji restoration, 33, 68
Mellen, Joan, 113
Merry Christmas Mr. Lawrence, 17, 61
Middle Cinema, 78
Mifune, Toshiro, 46–8, 54
Mirch Masala, 89
Mirza, Saeed, 90
Miyamoto, Mushashi, 34
Mizoguchi, Kenji, 15–16, 22, 25, 27–8, 46, 52, 54–7
Mochizuki, Yuko, 65–6
Modernization, 74
Mohapatra, Manmohan, 122
Mohapatra, Nirad, 73, 88, 122
Montage, 26
Morita, Yoshimitsu, 18
Mother, 56
Mujhe Insaaf Chahiye, 112
Mukhamukham, 88

Naruse, Mikio, 15, 22, 27, 54–9, 64
Nehru, Jawaharlal, 103, 135–6
New Indian Cinema, 78, 81–2, 84–6, 88, 91, 125
Niguruma no Uta, 65
Nihalani, Govind, 75, 87, 89
Nihon no Higeki, 65
Ninjō Kami-Fusen, 38
Nishant, 87, 123
Noh drama, 18, 21, 40, 45–6, 48–9, 52, 56

O'Flaherty, Wendy D., 113
Ofukuro, 65
Oshima, Nagisa, 15, 17, 57–8, 61–2
Our Fields, 171
Ozu, Yasujiro, 3–5, 15–16, 18, 22–3, 25, 27, 46, 50, 52, 54–9, 64, 88

Pande, Vinode, 124
Paranjpye, Sai, 76, 125
Pastoral Hide and Seek, 48
Patel, Jabbar, 123
Pather Panchali, 75, 93–106
Patil, Smita, 85, 123–5
People's Daily, 168–9
Peries, Lester James, 7
Phalke, D. G., 74, 77
Phaniyamma, 86, 121
Pokkuveyil, 121
Popular cinema, 4
Pornographers, 57
President, 111
Prisoner of Zenda, 142

Radio Ceylon, 155
Rajah Harischandra, 74–77
Ramachandran, M. G., 127, 133, 137, 140–7
Rama Rao, N. T., 127–9, 131–5, 137–9, 141–7
Ramayana, 107, 140
Ran, 17, 61
Rangoonwalla, Firoze, 97
Raosaheb, 85
Rashomon, 39, 54–6
Ray, Nicholas, 22
Ray, Satyajit, 3–8, 10, 12, 73, 75, 77, 82–3, 88, 93–106, 115, 136–7
Reddy, Pattabhi Rama, 86
Reedpipe Sounds, 172
Renoir, Jean, 22, 104
Richie, Donald, 4–5, 12, 30
River Without Buoys, 172
Rossellini, Roberto, 22, 104

Shahani, Kumar, 73, 75, 83, 88, 116, 120
Saigal, K. L., 150
Samskara, 86
Samurai films, 33–43, 69
Sanskrit drama/theatre, 74, 79, 103
Sara Akash, 117, 119
Sarkar, Kobita, 153
Sato, Tadao, 28–9, 31, 60
Seeta Rati, 122
Sen, Aparna, 85, 125
Sen, Mrinal, 73, 75, 78, 82–3, 105, 117, 136
Seppuku, 40–3
Seton, Marie, 99
Seven Samurai, 40, 43, 54–6, 60
Shah, Kundan, 76
Shah, Naseeruddin, 85

Shree 420, 152
Shakespeare, William, 45
Shantaram, V., 73
Shimpa stories, 16, 49–50
Shinoda, Masahiro, 15, 17
Sounds from Home, 172
South Pole Story, 54
Spooky Bunch, 189–90, 195–6
Stand-in, 164
Star Wars, 62
Subarnarekha, 116–7
Sugata Sanshiro, 39
Surechigai, 63
Swayamvaram, 121

Taipei Story, 192–6
Takamine, Hideko, 54, 58
Taking Tiger Mountain By Strategy, 163, 181
Tamilnadu, 73, 127, 130, 132, 139
Tanaka, Eijo, 25
Tarang, 88, 120
Taylor, John Russell, 9, 12
Television, 16, 23, 29, 60, 66–7, 205
Thodisi Bewafaii, 108
Throne of Blood, 18, 46
Tian, Zhungzhuang, 161, 187
Tokyo Story, 54–5, 58
Tolstoy, Leo, 25
Tora-San, 59
Tsubaki Sanjuro, 47
Tsui, Hark, 186

Tudor, Andrew, 31
Tunstall, Jeremy, 7, 9, 12

Ueda, Makoto, 31
Ugetsu, 54–5, 57
Umbartha, 123
Upanishads, 99
Universality, 6
Uski Roti, 118

Velaikari, 140
Von Sternberg, Josef, 16

Wayne, John, 51
Welcome to Shanghai, 18
When Winds Blow, 172

Xumao and his Daughters, 172

Yamada, Isuzu, 46
Yamanaka, Sadao, 22, 36, 37–8
Yang, Edward, 186, 192–6
Yeh Kaisa Insaaf, 112
Yellow Earth, 163–4, 173, 183, 190–2, 196
Yim, Ho, 195
Yoda, Yoshitaka, 31
Yojimbo, 39, 47, 56, 60
Yoshimura, Kozaburo, 28

Zen Buddhism, 34, 39, 40
Zhang, Junzhao, 161, 163, 187
Zhang, Yimou, 183

Contributors

MIRA REYM BINFORD is a film scholar who writes on Indian cinema and is the coordinator and organizer of the Asian Cinema Studies Society.

AUDIE BOCK is a highly esteemed writer on Japanese cinema and is the author of *Japanese Film Directors*.

PAUL CLARK, a research associate at the Institute of Culture and Communication, East-West Center, is the author of *Chinese Cinema: Culture and Politics since 1949*.

CHIDANANDA DAS GUPTA is a leading Indian writer on cinema who has published, among others, a book on the cinema of Satyajit Ray.

WIMAL DISSANAYAKE is assistant director of the Institute of Culture and Communication, East-West Center, and has published many books and research papers on film and communication.

MA QIANG is a film scholar attached to the China Film Co-production Corporation in Beijing.

TONY RAYNS is a British film critic and international film festival consultant who writes extensively on Asian cinema.

DONALD RICHIE, former curator of film at the Museum of Modern Art, New York, has written many books on Japanese film, among them, *The Films of Akira Kurosawa* and *Ozu*.

TADAO SATO is one of the most distinguished Japanese film critics and is the author of *Currents in Japanese Cinema*.

SHAO MUJUN is a senior researcher with the China Film Association, Beijing, China.

TERI SKILLMAN is a research intern at the Institute of Culture and Communication, East-West Center, and specializes in Indian film music.

MICHITARO TADA is a professor in the Research Institute for Humanistic Studies at Kyoto University, Kyoto, Japan.

ARUNA VASUDEV is a well-known writer on Indian cinema and is the author of *The New Indian Cinema*.